Afterwords

Afterwords

Hellenism, Modernism, and the Myth of Decadence

Louis A. Ruprecht, Jr.

State University of New York Press

The author gratefully acknowledges the kind permission of *Soundings, An Interdisciplinary Journal* to reprint material as well as a map in Chapter One (from "Nietzsche's Vision, Nietzsche's Greece," Spring 1990), and further material in Chapter Six (from "In The Aftermath of Modernism," Fall 1992). The author also gratefully acknowledges the kind permission of *Continuum,* an annual publication sponsored by The Continuum Publishing Group of New York, to reprint material in Chapter Three (from "After Virtue?," 1994).

Finally, the author gratefully acknowledges the kind permission of the Münchener Stadtarchiv und Glyptothek for the reproduction of plans and photographs on pp. 46–47 of this book.

Published by
State University of New York Press, Albany

©1996 State University of New York

For information, address the State University of New York Press,
State University Plaza, Albany, NY 12246

Production by Christine Lynch
Marketing by Theresa A. Swierzowski

Library of Congress Cataloging-in-Publication Data

Ruprecht, Louis A.
    Afterwords : Hellenism, modernism, and the myth of decadence /
    Louis A. Ruprecht, Jr.
      p. cm.
    Includes bibliographical references and index.
    ISBN 0-7914-2933-4 (ch. : alk. paper).—ISBN 0-7914-2934-2 (pbk.
    : alk. paper)
    1. Nostalgia. 2. Degeneration. 3. Hellenism. 4. Philosophy,
  Modern—20th century. 5. Civilization, Modern—20th century.
  6. Christianity—20th century. I. Title.
  B945.R853A3 1996
  909.08'01—dc20   95-20798
                                          CIP

10 9 8 7 6 5 4 3 2 1

CONTENTS

92357

For Jim

κοινὰ τὰ τῶν φίλων

The veneration of classical antiquity, as evident among the Italians—which is to say, the only sincere, unselfish and really generous veneration which antiquity has ever enjoyed—is all a magnificent example of Don Quixotism. And perhaps that is what Philology is, at it best. . . .

We imitate a chimera, and chase after a world of wonders which never really existed.

Such an impulse existed already in antiquity: the way men copied the Homeric heroes, the whole substitution of myth for reality. Gradually, Greece itself became an object of Quixotism. You cannot understand our modern world if you do not first consider the uncanny influence of sheer fantasy.

—Nietzsche; *Wir Philologen* 7[1] (1876)

ACKNOWLEDGMENTS

I could never have seen any of the things I will be trying to describe here—and thus really to have known them (the Archaic Greek word for knowing being *oida,* "I have seen")—had I not been fortunate enough to have lived in that magical country we call "Greece," off and on, for several years. It will not be possible to thank all of my many hosts, known and unknown to me in those long years, who gave so selflessly of themselves—that grand, old Homeric virtue of *philoxenia,* or guest-friendship. What they gave in the final analysis, and what I treasure most about my memories of the place, was the impossibly precious feeling for *time,* a gift whose full measure lies in the giving, as we in North America, in a country which is open twenty-fours a day, are fast in danger of forgetting.

I have a special debt to the American School of Classical Studies in Athens, which sponsored my first trip to Greece in the summer of 1986 as part of their intensive summer program in Greek archaeology. I subsequently had the privilege of working at the American School for two years as a visiting scholar. I am particularly indebted to Dr. William Coulson, the director of the school, to Dr. Nancy Winters, librarian extraordinaire, to Anne Stewart, an expatriated North American who knows their ruins better than most Greeks do, and to Dr. Robert Bridges, secretary to the school, and a dear personal friend, then as now.

In addition to these are countless other, more local debts, fondly remembered and gratefully acknowledged: to Elpida Hadjidaki, who graciously allowed me to work with her on a fascinating excavation called Phalasarna on the northwest tip of Crete. It was there in the course of three excavation seasons (1987–90) that I first learned about Greek pirates—*pirates,* not politicians and not philosophers—and began to be a little suspicious of the romantic whimsy for that allegedly harmonious and always-sunny paradise we imagine as the world of Greek antiquity. Quixotic, Nietzsche called it. And so it was.

Crete is not Athens, and pirates are not philosophers. It took living there, in Greece, for quite some time before I realized that. I am delighted to record an especially fond debt of thanks to Anastasia and Yianna Tzigounaki, from whom I learned my Greek, and much of "Greece" herself. They, along with their late mother Evanthia, and Anastasia's remarkably precocious daughter

Marika, provided me with a happy home and a quiet place to work, every time the urbanity of Athens got to me, and I retreated by overnight boat to the wilder climes of Crete. It was in Crete, in any case, viewed largely through their eyes initially, that I fell in love with the ideas I am studying still.

My rare good fortune also wears an American face. Many professors and friends have helped me in the challenging process of sorting out my as yet unsorted thoughts. I would like to thank the Charlotte W. Newcombe Dissertation Committee, administered by the Woodrow Wilson Foundation, which generously supported me for the entire second year (1989–90) of my dissertation research. They were the ones who made it possible for me to stay on in Greece, actually to complete the dissertation manuscript, and thus to take my degree.

My graduate studies were blessed, literally from the first day to the last, by an extraordinary range of colleagues, conversation partners, and friends. Old professors from Duke University—especially Peter Burian, Stanley Hauerwas, Stuart C. Henry, and Bruce B. Lawrence—have maintained a lovely and heartfelt interest in my work. They are, quite appropriately, some of the most important persons in my end-notes. Nancy Ammermann, Robert Carle, Barbara Elwell, Arthur E. Farnsley II, Thomas Flynn, Pamela Hall, Steve Olsen, Claude Pavur, Christine Pohl, Karen Root, Chip Sills, Jim Thobaben, Scott Thumma, and Stephen Tipton, all of Emory University, made my tenure as a student there an always challenging and always enjoyable one. Vernon K. Robbins and Jon P. Gunnemann were wonderfully patient and gracious readers, people who seemed to understand in an instant thoughts which had taken me months to say properly. They too stand behind many of my essential end-notes, and many of my thoughts. Paul B. Courtright, our departmental chairman ever since my return to the States in 1991, has been uncannily generous and supportive of this project, even though he did not yet know me when I happened upon most of these ideas, overseas. His unflagging support, his commitment to what I had to say, is one of the important reasons this manuscript is now seeing the light of day.

The late William Arrowsmith introduced me to a great many things worth knowing in the course of our two years translating Greek drama together. Most significantly, he introduced me to Nietzsche's uncollected notes for the essay, *Wir Philologen,* of which I make so much in this book. Arrowsmith translated some of the notes in *Arion* in 1963, returned to these occasional jottings in 1974, and finally included them in a new translation entitled *Unmodern Observations* in 1990. Since the notes for this essay provide the essential framework for my entire analysis here, my debts to Bill's genius and creative guidance are inestimable. I acknowledge his passing with great regret, as I acknowledge the remarkable passions embodied in his scholarly and personal life with gratitude.

The editorial staff at SUNY Press has been exceptionally sensitive to the twin demands of all academic editing—the need to get it right, and the need to get it said the way the author really wishes to say it. They have steered a careful course between the Scylla of leaving me too free to chart out my own often Odyssean path, and the Charybdis of rewriting the book for me. I am tremendously indebted to three anonymous reviewers who all agreed independently on a *major* restructuring that has infinitely improved the aesthetic and moral content of this book. And I am indebted to Carola Sautter, my editor at SUNY, quite simply for being who she is. She understands the necessities under which young scholars labor, and has been remarkably nurturing and supportive of this one.

Jeffrey Wilson, one of the most gifted and careful thinkers it has ever been my good fortune to know, has helped me enormously, even and especially where he has had some important misgivings about this project. He read it in its entirety, and while I have not been able to change everything he might have liked to see changed, I do hope that the book, in its present form, will be worth some further reflection on his part.

Teachers teach and students learn. Like most truisms, this one is more fiction than fact. It has proven to be quite wrong in my own case. Students—in my own classes and also in others—continue to teach me about many things I thought I already knew. This manuscript began to take shape in an explosive period of weeks during the summer of 1992 when I suddenly saw my way clear to begin to tell the story I wanted to tell. Roger Fowler, a former student, happened to be staying with me in those same weeks. I recall many late evening dinners in the garden where he and several other friends—Dominique Josef and Tracey Horn, most notably—helped me to understand where some of these thoughts were leading. While I remember those days with a peculiar fondness, especially now that several of those friends have moved away, I cannot nostalgize them. For Roger and Dominique and Tracey reminded me that nostalgia has no place in Romanticism, that tomorrow's magic is intimately tied to its endless potential for surpassing yesterday. Certainly in Roger's case this is so. He has recently engaged to be married, to another remarkable former student (and teacher), Kimberly Cotter. Their relationship, too, grew again in the fertile soil of that same summer.

My return to the States, after nearly two years away and in dawning anticipation of the appalling spectacle of the poorly-named "Gulf War," was facilitated by a dawning relationship with the editorial staff of that remarkable interdisciplinary journal, *Soundings,* whose editor, Ralph V. Norman, was both a wonderfully enthusiastic critic and a lovely correspondent in the old school. The *Soundings* editorial board first consented to publish a much shorter version of chapter 1—"Nietzsche's Vision, Nietzsche's Greece" was the title then— while I was still living in Greece. I recall proofing the galley sheets for that article on a boat from the Piraeus to one of the Aegean islands with a rare feeling for the impossible romance of it all. That feeling grows, if anything, more intense with the passing of time and the unfolding of this relationship. The *Soundings* staff has been remarkably generous in providing a venue for a great deal of my written work. They have also kindly consented to the reprinting of previously published material in chapters 1 and 6 of this manuscript.

One must go back, it seems, in order to go forward. That is one of the main messages of this book. I first discovered the life of the mind, if that is what this is, as a sophomore in college. My first religion professor in my first religion class was largely responsible for that. I am still thinking about things, and now writing about things, which he impressed upon me over a decade ago. He is impressing me still, on long walks over the Bridgehampton shoreline, and long hikes in the New Hampshire mountains, impressing me best of all with his total embodiment of the twinned virtues of wisdom and of love. Dr. Barney L. Jones has read every word I have ever written since first we met in the fall of 1981. His retirement from Duke University in 1984 has not changed that. His friendship has sustained my interest and energy at times when both were flagging. It would not be possible to say clearly enough how much my own perspective owes to the gracious gifts of his time and gentle insight. Suffice it to say here that I would not be doing what I am doing now had we not met fourteen long years ago.

My final and profoundest thanks in this endeavor go to James J. Winchester, who has patiently read and re-read, listened and re-listened, to more of this polemicizing than any friend should have to do. That he has done so with such unflagging good cheer is his first minor miracle. I think Aristotle was probably wrong about the philosopher's reticence in receiving gifts from other friends. And I am no longer so sure that this is what Nietzsche thought about the matter either. It has been Jim's remarkable scholarly insight—happily enough, now in the form of a book entitled *Nietzsche's Aesthetic Turn*—to present Nietzsche with a far more human face. This insight has, in its turn, taught me a great deal about the philosopher, about the Greeks, and ever so much more importantly, about myself. My personal and intellectual life alike would be simply unthinkable apart from the sustenance they receive at Jim's hands. So much of what I have learned since we met as graduate students, some ten years ago now, I have learned seated variously around his dining-room table, in the warm presence of a seemingly endless array of remarkable persons. With Tracey and Dominique and Roger absent from the table, new faces have moved closer to the center of my daily life—Arturo and Melanie Lindsay's, Barbara Marston's, Larry Slutsker's, even Carola Sautter's—all of whom I met through Jim. The constant center of all this continues to be Jim's cooking, his really astonishing virtues of hospitality, his practical gifts at making everyone feel equally at home, an essential participant in the grand adventure which is his round table. I owe an enormous debt of gratitude to his wife, Eve, and their daughter, Sophia, for being so generous and patient in sharing him as they have been. And it is to Jim that this book is fondly dedicated.

Louis A. Ruprecht, Jr.
April 1995
Atlanta

PREFACE
On Living *After* Greece

I

This is a book about the seductive power of *nostalgia.* We see ample evidence of this power in contemporary politics and contemporary theology alike. This book grows out of the conviction that such nostalgia—grounded in a misplaced myth of origins and a perverse theory of decadence—is both deeply tempting in moral and political philosophy (to say nothing of theology) *and* that it is deeply misleading as a strategy for political or moral reform. It leads us to waste our better energies vainly tilting after windmills, windmills of our own imagining. By *mis*naming our problems, and by grounding them in a wrong-headed notion of "the glory that was," we are invited to look for curatives in the wrong places. As Plato knew well, a little *pharmakon* can help us; too much will kill us more surely than the sickness it was intended to cure. When Socrates drank the hemlock, he was fascinated by the phenomenon of what he was feeling, the strange mixture of pleasure and of pain. Such complex seductions can be fatal; this modern posturing can be so as well.

Plato's *Republic* is a classic statement of this anti-nostalgic point of view. We know that Plato is at war with the poets in the *Republic,* with Homer especially. Yet it is commonly noticed that Socrates continues to quote Homer and Hesiod and the tragedians when it suits his purposes. I have long puzzled over this inconsistency, an inconsistency far too obvious to have escaped the philosopher's attention. And so I am encouraged to ask anew about the meaning of this curious declaration of war against the poets. It is actually, I think, a philosophical declaration of war against poetic nostalgia.

The poets, it would seem, view the world from the perspective of *decadence.* They give us a portrait of a Golden Age, and then they tell us that it is gone for good. Gold Age, to Silver Age, to Bronze Age, to our age . . . that is a myth of decadence. In the *Republic,* Socrates speaks once through the mouth of the Muses—ironically. When he is speaking this way, as a poet, he speaks of human society's ideal origins,[1] and he speaks of the *inevitable* deterioration of the just city.

To say it again: the poet, like the Muse, and very much like the scriptural religionist, provides us with a myth of ideal origins, origins which are then lost through what is believed to be *inevitable* decay.

1

The dialectician answers this all with a genealogy. He gives us a narrative of origins[2] that is exotic for its sheer primitivism, as well as for its oddly amoral character. The first city was no ideal city, according to Socrates—Glaucon calls it "a city of pigs." Still later, the dialectician gives us an allegory, a story of a Cave where, once again, our common origins are narrated as a problem to be transcended, not a paradise lost, waiting to be regained.[3]

The philosophical movement is thus centrifugal, not centripetal. We are invited to dream a world that has never been, and may never be, not a world which we once had, and then lost. It is my contention that our political coming-of-age may indeed be bound up with the outgrowing of political nostalgia, with freeing ourselves from such paralyzing and pernicious myths of origin.

This is a bracing, and at times quite troubling vision. It is somehow more comforting to rely upon narratives and myths in the construction of a moral vision. Yet history simply does not lend itself to the artificial simplicity of poetic narratives and originary myths. Growing up sometimes involves giving over the fairy tales. I believe that such a giving over is not a giving up. It is necessary, in the way most political and religious truths mean to be.

Narratives have clear beginnings and endings (they also have complex middles, as we shall see). That is part of their artifice, and grand simplicity. The problem with a great deal of modern discourse is that we lack any clarity about precisely when we think the story of "modernity" began, and thus what we think "modernity" actually entails. If we date the modern age to the intellectual tumult that separates Montaigne from Descartes,[4] then these issues look one way. If we date the birth of the modern age somewhat earlier, tracing it to certain intellectual developments of the High Middle Ages,[5] then the issues look rather different. Across a variety of disciplines and a host of theories about the advent of modernity, one constant is the central place occupied by classical antiquity. Something of the remarkable intellectual synthesis that was the High Middle Ages owed it origins to the rediscovery of Aristotle via the mediation of Islamic scholars and scribes. We know of Montaigne's and Descartes' immersion in the Classical tradition (Roman in the one case, Greek in the other). Modernity, in this case conceived as a profound absence, is precisely the absence that comes of living "after Greece."

What this book[6] has to contribute to this debate, I hope, is the insight that the moralists have looked in the wrong place for the enduring legacy of Classical thought. Those moralists, like Alasdair MacIntyre,[7] who wish to find in Classical Greece a vision of moral community and moral harmony that escapes us in the modern world are simply ignoring the political and historical facts. They are looking in the right place, but for the wrong thing. Classical Greece was no moral high water mark, by any stretch of the narrative imagination. The pre-Classical and Classical traditions of tragic and erotic thought, however, continue to be a rich resource for many modern perplexities and problems. I have devoted much of my scholarly energy to re-thinking precisely these traditions.

II

There is doubtless a certain irony in titling this, my second book, "*After*words." That might seem a title better suited to the conclusion of an academic career than to its inception. Put even more strongly, the hubris involved in titling one's early books this way might even be considered, as it proved to be in Nietzsche's case, a prophecy and a premonition—namely, that this will indeed be a series of "last words" . . . , my own. *In* the academic world but not *of* it, this book might be viewed as the testament of a young scholar—*too* young, for the kinds of global arguments he is making—on his way out of the academy. That is not my desire, although I deliberately write with passionate conviction and more than an occasional polemical edge of my own. The times demand that, it seems to me. These are polemical days in scholarly and political and religious circles. Republicans and Democrats squabble about the future of Liberalism. Conservatives and moderates in the Southern Baptist Convention squabble about the inerrancy of scripture. Philosophers of all stripes squabble about the meaning of truth and truthfulness in moral matters. I did not start any of these fights, anymore than I have invented the polemical language of antimodernism. But I consider the ideas which are at stake in these debates well worth fighting about. My rhetoric is, among other things, a quite conscious and deliberate attempt to win my way into this debate—in the hopes that, once that has been established, I might have the time, perhaps even the audience, to continue to work on more constructive intellectual alternatives to some of our reigning academic and ethical orthodoxies. Simply put, I hope to replace what I have elsewhere called "the tragic posture"[8]—a constellation of pervasive attitudes which are deeply characteristic of our modernness—with something more genuinely akin to "the tragic vision" as the preclassical Greeks articulated it. My first book was about the tragic vision, particularly as Hegel and Nietzsche—building upon Sophocles and, in Hegel's case, the gospels—envision it. This is a book about the tragic posture, a modern posture defined by a fascinating range of "after-words."

I remain troubled by the fact that this book has a rather negative, and highly critical, tone. I see no avoiding that right now. This is a fairly polemical set of arguments, and was so long before I began my graduate study. I envision this book as a sort of ground-clearing, a sweeping away of a whole range of modernist assumptions—primarily assumptions about "the Greeks," which in turn lend a peculiar perspective on our alleged "modernness"—which I have always found rather shallow and self-serving. That clearing is performed in the earnest

hope that, once accomplished, more serious reflection upon these serious matters may again take place. That more constructive process of critical thinking—
an attempt to show how Greece's richest legacy lies not in moral and political
philosophy at all, but rather in tragic and erotic literature—will be the task, I
hope, of yet one more book . . . and of a lifetime.

Perhaps a brief remark is in order about the conceptual history of this project. It began as a much denser, and significantly longer, doctoral dissertation
in which I tried to explain what I thought the tragic posture was, and how inadequate it appeared when compared to what the Greeks themselves had said
about similar matters. In essence, I now see (as I ought to have seen more
clearly at the time) that I was trying to do two things at once. Those tasks are
now separate. This is a book—again, a highly critical book—about the tragic
posture. Alasdair MacIntyre in moral philosophy and Stanley Hauerwas in
Christian ethics are taken to be among its most eloquent and influential
spokespersons. The two books which sandwich this one are about the *tragic vision*, on the one hand, and its relation to the rich *erotic* tradition of the preclassical Greeks, on the other. Hegel and Nietzsche are my primary influences in
charting out the tragic vision, although Nietzsche also figures prominently in
the argument I am trying to make here.

My sense of what we might, for lack of a better word, call "the erotic vision"—that which mediates the realms of tragedy and of philosophy—is deeply
informed by Plato, whom I consider a probing and insightful poser of erotic
questions. These three tasks, then—tragic posture, tragic vision, erotic vision—
while clearly separate, are still intimately related, and there will clearly be some
overlap. In order to distinguish them more clearly, perhaps a further word is in
order about the genealogy of this project, about how it has acquired the provisional shape it now has.

III

I have enjoyed the happy opportunity to teach in a rich and diverse depart-
ment of religion, where I enjoy the most enviable schizophrenia (something
which is not nearly as schizophrenic as is normally alleged—one of the motifs
with which I will be playing throughout this manuscript) of teaching courses
on the theological and ethical traditions we now know as "Christianity," as well
as courses in which I try to take Classical Greek and Roman paganism seriously
as a religious tradition with real coherence, and an enduring claim upon our
sense of ourselves in an ill-defined place called "the West." Indeed, the Christian tradition itself—as a coherent outgrowth, like Rabbinic Judaism, of the
Hellenistic Jewish world—became what it is today largely through its inges-
tion and internalization, not its elimination, of Classical and Hellenistic tradi-

tions. This book, which is designed to be a critical analysis of what we say about ourselves as modern people, is grounded in these twinned and inseparable poles of my own thinking—the Judaeo-Christian on the one hand (a terminology which, despite its obvious shortcomings, I continue to find instructive and heuristically appropriate in North America) and the Greek (or Greco-Roman, an equally vague and ragbag category which nonetheless clearly means *something*.)[9] What I make of most modern arguments depends on my own Classical and historical training. This is the foundation for my skepticism regarding modernism's many afterwords, the notion that we are coming apart, somehow, living *after* an earlier age of coherence and real meaning.

I begin my course in Christian ethics with the so-called "social gospel," with readings designed to exhibit what North American Christians were saying about themselves and about their faith's social and ethical implications—all of this at the turn of the century. Now, near that same century's end, I am increasingly struck by the similarity of contemporary moral arguments made by those who bemoan our alleged loss of a sense of the commonweal in the face of what is termed an "erosive" and "liberal" individualism. 'Individualism' is not a bad word, I wish to remind these modern thinkers. That is the central message of Nietzsche's early Classicism, as well as my message in chapters 1 and 2. It was certainly *not* the message among Greek thinkers, such as Aristotle, who are currently being invoked to make the antiliberal, antimodern case.

One of the themes which I will try to underscore in this book is my belief that there is nothing new under the sun, intellectually speaking, that some of the most apparently radical or reformative ideas which animate social and ethical debate today—such as the remarkably popular book, *Habits of the Heart* and its emphatic blurring of the line between public and private matters—are not so new at all. Indeed, the *Habits* people, as well as the communitarian and feminist theologians who sound many of these same prophetic notes, are, in some profound ways, returning to the turn of the century, to the language of the Social Gospel. Beverly Harrison's story of Christian origins,[10] like Stanley Hauerwas',[11] is very much like Walter Rauschenbusch's.[12] Their agenda of social reform, particularly its emphasis on economic justice and the distorting forces of industrial capitalism—is quite similar as well. That insight—that it has all been done before, in its own way—might help us to recover a sense of humility which is so glaringly absent from many of the rather strident moral debates, and the more outrageously antiliberal arguments, we hear in North America today. Surely it calls into question our peculiar scholarly penchant for privileging our own sense of crisis.[13] Modernity, to say it again, is not new.

I have been much impressed by the emerging insight that a coherent "Christian ethic" requires a careful distinction between two sorts of "first questions" which need to be answered in turn. The question "What is Christian?"

has a certain obviousness about it. Yet it takes a peculiar form in light of a second question which needs to be spelled out clearly, since it is implicit in what so many contemporary theorists are trying to say—namely, "What is modern?" It is particularly striking how radically inconsistent competing answers to these questions can be among thinkers who all claim to be doing the same kind of work. In this prefatory word, I would like to sketch out some tentative trajectories of my own thinking about these matters, since this manuscript as a whole is designed to render an alternative account of the answer to the second question, the question of our modernness. The best I can do at this point is to call our times "peculiar," well aware as I am that there are no times which have *not* been.

IV

Responding to the dilemmas of the modern age is not simple, I am arguing, in part because there is no simple answer to the prior question of what we mean by "modern." The balance of this book will be devoted to an attempt to unpack what a variety of scholars have said about this vexing question. What is it about these peculiar times? I find the amount of "modernist" literature almost overwhelming; the word is on the tip of every scholarly tongue—yet I seldom know with any clarity what (or when) anyone specifically thinks the word means. Perhaps it will be a good first step to say what I do *not* think our "modernity" entails.

This book is grounded in the belief that our modernity is neither as new and novel, nor as calamitous and disjunctive, as is customarily asserted. That is a large claim, probably worth repeating. Now new. Not novel. Not a calamity. Not radically discontinuous with the *pre*modern, whatever *that* was. I have been much impressed by the presence of so many "after-words" in modern discourse. It has become a compelling, if not compulsive, topic of conversation to discuss what it is precisely that we come *after*. "The imagination," says Wallace Stevens, "the imagination is always at the end of an era." Scholars love a good crisis, in order to have something exciting to talk about. So it is that we are told we live in age which is "after" or "beyond."

We live *after* a coherent sense of community, *after* the Greek *polis*, *after* virtue, which is to say *after* Nietzsche and thus probably *after* the possibility of morality itself. We live *after* Christendom, perhaps *after* the possibility of religious belief, in what we like to think of as an "*after*math." Finally we may even live *after* modernity itself, whatever that was, in an age we now pretentiously label "*post*modern." The sins of pride and pretense run deep among philosophers and theologians. I will devote a chapter, respectively, to each of the ideas I have listed here. That is the narrower purpose of this book.

I do not see our modernity as the necessary loss of meaning and the collapse of religious faith or of religious institutions. Thus, I cannot agree with Stanley Hauerwas that we live "*After* Christendom," or that we are "living amid fragments." The old myths and scriptures still mean, even if they do not mean to us in an era of "higher criticism" precisely what they have meant to others. Every generation has retold the old stories, and reinterpreted them in the light of contemporary problems. That is what theology is for. Our scholarly skills can help us to do so without nostalgia, without romanticizing the past as a bygone era of moral harmony which eludes us now.

Nor is our modernness characterized by a rampant and incoherent individualism. Individualism is not a bad word, and I think the various scriptural religions are very much in the business of promoting individual voices and of nurturing individual human excellences. Not at any cost and not to any extreme, to be sure. The claims and requirements of the community *do* place limits, *necessary* limits, on any individual's so-called "rights." But communities remain the places for the promotion of individual human flourishing. Their goal is the promotion of self-sufficiency. This Aristotle knew well, as I try to show in chapter 2.

I am not particularly impressed by those who bemoan (and even less so by those who celebrate) the fact that our world has grown so much smaller, that we are all so "global" and "cosmopolitan." The United States of America, the single most powerful and pervasive empire in the world right now, is also at times an embarrassingly parochial place. We seem to suffer from an unusually high level of cultural *in*sensitivity, and incredibly poor knowledge of the places into which we send our military, our businesses, our own very distinctive culture. The ideology of the melting pot perhaps makes us believe too quickly that we can, and do, take it all in. Perhaps. But it need not do so. The only thing which frustrated me more about the "Gulf War" than the casualties (and our outrageous inattention in reporting them) was our complete absence of knowledge of that region. No one thinks of Iraq as a place steeped in biblical history, to say nothing of its being one of the cradles of something we call "civilization." It is a telling fact that biblical archaeologists were among the most vocal opponents of the carnage. Most U.S. citizens, who claimed to be so ready to kill in the name of protecting Kuwait's sovereign borders, did not know where these borders came from, or when, or who drew them. *Europeans* drew them, after the First World War and the collapse of the Ottoman Empire.

The invocation of something called "empire" is interesting, because the word bears connotations at least as much cultural as they are military. The empires we study were not institutions designed solely for the organization and advancement of military machinery. The empires which continue to matter to our own historical consciousness are those which made an historical, and thus a *cultural,* impact on the world they left behind. Many of them—the Alexandrian, the Roman, the Byzantine, the Ottoman—were profoundly multi-ethnic polit-ical organizations. A pressing "modern" question is whether they were also multicultural, or whether a certain kind of civic belonging carried with it the pretense of henoculturalism, if not monoculturalism.

What needs saying first is that this fixation upon matters "multicultural" is a deeply North American concern. And what seems at least arguable at this point is that we are engaged in a fascinating experiment right now, trying to do something which may well have *never* been attempted before—namely, the creation of an imperial system which is both multi-ethnic and multicultural. So it is that nostalgia of any form will not help us. We are being asked to envision a world which has never yet been.

Rome is an empire which impresses me more the more I study it for its cos-mopolitanism, which is to say, its ethnic and cultural awareness—things which put European and North American empires to shame. As citizens in a nation of unparalleled military power and influence, we bear the unique historical bur-den of that responsibility. I take very seriously the historical accident which places me in this nation at this peculiar time. In one century, or perhaps five, the United States will not be what it is now. And it is not so very long ago that our forebears were living in one-room log huts. We were a comparatively poor country until comparatively recently. We forget so quickly, and suffer from the pretense of believing that the way things now are is the way they have always been, the way they need to be. My commitment to "higher education" in North America is very much motivated by the unique responsibilities which United States citizens face in these days of North American ascendancy. Our duty—so long as we are here, and so long as we are so powerful—is to chase down foot-notes, to read critically, to cultivate a healthy level of intellectual mistrust—mistrust of nostalgic postures, whether political or religious—to ensure that our democratic institutions promote the disciplined putting of a certain set of ques-tions—even and especially before we are prepared to kill in such horrible num-bers as we did in the "Gulf War." Wisdom is a skill which requires practice; it atrophies when it is not exercised.

There is a profound sense of apocalypticism and of crisis which animates much of the modernist debate. The world, thanks to Europe, has experienced two world wars of seemingly infinite destructiveness, and at least one holocaust (a word which I decline to capitalize). I must confess, with some pain and mis-giving, that I am not certain how new and altogether unique I think these events were. Surely for us they seem to be. But, then, it is *our* century. I *do* recognize that the body-counts are new, that the military technology means that the num-bers get bigger, and the bombs get smarter, every year. But the experience of "total war," and of deliberate ethnic cleansing, do not seem to me to be the unique legacy of the twentieth century. They certainly do not define our "modernity." I do not *know* how different our own crises are. I only know that the world wars and the holocaust—Auschwitz and Hiroshima are two modern buzzwords—loom over this century, as they loom over "modern" moral and theological debate.

What we need badly is a good grounding in history, a more panoptic sense of the historical moment in which we all happen to find ourselves. This century began as a profoundly *European* one. It will end in a decidedly *North American* manner. In both cases, technology makes this so. Marshall G. S. Hodgson, to whose work I will return in chapter 5, went to great lengths to demonstrate how China's extraordinary inventiveness fueled the emergence, and then the ascendancy, of the European nation-states in the sixteenth century and thereafter.[14] It is a matter worth pausing over to realize how much *American* inventiveness in the past century and a half has changed the world we now know. Centuries hence, our own inventiveness may well be seen to have helped to create the new ascendancy of Japan or China, in their turn.

One can tick off a seemingly endless list of inventions, apart from which our world today is unthinkable, and thus "unmodern": steam engines, electric lights, automobiles, airplanes, phonographs and then magnetic tapes and then compact laser discs, lasers themselves, microchips and then computers, cinema, rockets capable of flying to the moon and lunar modules capable of landing on it, the atomic and hydrogen and neutron bombs. If you were as impressed, and horrified, as I was by PBS' "Civil War" series, then you might well wonder if the United States did not also leave the world with a legacy of total war, in which casualties of an impossibly high order became first acceptable, and then common. Surely the European nations watched in horror as this conflict went on year after year, glad to be far away from it. But then this American invention was perfected there, in Europe—first at Verdun and the Somme, and then when civilians were drawn onto the battlefield in the saturation bombing so characteristic of the Second World War.

Most all of these inventions have had a profound *cultural* impact. People all over the world listen to North American (and some British) pop music—on technologies *we* invented. Everyone seems to be wearing Levi's and college sweatshirts (even when they don't know where Harvard is) and baseball caps (even when they don't know how to play) and business suits (even when they are too hot and restrictive to be reasonable). English has become *the* international language—in much the same way that French was in the last century, and Latin was in the European Middle Ages, and Greek was in the eastern Mediterranean, after Alexander's conquests and throughout the days of early Christian expansion.

Is ours a "new age"? I honestly do not know. I continue to have my doubts. But it is a ridiculous question, since it is not ours to know. The word 'modern'

comes from the Latin *hodiernus,* which simply means "contemporary." Therefore, by definition, I do not know what it would mean to be "postmodern"—
how, after all, can one live *"after* today?" I will return to that dilemma in the
fifth chapter and again in the sixth. For my part, I have no more desire to retreat to some vaguely defined Golden Age than I wish to leapfrog ahead into
some equally vague notion of postmodernity. I have my hands full, in the here
and now.

V

At this point perhaps I may return to an earlier question—of what "Christian"
means—and what the Christian tradition has to contribute to debates about our
always new, always bracing "here and now." The question of Christian identity
is not my primary concern here. The prior question—of "modern" identity—
is. Yet a few tentative observations are probably in order, since I will use Christian history in the fourth and fifth chapters to concretize some of these claims.
Christianity is a test case, a test case of scriptural religious identity in the modern world.

If nothing else becomes clear, and really prominent, in a majority of modernist literature, it is the following curious paradox: Modern people are, almost
by definition, antimodern. They pose the "here and now" as a *problem,* a problem to be solved. It is a curious way to think about the world. Another paradox
grows out of this one. My own interest in religion in America began in my fresh-
man year in college (1979–80) when Jerry Falwell's "Moral Majority" was so
much in the news. *Fundamentalists are also profoundly antimodern,* and have
(at least in the Christian tradition, and at least in North America, where the term
was coined) attempted to define the Christian faith as the key *alternative to* our
allegedly incoherent "modern" way of proceeding. I am impressed by the content of some of what the fundamentalist theologians have to say, precisely because it parallels so neatly what a host of other (anti)modernists are saying. It
is not only the technology of our modernity which the fundamentalist movement in North America is willing to use for its own purposes. They use the modernist self-understanding, too. I turn my attention to this paradox primarily in
chapter 5. I do not share their first premise: *namely, that modernity is a unique
problem to be solved.* This very curious paradox—the paradox of modern antimodernism—is well worth reflecting upon.

So, we have inherited this curious intellectual landscape in which *most*
moderns, and nearly *all* fundamentalists, are antimodern. Many of those Christians who are not fundamentalists, especially in the so-called "Liberal"
churches (whichever ones those are) seem to be nearly anti-Christian, given
how much of the "tradition" they are prepared to give over. Another level of al-

leged modern schizophrenia: *Christians who are anti-Christian*. The extraordinary challenge which feminist theology raises for the Church is a good case in point. It remains unclear to me exactly why those women who have not elected to leave the Church, as Mary Daly has done so emphatically, remain in the Church, given how much of the tradition they find oppressive, and sexist, and wrong. I am glad, and powerfully impressed, by their courageous refusal to leave, yet I think they often owe us a more positive account of specifically why they stay.

They, along with many other Christians I suspect, are much less threatened by the feeling that things are up for grabs. Things always have been up for grabs. The gospels are up for grabs. They probably always will be. And in the midst of that belief—that men and women are born to trouble as the sparks fly upward, that *self-consciousness* is both the unique problem and the unique promise of the human way of being—Christians try to live faithfully in accordance with their beliefs about the limits of human understanding and the absoluteness of God.

You cannot read the literature in the New Testament without being powerfully impressed by the sense that here, too, was a world in which nearly everything was up for grabs. Christianity is not a "European" religion, historically speaking. It came "west" at a comparatively late date. By the time it did so, Israel was a nation, an empire, no longer. It had successfully thrown off the yoke of "Greek" oppression in the Maccabean revolt (144–142 BCE), but the new Judean dynasty of the Hasmoneans lasted less than a century. The Romans came in 66 BCE and made Judea a province on the outskirts of their vast eastern empire. Despite two Jewish revolts of horrible destructiveness (66–70, 132–135 CE), it seemed pretty clear to most of the Jews in Roman Palestine that the Romans were here to stay, and that the *political* kingdom they had been expecting was apparently not what this was all about. These are the political questions, and the spiritual dilemmas, of Hellenistic Judaism, the context out of which Christ's teaching, and Paul's, and then the Christian movement itself, emerged. Matters of cultural assimilation (the Greek question), political self-understanding (the Roman question), the nature and continuity of the covenant (the messianic question), the role of Jerusalem and the Temple (the imperial question), were paramount—as they had been in countless ages past. As you chart out this new movement's growth, it is clear that Christianity became ever more Greek, ever less Jewish, until it seems finally no longer Jewish at all. The emphatic *universalism* of their message in any case is clear from the outset:

- the Messiah has indeed come,
- but he was not the political and military leader we expected,
- in fact, he left without saying when he will return

- but he left us with the commission to preach *to the whole world*
- because Judaism's God, the only God who ever was or will be, is now positioned to become the God of everyone, again. In Hosea's lovely phrase, "not my people are my people, says the Lord."
- in the eyes of some committed and rabbinically trained Jews in the first century of the Common Era in Roman Palestine, it looked as though it was time to let God go, and to let God *be* God, for *everyone,* even for their traditional enemies (the book of *Jonah* is an instructive example of this same idea).

When I say that everything was up for grabs, I do not mean merely that there was political turmoil, although clearly there was that. Rather, the Jewish world, under Roman rule, was becoming much larger. Greek culture was inescapable, much as North American culture is now. Greek language was a practical necessity, as English is now. If a singer wants to sell records today, he or she records in English, no matter what country he or she is from. If you wanted to preach a message of God's *universal* "good news" then, you had to do so in Greek, even if you were from the middle of nowhere, in the east, in a Roman province called "Palestine." We "moderns" have not invented such problems and concerns. Yet we sometimes speak as if we have done so. Our failure is a lack of historical understanding, a failure of awareness about what we are doing elsewhere in the world. Greeks and Romans knew better than we do, it seems to me, how disruptive (*and* simultaneously inescapable) their way of life could be. Christianity, after all, really took off in Greece and Asia Minor, not Palestine.

For the purposes of my argument in this book, I treat Christianity as more of an historical phenomenon than as a simply biblical one. Narratives, even biblical narratives, can distort and deform important insights. That historical narrative will be paramount in chapter 4. Modern theologians seldom really deal with the Bible in great detail, unless they are self-styled "fundamentalists." That is because theology's task always has been, and always will be, the translation of biblical ideas into contemporary idioms, for the addressing of contemporary problems.

In my own thinking, I tend to gravitate to Jesus' character and teaching more than I do Paul's, but for the purposes of this book I will concentrate on what I take to be Christianity's central image: the essential gesture of *forgiveness*. Apart from that fundamental image, it seems to me that Christianity itself is nearly unthinkable. It seems to lie at the heart of the message of reconciliation the earliest Christians preached. It is an extraordinary message. God has given us a gift—the Greek word is *charis*—and our duty is to accept it and pass it along. To love one enemies is hard enough personally, but *Israel* is also being told to love *its* traditional enemies—Greeks and Romans, primarily. It is almost as if North Americans were being told to love and include Iraq in their moral economy—imagine preaching this, in North America, if Iraq had done to us what we did to her, and then occupied us in addition. God, these people were so rash as to claim, is changing the game. Things are not as we expected at all. Gone is any nostalgic desire to recover a lost paradise; the theological gesture is profoundly forward-looking, envisioning a world which has never yet existed.

The moral task—perhaps at least as difficult as the forgiving itself—is to feel forgiven (and, naturally, "to sin no more," a lingering and long-standing moral dilemma for the Church). This idea seems to represent a profound step beyond Greek moral thinking. Aristotle's "great-souled man"[15] is very liberal with the bestowing of gifts, as I will show in chapter 2. But he does not want to need anything, himself. His radical autonomy seems almost isolationist at times. Not so the Christian. He or she is called to be at least as gracious in the receiving of gifts as in the giving of them. And it is extremely difficult to have the grace of receiving a gift well.

Here is where feminist theologians have made a crucial contribution to Christian theology and to moral thinking, in my judgment:

> I shudder to think how many times during my years of theological study I came upon a warning from a writer of Christian ethics not to confuse real, Christian love with "mere mutuality." One senses that persons who can think this way have yet to experience the power of love as the real pleasure of mutual vulnerability, the experience of truly being cared for or of actively caring for another. Mutual love, I submit, is love in its deepest radicality. It is so radical that many of us have not yet learned to bear it.[16]

I am struck by the stridency in a great many contemporary moral debates, at least in North America where I live, and especially in our theologies and our politics. We moralize everything—our art, our religions, even sex and romantic love. That same kind of moralistic presumption seems to lie at the heart of too many modernist claims.

VI

Perhaps the most jarring and outlandish notion in this book will be this idea—namely that, our technology aside, we are no more "global" or "cosmopolitan" or "multicultural" today than the ancients were. Worse still, implicit in my argument is the suggestion that we may be *less* so, by and large.[17] Our airplanes, telephones, computers, and rockets have not altered that fact very much, as nearly as I can see. They have, in all likelihood, contributed to the main problem, which is the problem of presumption in self-understanding, to which I turn in chapter 5. When academic knowledge is itself mass-produced, *we haven't the time* to acquire the global perspective and sense of wonder at the world's vastness which any credible intellectual ought to have. The merest glance at Herodotus and Thucydides, at Shakespeare and Marlowe and Jonson, puts a great deal of "modern" academic writing to shame. These people *know* that there is a vast world out there. They know how different it all can be. Yet they *also* know, as Hegel knew, that there is no such thing as "pure difference." If something were totally and completely different, then it would remain a mystery to us, would in fact be totally alien and therefore unintelligible. Even so particular a thinker as Aristotle knows this: "Anyone may see, in the course of travelling," he insists, "the bonds of recognizability [*oikeion*] and even friendship [*philon*] which link every human being to every other."[18] Herodotus' Lydians and Egyptians, Shakespeare's Venetians and Romans and Greeks—all are exotic and alien, dressed in the glittering fabrics of the far away, yet they are somehow as near to us as our own skins. That is not simply because Herodotus has made over his Egyptians in Greek dress—he *travelled* there, extensively, after all—or that Shakespeare has taught his Greeks to speak the Queen's English. The artistic facts are a little more subtle than that.[19]

I will say many times that "the problem" with us is the way we *assert* our differences rather than argue carefully for them. We have told ourselves a story about our "modernness"—a story of fragmentation and confusion, which is to say, the myth of decadence—for so long that we have actually begun to believe it. By "us," I mean primarily the intellectual community. Academics seem to be in the *business* of trying to get a handle on what is "different" about "us." Sociologists certainly are. I do not want to write off such intellectual projects—I am, after all, an academic myself. Neither do I wish to write only for such a community. It is one of my sincerest hopes that this book will find friends *outside* of my own discipline—which is religious studies—and *outside* of those too-high university walls and Gothic cloisters. One of my surest convictions is that the increasing departmentalization and specialization of the modern university—and here the problem is the "scholarship" and the "university," not "modernity"—has made it increasingly difficult for people who really should be talking to one another to do so. Too many local conversations, totally unchecked by contact with "those outside." Too many books being written, too little time to read them, and too little real substance, real spirit, in what they say.

Many will want to argue that I have ignored the "inside" this way, that I have conveniently side-stepped my academic obligation to read more than I have done. There is a potential problem in that my book lacks the footnotes, and the erudition, and the scholarly breadth to defend the grander and more outrageous claims I am making. I know of no easy answer to that objection other than to say that I reject the premise. I cannot write that way, and I suspect that very few people really can. The life of the mind—a life that I have been very lucky to enjoy for some years now and for which I am sincerely grateful—is like a love affair, in its best moments. Yet it takes place, at the same time, in the musty loneliness of the library, ideally with one or two well-loved and well-worn books close by. I will be making a great deal of that endless alternation—between society and solitude, the Agora and the Acropolis, the marketplace and the mountaintop—in this book. Human life is always lived between these poles—even and especially a scholar's life.

I know of no simple way to "justify" the lives scholars lead. We do not really "produce" anything tangible for long periods, and it is often unclear what we are doing at all. The best justification I have ever been able to articulate is that my "job" involves reading a hundred books or more, in order to be able to point out to my students the six or seven which are absolutely wonderful and essential.

That is also a part of the task of this book. It is, in large measure, a response to six or seven books which have become very precious to me. They are books which I have read many times, books which have helped me to think about things new and old—myself most of all—in new ways. I have used them to help orient myself amidst the dazzling and rather dizzying array of modern self-portraits, one or two books at a time, and I have tried to bring each of these books into dialogue one with another, and all with the (Greek) past.

In a prefatory first chapter, I want to introduce some notes for a little-known essay called *Wir Philologen* on which Nietzsche worked sporadically between 1874 and 1876. It was never completed and thus never published, though I for one wish it had been. I spent a lovely month translating the essay while I was living in Athens, privileged to be seeing things about which Nietzsche himself could only dream and write. Nietzsche is antipathetic to nostalgic or romantic construals of the past, and I must confess that I find his account of the Greeks' enduring significance far more instructive and truer to the historical and archaeological record than most antimodernists', at times, overdrawn polemics and postures. Nietzsche has helped me to dwell with the Greeks, to think about them in ways which will be evident on nearly every page of this book as well as its epigraph.

In the next two chapters, then, I am reading Aristotle's *Nicomachean Ethics* (actually his *Politics,* too) along with what several people have had to say about them. First and foremost, there is Alasdair MacIntyre, whose enormously influential rereading of the Aristotelian tradition in *After Virtue* first got me started on these topics some nine years ago. There are other voices in this rediscovery of Aristotle, but MacIntyre's seems to me to be drowning out the rest—all except one, as we shall see.

Turning from philosophy to theology, I devote the fourth chapter to Stanley Hauerwas' *After Christendom?* and then a longer chapter, the fifth, to Bruce Lawrence's recent study of global fundamentalism, appropriately entitled *Defenders of God*.[20] I have been richly blessed to call both of these men teachers, and now friends. I trust that it is understood that my disagreements with them are, while quite possibly still the ranting of an upstart student, also intended to be an indication of how much they both have taught me, and how much their presence in my life means to me now. Each of them has read and responded sensitively to all of the criticisms I have made in this book, placing me even deeper in their debt.

Finally, in the last chapter, I take the time to muse over Charles Taylor's *Sources of the Self*,[21] perhaps the most probing, and exhausting, book in this short list, as a way to summarize many of the issues with which I am wrestling throughout. In his work, we see an essential Nietzschean premonition come to fulfillment, the premonition of antimodernism. In Taylor's work, the essential *posture* of such antimodernism become clearest.

When I take the time to mention each of these books' popularity, I am not trying merely to be topical. Nor, by contrast, do I mean to be casting a sneering glance down the length of a too-long scholarly nose. *The New York Times,* despite MacIntyre's strident objections, is no "parish magazine of affluent and self-congratulatory liberal enlightenment."[22] It is a serious journal in the serious business of discussing serious topics. I have always been impressed by their editorial mission, particularly in the two years when I lived abroad, and clung to that paper, when I could find it, like a lifeline. Rather, I take these books, and their popularity, to be significant pieces of evidence in the self-portraits modern thinkers paint. What the *Times* editorial staff worries about is what we all worry about, to one degree or another. If these books that I am reading have had a place there, then all the more reason to assume that they are significant elements of the story we tell ourselves—in "the modern age." These books have been the shapers of a language and the creators of a vocabulary that are now an essential part of the modern brainscape. They, too, constitute a part of what it is for *us* to be "modern."

In addition to these books, there are others which stand behind most everything I have written here. First and foremost is Martha Nussbaum's *The Fragility of Goodness*[23] (and more recently both *Love's Knowledge*[24] and *The Therapy of Desire*[25]), books about which I have written elsewhere, and which continue to amaze me each and every time I take them up. Then, too, there is a short essay called "The *Iliad,* or The Poem of Force," composed by Simone Weil in 1943. I can still point out the classroom on the East Campus of Duke University where I read that essay during my sophomore year in college. I have been living "after" that long night ever since. The way I understand the phenomenon we call "Greece" is deeply indebted to both of these remarkable women, as I hope to show clearly in what follows.

Finally, there are the Greeks themselves. Trying to define who and what they were is the subtext of this entire book. It is the explicit goal of the book which preceded this one, as well as the one which will follow it. I suspect that I will spend a lifetime sorting that question out, and I do not expect to have definitive answers, now or later. My allusions to the Greeks—to Homer, to the poets, to the historians, to Plato and Aristotle—are all pretty self-explanatory. What I am trying to show is that when we look back at them, free of the modern prejudice about how radically "different" they were, then we can, with Martha Nussbaum, "see how true they are to us—that is, to a continuous historical tradition of human ethical experience." "The problems of human life," she adds, "have not altered very much over the centuries," and the Greeks will always be a key resource in evaluating "our own persisting intuitions about value."[26]

When I jump back and forth this way, reading our most eloquent modernists *against* the Greek tradition, and thus against the grain, I mean to make us pause over this word—'modern'—which has been so trivialized through academic overuse. The word is not, and should not be made into, a proper noun. When we call ourselves "modern" today, we *seem* to want to say that we are "different" somehow, radically and paradigmatically so. A closer look at who the Greeks actually were and how they really lived makes it a little harder to say, with any kind of precision, what we think is so different about us and our age. There is very little articulacy about what it is that we allegedly come "after." In the decadent narrative of decline and fall which all of these modern thinkers share to some degree, Greece is a kind of Ithaca—the measure of a distant fall from grace and innocence, the object of all our spiritual aspirations for a homecoming. My conclusion will be that, in most important ways, we never lost the island. It still lies off to starboard, glistening in the mist. It lies *ahead* of us, not behind. Our inability to see it, or else to confess that openly, is where we are beginning to fail—as scholars and, infinitely more important, as people.

Notes

1. *Republic* 546a.

2. *Republic* 369b.

3. *Republic* 514a.

4. As Stephen Toulmin does, in *Cosmopolis: The Hidden Agenda of Modernity* (The University of Chicago Press, 1990).

5. As does Louis Dupré in his *Passage to Modernity: An Essay on the Hermeneutics of Nature and Culture* (New Haven, CT: The Yale University Press, 1993).

6. In tandem with my first book, *Tragic Posture and Tragic Vision: Against the Modern Failure of Nerve* (NY:Continuum Press, 1994).

7. Most notably in *After Virtue,* 2 Edition (South Bend, IN: The University of Notre Dame Press, 1984). I will examine his arguments in Chapters Two and Three.

8. Ruprecht, *Tragic Posture and Tragic Vision,* 11–25.

9. For a powerful indictment of the continued use of this Hebraic-Hellenic dichotomy, see Vassilis Lambropoulos, *The Rise of Eurocentrism: Anatomy of Criticism* (Princeton: Princeton University Press, 1993). While Lambropoulos has helped me to see how a high a price *Hellenism,* not Hebraism, has paid by being endlessly compared and contrasted in this way, I think the terms continue to have an important heuristic value—as descriptive terminologies when applied to the Hellenistic Jewish world, to say nothing of the contemporary North American educational context.

10. Beverly Wildung Harrison, *Making the Connections: Essays in Feminist Social Ethics,* ed. Carol S. Robb (Boston: Beacon Press, 1985), 216–22.

11. Stanley Hauerwas, *After Christendom? How the Church Is to Behave if Freedom, Justice, and a Christian Nation Are Bad Ideas* (Nashville, TN: Abingdon Press, 1991), 23–44.

12. Walter Rauschenbusch, *Christianity and the Social Crisis* (Louisville, KY: Westminster/John Knox Press, 1907, 1991), 44–142.

13. See Frank Kermode, *The Sense of an Ending* (Oxford University Press, 1966), 30–31, 94–98.

14. Marshall G. S. Hodgson, *The Venture of Islam: Conscience and History in a World Civilization* (Chicago: University of Chicago Press, 1974), III, 176–208.
Hodgson calls them "the gunpowder empires," in fact, and sees them as the *necessary* prelude to "modern times.:

15. *Megalopsychos, Nicomachean Ethics* 1122a20–1125a35. See also Aquinas' *Commentary on Aristotle's Nicomachean Ethics,* translated by C. I. Litzinger (Notre Dame, IN: Dumb Ox Books, 1993) 227–51.

16. Beverly Wildung Harrison, *Making the Connections,* 18.

17. Strabo, writing in the first century, is really pertinent on this point in a fascinating discussion of his contemporary academic historians. "Although they set out to prove that the men of earlier times were more ignorant of regions remote from Greece than the men of more recent times, they showed the reverse, not only in regard to regions remote, but also in regard to places in Greece herself." (Strabo, *Geography* VII.3.§7). For the Greek text of Strabo, I am using the Loeb Classical Library edition

edited and translated by Horace Leonard Jones (Cambridge, MA: Harvard University Press, 1924, 1979), III 194–95.

18. *Nichomachean Ethics* 1155a21–22.

19. My thinking about these and other matters has been decisively shaped by Marguerite Yourcenar, particularly her historical novel, *Memoirs of Hadrian,* translated by Grace Frick (New York: Farrar, Straus & Giroux, 1954), most especially her "Notes on the Composition of *Memoirs of Hadrian,*" 319–47. See also Georg Lukács, *The Historical Novel* Trans. Hannah and Stanley Mitchell (London: Merlin Press, 1962) 60–61, 89–90.

20. *Defenders of God: The Fundamentalist Revolt against the Modern Age* (San Francisco: Harper & Row, 1989).

21. *Sources of the Self: The Making of the Modern Identity* (Cambridge, MA: Harvard University Press, 1989).

22. Alasdair MacIntyre, *Whose Justice: Which Rationality?* (South Bend, IN: University of Notre Dame Press, 1988), 5.

23. *Luck and Ethics in Greek Tragedy and Philosophy* (Cambridge: Cambridge University Press, 1986).

24. *Essays in Philosophy and Literature* (New York: Oxford University Press, 1990).

25. *Theory and Practice in Hellenistic Ethics* (Princeton: Princeton University Press, 1994).

26. Nussbaum, *The Fragility of Goodness,* 15.

A Premonition

1

After Nietzsche?
When Un-modern Turned Anti-modern

> Yes, hateful slander existed
> even in ancient days:
> partner of flattery, sly evil-doer.
> It casts brilliant things in shadows
> and brings to light
> a rotten glory
> better left in the dark.
> —Pindar, *Nemean 8*

In creating a compelling story of modernity—which is to say, the nostalgic passion-play of a decline and fall *into* modernity—it is essential to determine how to begin. The most cursory survey of the dramatic literature of modernism displays an astonishing array of possible beginnings. So it is that Luther or Calvin, Montaigne or Descartes, Newton or Napoleon, Kant or Hegel is posited as "the first modern thinker." I am *not* making this claim about Nietzsche. Indeed, this book is designed to call precisely such narrative periodizations into question.

I wish to begin with Nietzsche, not because I take him to be the first modern thinker, whatever that would mean, but rather because I think that we can trace out an important trajectory in his career which will illumine much of my subsequent thesis. We see Nietzsche erupt onto the scene in the early 1870s with an eloquent attempt to think against the contemporary grain, to think outside of his own times in a manner he calls "unmodern." Later, in the wake of his growing disaffection with his reception (or nonreception) in Europe, Nietzsche begins to think *against* his times, to envision what he begins to call a philosophy of the future, and a world yet to come. Nietzsche transformed himself from an unmodern thinker to an antimodern one in the space of a single decade. And his perspective on the Greeks lies at the heart of this dramatic change. These facts bear closer scrutiny than they normally receive. From unmodern to antimod-

23

ern, via the Greeks—this is the pattern which we will see again and again in the course of this book.

I

Much has been made recently of Nietzsche's later "perspectivism"—the conviction, that is, really quite logical for a thinker who has called the value and intellectual utility of truth into question, that where we stand in fact largely determines what we can see.[1] "The concepts 'true' and 'untrue' have, it seems to me, no meaning in optics"[2]—this Nietzsche tells us explicitly, rather late in his career. One is tempted to say "*in the realm* of optics." But this is not what Nietzsche says. The omission is, in fact, a large part of his point. There *is* no other realm. All the world's an optics, a perspective, an (optical) *illusion*. Now this was surely pretty radical stuff in Nietzsche's day, and seems to have been an insight to which he came at a remarkably early date.[3] It is already implicit in the notes and complete essays for his enormous cultural project normally translated as "untimely meditations."

Yet Nietzsche's views can be radicalized still further. It was, in point of fact, his chief intention to do so. It is not merely the case that where we stand determines what we see, what we are *capable* of seeing. Many thinkers have said that much. Rather, we ourselves are able *to choose* what we see, as well as what we do not see, that which we have opted to ignore. And this fundamental choice may often prove to be the most important choice of all. Less a selective blindness, this is really a call to genuine insight, to spiritual selectivity—the mature doctrine of necessary fictions,[4] and the general "aestheticism" which is so deeply characteristic of his later thought.[5]

This matter needs to be concretized; it was in fact an extremely concrete matter for Nietzsche when he first confronted it. The issue centers around a crisis which came fairly early in Nietzsche's career, a crisis which focused less on Nietzsche's vision of the university system and its failure to live up to his own soaring educational vision,[6] than on his view of the "modern" cultural crisis, particularly in Germany, and its implicit, vital link to the ancient Greeks.

The matter is a broad one, and will take some time to sort out properly. It is further complicated by what we know of Nietzsche's personal history and intellectual development in this same period. The years of his appointment to a chair in classical philology at Basel from 1869 to 1879 were explosive, formative ones for the young professor.[7] He was the *only* young scholar ever to be nominated to such a position without having first completed his own writing program. He was only twenty-four at the time. The singularity of his career was matched by the singularity of his educational vision. He was an accomplished scholar already, trained in the minutiae of the philological discipline; but more than this, he was a scholar of profound *vision,* and an even more stunning intuition into the real nature of the past. (This reference to "reality," like his allusions to "truth" in this same period, bear a complex relation to Nietzsche's later writings. They seem to be bound up in intuitive value-judgments which are thought to promote an abundance of life. He clearly believed that the Greeks were masters at this.)[8] Nietzsche seems to have realized, as most of his philological contemporaries had not, that in order to unmask the past, in order to appropriate it to the cultural demands of the present, in order to make Greece a *living* commodity in the German-speaking countries to the north, then certain things (like the moral writings) needed to be ignored which had been occupying scholars' whole attention. And other crucial realities needed to be called up from the depths, things of which most scholars remained blissfully unaware. That is the central insight in *The Birth of Tragedy Out of the Spirit of Music.* At a relatively early date then, this perspectivist offered the philological community a whole new perspective on the Greeks they all claimed to be studying. It is a perspective which, for all of its own attendant problems and developments, is still sadly lacking in most contemporary Anglo-American narratives.

Matters are complicated by two related issues. On the one hand, as the scholar *cum* free spirit, Nietzsche playfully insists upon his right to change his perspective, to make rhetorical and poetic—rather than scholarly—sense. He is intent upon uncovering new truths, on casting his glance into every dark corner which has been occluded in the shadows cast by the harsh lights of staid academics and bad philology. But more importantly, *Nietzsche's mind was changed on a number of central issues in precisely this same ten-year period.* Thus there remains some real question of continuity, and of potential inconsistency, within his chief philosophical writings, early and late.

That seminal decade in Basel saw Nietzsche through many of the defining crises of his intellectual life: the troubling break with Wagner, the only real genius Nietzsche ever knew at first hand, after several appalling spectacles in Bayreuth;[9] the philosophical break with Schopenhauer,[10] whose deep pessimism came gradually to seem more a symptom of the times than their antidote; the disappointing failure of his first book, *The Birth of Tragedy,* in 1872 and 1873;[11] and perhaps most profoundly, his gradual disaffection with and rejection of, not merely the scholarly community of which he had tried so long to be a part,[12] but also—most painful of all to him—"German culture" itself.

The programme of essays which Nietzsche began to collect under the rubric of *Unzeitgemässe Betrachtungen* ("Unmodern Observations")[13] span this crucial period of crisis and, while variously outlined in his notes to himself,[14] were conceived on a massive scale. Intended to number thirteen in all, they would have explored topics as diverse as religion and culture, sociology, psychology, musicology, and, consistently, education . . . all in the name of revitalizing Germanic culture, prompting a new renaissance under the aegis, once again, of the ancient Greeks. Given this intention, given as well where Nietzsche himself first chose to cast *his* scholarly glance, the massive notes which he collected for an essay entitled *Wir Philologen*[15] take on a singular importance—as his most sustained early conversation with the preClassical Greeks, and at the same time, with the Classical philologists of his own day. It was Nietzsche's dawning convictions about what was right and what was wrong in the philological perspective which animated some of his best insights in this period. By 'philology' Nietzsche refused to be confined to the hyperlexicality of classical scholars, pouring over their endless emendations and desiccated manuscripts. "It would be a shame," he quips, "if antiquity should speak less clearly to us because a million words stood in the way!"[16] Philology, Nietzsche insists, ought to be a spiritual and educational exercise, aimed at self-overcoming and the creation of genuine culture in oneself and in one's times. He consistently defines this virtue in this period as "a unity of style"[17]—all of one's spiritual powers integrated in the singularity of an aesthetic quest. And the Greeks remained Nietzsche's lodestar throughout his creative life—as a source both of spiritual inspiration *and* an impetus to surpassing cultural achievement in his own age.

> If Greek culture is really understood, we also see that it is gone for good. Thus is the philologist *the great skeptic* in our cultural and educational circumstances. That is his mission.[18]

The philologist as *skeptic,* not *Übermensch.* Here, if anywhere, are insights—again, formulated very early—which Nietzsche never gave over.

II

What, then, was the main point of *Wir Philologen*? What was *Nietzsche's* perspective on the classical tradition? Difficult questions to answer. Nietzsche characteristically fights on many fronts at once, and the notes for this essay are characteristic in their breadth and intensity. But the question *can* be answered, and it seems to me that the answer is crucial for a more-than-superficial understanding of Nietzsche's development in this period. The essay is, for me, one of the most important things he ever wrote, and would have been among his loveliest books, had he ever seen it to completion.

What I want to argue is that *Wir Philologen* is far more than a parting shot fired across the ship of academic state—an academy which Nietzsche was, even then, determined to leave behind. Still less is it merely a pictorial, imagistic presentation of the philologist-as-*Übermensch,* the pedagogic soul of a rejuvenated Germany, over against the petty, technical expertise and bourgeois cultural philistinism of his academic contemporaries.[19] That is where Nietzsche's individualism turns crassest, becoming what Alasdair MacIntyre will, in the next chapter and using pseudo-Aristotelian terms, call "beastly." Rather, I see *Wir Philologen* as a sustained and sophisticated reflection on the ways in which perspectives on the past and present are intimately related. "Philologists are such people as would use the stunted feeling of modern men concerning their own vast inferiority, all to earn a living," Nietzsche warns. "I know them. I am one myself."[20]

I have already identified this collection of scholarly *prejudices,* past and present, as "the tragic posture."[21] I would now like to read *Wir Philologen* as Nietzsche's single most sustained engagement with this distinctively "modern" posture, and thus as the most unmodern of his many observations—all of it undertaken in the name of a vision which seemed more authentically "tragic" to him, a vision which was, moreover, *Greek* to the core. Reading Nietzsche this way, and reading this essay in particular, we may be better able to see what in Nietzsche's perspective did not change, what did change, decisively—and often for the worse—as well as where and in what manner Nietzsche's vision is singularly relevant to a variety of contemporary perplexities and problems. He is still "unmodern," even to so late and so postured a "modernity" as our own.

What perspective does Nietzsche invite us to take on the tragic posture? A dramatic analogy best makes the point which wants making here. There is something deeply compelling, but also deeply artificial, about all great art, dramatic art first and foremost. A single *perspective* is given to us, and we are not really permitted to look at the theatrical world in any other way. The play begins in a manner which will help the poet, and us as well, get to the very ending he or she has in mind. "That which is taken for a beginning is always a deception," Nietzsche reminds us.[22] The play is a closed circle whose beginning *destines* us to a certain kind of end. I have made this point before, and will surely do so again. That is the secret, and the subtle artifice, of all good storytelling. It is this essential deception which is part of the artist's mission—aesthetic fictions, again.

> The Greeks were terribly plagued by a love of fables. . . . Every poetic people has such a passion for lying, along with a commensurate innocence. The neighboring peoples must have found this unbearable.[23]

Nietzsche's main point is elegant and simple: in a narrative, every beginning and ending are of a piece.[24]

What, then, is wrong with the stories the modern philosopher and philologist are telling? They are so deeply pessimistic about the "modern" situation—

a prejudice which is part and parcel of the tragic posture—that they have constructed a romantic image of the past *against which* to measure their own decline and fall. The past had in tremendous abundance the very things we no longer have. Their cultural richness is an indictment of the spiritual sterility of modern times—as though Schopenhauer and Wagner did not exist, as most classical philologists were content to pretend that they did not. Wagner's promise, in Nietzsche's early judgment, lay in his *cultural* power, his potential to give a tradition of authentically national theater—as a total, unified dramatic experience—back to contemporary German-speaking culture. Hence the depth of Nietzsche's disappointment at Bayreuth: a whole cultural, and modernist, dream was dying in a decadence more profound than Nietzsche had yet understood it to be.

Another dimension to the pessimistic modernism which Nietzsche was combatting was its *fatalism*. We will return to this notion in some detail in the third chapter. Pessimism tends to exploit this same concept—"modernity"—as somehow the inevitable *fate* of the contemporary world. Things have not changed so very much in the past century; we are still fatalistic modernists by and large, at least within the iron cage of the academy. There is simply nothing to be done about modernity. It defines who we are, more often than not, for the worse. "Is tragedy possible," Nietzsche asks us rhetorically, "for him who no longer believes in a metaphysical world?"[25] The modernist answer seems to be, No. The gods have all died, and tragedy died when they did. The only theater left to us—apart from Wagner's megalomaniacal self-indulgence—will be a theater of the absurd or else, as Hegel feared, satire and farce which, however well-intentioned, mark out the vast terrain of cultural decay.

Such a portrait of the modern situation as a Fall from the pristine purity of the past invokes tragic language explicitly. We are all reeling in the midst of a tragic cultural crisis, so the argument runs. It does so because it believes, rather disingenuously, that tragedy is about "unhappy endings" pure and simple—as we are allegedly "ending," unhappily, now. This view Nietzsche rejects out of hand.[26] He does so both factually and philosophically. Factually, Greek theater gives the lie to any such teleology. "Fragility, not Teleology," was the battle-cry of the tragic stage, as we will see more clearly in chapter 3. Aeschylus, so far as we know, wrote only trilogies. That is to say, a deep crisis in the moral order is presented in the first play, but it is resolved in the third. Sophocles, too, began by writing trilogies, none of which survive intact, but then he later took to writing single plays. All the more telling, then, that three of Sophocles' seven surviving plays also *end well*. Nietzsche himself made much of this fact in *The Birth of Tragedy*.[27] It is only with Euripides that disaster begins to play a larger role in tragic drama. I suspect that this is precisely what Nietzsche considered so Socratic, and therefore decadent, about him (much as Aristophanes did in

The Frogs). That had become pretty much a canonical orthodoxy in the preceding generation, blaming the "end" of the Greek theater on Euripides.[28] What is surprising, and really very unusual, is to see Nietzsche accept an academic orthodoxy so uncritically.[29] It is precisely Euripides who troubles scholars so because he has left us a number of tragedies (or rather "tragicomedies" in our modernist double-speak) which defy scholarly classification *precisely because of the way they end.* The *Helen,* the *Iphigenia at Tauris,*[30] and the *Alkestis*—all raise the same issue because all end well. To say it again: Greek tragedy is not, and never was, about unhappy endings or simple disasters. Aristotle observes quite clearly that, given the choice, anyone properly put together would prefer a happy ending where it is possible.[31] Tragedy is, in fact, not particularly interested in endings at all. It is modern people who are interested in that.

This leads us to the related philosophical issue. In fact, tragedies do not *end* badly. They *begin* badly. They begin at a point of outrageous human suffering, of a crisis in expectation and in the moral order. And regardless of how they end, the tragic genre is an inherently *affirmative* genre. We are all elevated somehow by the strangely pleasurable suffering we have witnessed.

> The passion in Mimnermus, the hatred of age.
> The deep melancholy in Pindar: only when a ray of light comes down from above does human life shine.
> The world is to be understood out of *suffering*—that is the tragic in tragedy.[32]

Tragedy presents us with a deep paradox: we are witnesses to pain and suffering on the stage, and yet we derive pleasure in the process. It constituted a lifelong philosophical endeavor for Nietzsche to come to terms with this fact, to appreciate the essential dramatic miracle we have all experienced. Greek tragedy stands at an infinite remove from simplistic categories like "optimism" and "pessimism," since it is not finally interested in the way plays "end." Resolved or unresolved, tragedies are about *a certain kind* of spiritual crisis—what Hegel called a *Kollision*[33]—something from which, however agonizing, meaning can be found (found, not made, as the more simplistic narratives of our day would have it).

Now the inconsistency between these penetrating insights and Nietzsche's untrammelled hostility vis-à-vis the Christian tradition should be clear. For the dominant assumption, in Nietzsche's day as well as in our own, is that Christianity is an "antitragic" faith by definition—that it cannot allow tragedy the last word in human affairs because it is too invested in a narrative order which must "end well." If there is any truth to Fitzgerald's dictum that Americans "all believe in the green light," then Nietzsche views the claims of Christians as even more superficial (in the case of Stanley Hauerwas, as I will argue in chapter 4, he may well be right). They believe in lights they cannot see. Christianity is grounded in a hopelessly optimistic (an interesting oxymoron, that) view of the world, too deeply committed to the principles of resolution even to appreciate the tremendous challenge which tragedy presents to its view of the world. To open oneself fully to the pessimism which tragedy preaches would be to move "beyond" Christianity, or rather beneath it, just as surely as Christianity attempts to move "beyond tragedy." Now such a view, while oddly compelling at first glance, is more deeply indebted to the posture than it is to careful argument. It is surely a bit too simple when dealing with a faith which preaches at its heart a crucified god.[34] And in any case, this postured refusal of Christian theology relies on the very sloppy categories of optimism and pessimism, as well as this fixation upon (unhappy) endings, which are the chief trademarks of the tragic posture. They are all things which Nietzsche, at his best, rejected out of hand.

III

So much, then, for the chief intellectual assumptions which constitute the tragic posture as I have defined it. If I have gone into greater detail rehearsing those four points here, it is only because I think that Nietzsche was so deliberately engaged in thinking about all four. How does the Nietzsche we meet in *Wir Philologen* line up over against this posture?

Extremely well, it seems to me. In fact, the notes for this essay represent the most systematic engagement with this constellation of ideas known to me in Nietzsche's *Nachlasse*. The two starting points—beginnings and endings, past and present—are most easily dealt with. They are, after all, the *leitmotif* of the entire essay. Winckelmann and Goethe had essentially rediscovered Greece for Germany[35]—and in rediscovering her, they had also revaluated her, recasting her in a vaguely German image, while animating her at the same time with new spiritual life.

But the legacy of this rediscovery, at least within the German academy, had not been a particularly happy one. The philological community was willing to see only a fantasy world of their own devising,[36] a world less true to the past than it was a utopian sublimation of classicist desire—classicists who were themselves entirely unsatisfied with the "modern" world in which they lived. This is the "Quixotism" of classical thinking to which Nietzsche objected so strongly. "There are things about which antiquity instructs us," Nietzsche says, "which I am hardly able even to say openly."[37] Greece was, in the final analysis, an *aesthetic* and not a political or moral ideal.[38] Nietzsche notes this pithily, in a passage from the Seventh Notebook which had such importance to him that he italicized all of it:

> *The philologist needs to understand three things, if he wants to prove his in-nocence: antiquity, the present, and himself. His guilt lies in the fact that he understands neither antiquity, nor the present, nor himself.*[39]

As I have said many times now, interpretations—or less kindly, *prejudices*—about antiquity and modernity are always of a piece. Beginnings and endings hang or fall together.

The reasons for this are not far to find; we have alluded to them already. Philology has created a mythical haven for itself, an Ithaca to which it longs for return. It is a perspective which refuses to look at what it does not want to see. A romanticized classical antiquity and a pessimistic rejection of the present as somehow "modern" are flip sides of a common coin—an academic escapism of the worst sort. "The *flight from reality* to antiquity: isn't the interpretation of the past falsified in precisely this way?"[40] He continues: "Greek antiquity is a collection of classical examples for the clarification of our whole culture and its development. It is a means to understand ourselves, to correct our times and thus to overcome them."

What, then, stands in the way of completing this essential cultural task of overcoming? "The pessimistic foundation of our whole culture," Nietzsche replies.[41]

What I find most intriguing about Nietzsche's engagement with the tragic posture is how nicely it traces out the areas of real development, and occasional degeneration, in his mature thought. His primary insight—that the Greeks are surpassingly important, but for reasons which are as unmodern as they are for-eign to the philological community—stands. He had been dissatisfied from the very start with Winckelmann's self-satisfied talk of the "noble simplicity and quiet grandeur"[42] of the Greeks. His attempt to recover the *Dionysian* elements of theatrical experience is a product of this dissatisfaction.

Nietzsche himself, however, bows to the postured disdain for "modern" times later in his career. What began as a rather narrow disenchantment with cultural philistinism and the politicization of post-Hegelian Germany grew into a far broader rejection of German culture and the Teutonic style—a style which he characterizes as corrupted by a strict diet of local newspapers, Wagnerian music, and warm beer. Still later, Nietzsche's rejection becomes nearly univer-sal: he calls all of Europe, and finally the entire modern world, into question. His mature doctrine of *décadence*,[43] what he calls his "nose for decay," is itself postured and overdrawn, according to his own earlier standards. He is no longer *un*modern; he has turned *anti*modern. And that is where his classicist polemics give way to the tragic posture.

By contrast, Nietzsche's reflections on tragedy and the nature of tragic suffering represent the most consistent dimension to his thought which, if anything, achieve ever-greater prominence, eloquence, and conviction. Nietzsche calls himself the first tragic philosopher. The tragedy he envisions embodies suffering, to be sure, but suffering of a very definite kind. Tragedy is an *ennobling* estate. "Tragedy is the form that promises us a happy ending," Walter Kerr observes. "It is also the form that is realistic about the matter."[44] The Greeks do not deceive themselves; suffering is itself an eminently Hellenic motif.[45] But in their best moments, the Greeks took suffering and turned it into some of the finest poetry the world had yet known.

> By Homer's time, the Greek spirit was largely complete. . . .
>
> With them, we understand how bitter and cruel life appears! They do not deceive themselves. But they play around life with the drama of lies. Simonides says to take life as a game. Seriousness was all too familiar to them— as pain. Human suffering is a pleasure to the gods, since they will get a song out of it.
>
> This the Greeks knew: that only through art can pain become pleasure: *vide tragoediam.*[46]

Whatever else this means—and it meant *many* things to Nietzsche, at a variety of moments in his own life—it indicates decisively that tragedy is not about optimism or pessimism, pure and simple.[47] These categories are inadequate. And that is one of the most enduring and consistent themes in Nietzsche's thought.[48]

This takes us to the final issue of Nietzsche's problematic and exceedingly complex relationship to the Christian tradition. He is, in these early years, still a far cry from the cheap anti-Christian polemics of his later works.[49] It is quite odd, then, that the same man who speaks so eloquently of tragedy as a way beyond the optimism/pessimism dichotomy should himself fall back on these same categories when it comes to discussing the Christian tradition. The spirit of Christianity—a ressentimental spirit of *décadence*—overcame the tragic integrity of the heroic and classical world, he says.[50] This same tragedy—and here the word *does* connote unhappy endings—played itself out again when the spirit of a rejuvenated antiquity we call the Renaissance, was done to death *by* Christianity, this time in the guise of the *German* Reformation.[51] "Rome against Judea; Judea against Rome"[52]—*that*, Nietzsche insists, is a timeless antagonism.

All the more remarkable, then, is this note, which flies in the face of so much which Nietzsche had already said, and would go on to say with ever-increasing vehemence.

> Christianity has overcome classical antiquity—that is too easily said. First of all, Christianity is itself a part of antiquity; secondly, it preserved antiquity for us; and thirdly, it was never really at war with the pure spirit of antiquity.[53]

Christianity *as a part of* antiquity, as the preserver of antiquity . . . one idea which consistently occupies Nietzsche's attention in this period is how one gains access to the Greeks. And in this period he wrestled frankly with his clear knowledge that our only access to the Greeks comes by way of Christianity, as well as what he calls "Alexandrian culture." That is to say, the only books we still possess are those that Alexandrian scribes and medieval monks thought fit to copy over. So it is that a decadent culture is in the same sense, inescapable. It has mediated all that we know of the Greeks to us.

> "Enlightenment" and Alexandrian culture is the matter—in the best of cases!—that philologists want. Not Hellenism.[54]

Over against this scholarly prejudice and narrowness of vision, Nietzsche notes another way of gaining access to antiquity. He sees something of this in Goethe: "This is the way Goethe grasped antiquity: always with a competitive spirit. But who else?"[55] That is to say, apart from scholarly decadence, there is another (Goethean, agonistic) incorporation of preClassical ideals, a virtual leapfrogging of the Christian-Alexandrian moment, in order to get from modernity *back to* Classical antiquity. We use the very best of the Alexandrian and Christian syntheses . . . in order to overcome them. Now, Nietzsche's reasons for admitting here what he himself elsewhere denies are also illuminating:

> Better to say that Christianity continued to be braced up by antiquity, needed to let itself be overcome by the spirit of antiquity—that is, by the spirit of the Imperium, of the community, and so forth. We suffer from the extraordinary impurity and confusion of *human affairs* . . . [56]

The problem is also the impurity and confusion of the *humanities,* the sloppy philology which insists on speaking of Greek and Latin antiquity in a single breath, of Athens and Rome as if they were of a piece. That academicians, theologians particularly, continue to do so will become clearer, I hope, in chapters 4 and 5.

> *Our relationship to classical antiquity is the real reason, the essential reason, for the sterility of modern culture:* this whole modern concept of culture is something we get from the Hellenized Romans. We must distinguish within the phenomenon of antiquity itself: when we get to know its really productive period, we also *condemn* the whole epoch of Alexandrian-Roman culture. *And*

yet we condemn our whole attitude toward antiquity and our entire Philology
at the same time![57]

IV

"We must distinguish within the phenomenon of antiquity itself." That is the
methodological heart of Nietzsche's perspectivism, *his* perspective on the phenomenon of antique culture. 'Greece' was never synonymous with 'Athens'—
not even culturally—until a very late date. That is an Alexandrian prejudice.
"Greece" is a scattered collection of islands and local cultures with no center,
a menagerie of artistic styles and perspectives which are not easily harmonized:
from Asia Minor, through the eastern islands of the Dodecanese and the central
Cyclades, and finally westward to the mainland, with Crete beckoning to the
south. We will be moving away from Athens, southward toward the Aegean islands, in a moment.

But first, to say it again: Greece embraces not a single antiquity, but several—Nietzsche's Greece chief among them. This Greece is not many things
which we might expect it to be. First and foremost, it has nothing to do with
Rome. Rome did not preserve the best parts of classical antiquity, for Rome was
already *décadent*.[58] "How much power does man have over things?—that is the
central educational question," Nietzsche insists. "Now, to demonstrate how
completely different it all can be, point to the Greeks. We need the Romans to
show how things got to be as they are."[59]

> The Greeks are the only people of genius in world history. Even as learners,
> for they understand learning best, knowing enough not strictly to decorate and
> to glitter with borrowed adornments—as the Romans do.[60]

Not only are Greece and Rome *not* synonymous, but Rome actually *contributed*
to Greece's undoing. There are fascinating moments in which Nietzsche seems
to suggest that the *pax Romana,* far from being the triumph of the late Hellenistic age, merely made the Greek world fat and lazy. Where struggle has
become a thing of the past, there a form of cultural vitality has grown old.
Moreover, Rome tilled the soil and made it ready for Christianity—which, as
we saw, in Nietzsche's later view perpetuated the worst of it all. Taken together,
Rome and Christianity did the very *memory* of an older, healthier Greek antiquity to death. Gaining access to this past anew is the essential educational and
philosophical task.

Another thing which Greece quite clearly is not—and again the legacy of
Rome misleads us—is a political or military high-water mark. According to
Nietzsche, after the seemingly miraculous victories against the Persians—first
at Marathon, and then later at Salamis and Plataea—Athens had started down

the path, not to world-historical importance, but rather toward inevitable military defeat and cultural irrelevance. Her best days were already behind her, though her empire had hardly begun. Taking the aesthetic turn so characteristic of his later thought, Nietzsche insists that Greece was an *aesthetic* ideal, never a moral or political model for our own, or any, times.

> The political defeat of Greece is the greatest failure of culture, for it brought in its wake the hateful theory that one may only nurture culture if one is at the same time armed to the teeth, that it is all done with boxing-gloves. . . .
> In this manner, Sparta [we should add Rome also] was the ruin of Hellas. It forced Athens to establish a centralized confederacy and to cast her lot completely upon politics.[61]

These are comments clearly directed against Nietzsche's contemporaries. Prussian troops held to define a nation which was quick to interpret military victory (against France in 1871) as a validation of its own cultural superiority.[62] Culture, Nietzsche insists over and over again, is not concerned with *that* kind of power.

Nor is it about racial integrity, which was another alarming aspect of the contemporary German cultural scene, what Nietzsche censured most explicitly as "philistinism." Using the offensive notions of racial "purity" and "blood" to his own rhetorical purposes (and against those anti-Semites like Wagner and his own brother-in-law[63] who liked them), Nietzsche explodes the philological, Aryan myth of ancient Greece in the most deliberately jarring terms.

> *First habitation* of Greek soil: Mongolian origin, with tree- and snake-cults. The coast bordered by Semitic raiders. Thracians here and there. The Greeks took all of these ingredients into their blood, and all the gods and the myths with them (much of the Odysseus-myth is Mongolian). The Doric incursion was a later military thrust, after which all the antecedent elements gradually coalesced.
> What are "the Greek races?" Is it not enough to say that Italians, coupled with Thracian and Semitic elements, became *Greeks*?[64]

Here, in a single brilliant sketch, Nietzsche manages to antagonize the racist theoreticians of his own era, underscores his own respect for Renaissance-culture and *Italian* (rather than German) philology, and de-emphasizes the importance of military power in the cultural course of things. These were, then as now, "unmodern" observations in the best sense.

Even racially, Nietzsche is saying, the Greeks were never one thing. It is ridiculous to look for that kind of unity. Any unity we find is one we impose ourselves—the first law of perspectivism. "We must distinguish within the phenomenon of antiquity itself." Philology is, as it must be, shot through with

Figure 1.   Front view of Fallen Warrior, Temple of Aphaia, West Pediment.

perspectivism: there are many different Greece's, and the philologist needs first
to decide *which* Greece he wants—and *why*. One of the chief convictions which
animates Nietzsche's whole essay is the intuition—which flew in the face of
academic orthodoxy then, but has since been completely vindicated—that
"Greece," or at least the first in a long line of Greece's, was far older than anyone had yet realized. In an early letter (1872) to Erwin Rohde, Nietzsche is quite
clear about this:

> Oh, that I would never again hear that effeminate image of the Homeric world
> as a youthful place, the Springtime of the world, etc.! In the sense that is ar-
> gued, it is simply wrong. That an uncanny, wild struggle—emerging out of a
> darker, gloomier, more savage time—preceded him, and that Homer stands as
> a conqueror at the end of this desolate period—that is among my surest con-
> victions. *The Greeks are much older than we think.* You can talk about Spring
> only if you put the Winter first. This world of purity and pristine beauty did
> not simply drop down from heaven.[65]

And again, three years later, in the notes for *Wir Philologen:*

> Men today marvel at the gospel of the tortoise and the hare—ah, those Greeks
> simply ran too fast. I do not look for happy times in history, but rather for times

Figure 2.   Temple of Aphaia, West Pediment, Glyptothek München.

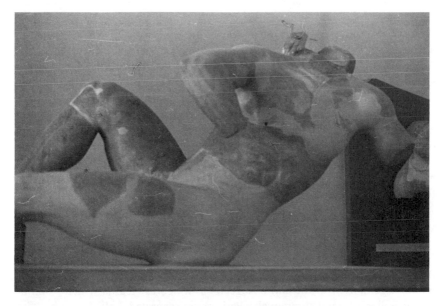

Figure 3.   Front view of Fallen Warrior, Archaic Parthenon, Akropolis Museum, Athens.

which provide soil suitable for the cultivation of genius. This I find in the times prior to the Persian Wars. One cannot learn enough about them.[66]

The implications of this perception are profound. Some of them we meet consistently in Nietzsche's later thought: the way he privileges the pre-Socratic philosophers and calls Socrates decadent by comparison; his preference for Aeschylus and his insensitivity to Euripides' manifold dramatic gifts; his polemical and nearly universal Roman/Christian scorn. But there is something else at stake for Nietzsche here, something which lies at the heart of the tragic posture, something which is both unmodern *and* antimodern, by turns. It is the single most important aspect of the essay, tossing the gauntlet down at the feet of the philological establishment, and at the same time charting out a vast territory for a lifetime of creative thinking.

You believe that Philology is at an end—and I believe that it has not yet even begun.

The greatest events which Philology has yet experienced are the successive appearances of Goethe, and Schopenhauer, and Wagner. One can manage a glance backward which penetrates much further now.

The 5th and 6th Centuries are now ready to be uncovered.[67]

V

There is an island in the Saronic Gulf, directly south of the Piraeus harbor in Athens. It is a relatively large island which dominates the horizon from that perspective. Even today the rather shallow soil, which is nonetheless ideal for certain fruits and pistachios, and the soft rolling hills which make a picturesque setting for the poets and painters who have settled there, all combine to provide a stunning contrast with the rocky mountains of Attica, and the overbuilt chaos of Athens herself. The island served briefly as the capital of a soon-to-be liberated Greece in 1826, before once again yielding pride of place to Athens. The history of the island has, in fact, *always* been deeply intertwined with Athens, from prehistoric times.

That island is Aegina (Map #1). The archaeological record tells us that when Aegina was prospering economically, then Athens had fallen on hard times—and vice versa. This appears to have been the case from the Early Bronze Age. The Aegean, in a sense, was not big enough for them both. In the Archaic and Classical periods, when Athens was asserting her cultural and economic hegemony over the entire Aegean basin, it was Aegina which stood in her way, literally and figuratively. Pericles, exasperated, called Aegina "the eyesore of the Piraeus." Why?

Map 1. Locating the Island of Aegina. Reprinted with permission of *Soundings, An Interdisciplinary Journal.* (Knoxville, TN).

The question can be answered variously. And in answering it, it seems to me that we are drawing on knowledge only barely available to Nietzsche, if he knew of it at all. Yet remarkably, Nietzsche *sensed* it in the Greek history he wanted to tell, a history which he *intuited,* like Goethe, so sensitively and so well. The economic competitiveness of the area—that agonism which promotes the spiritual health of a culture, and which Nietzsche refers to as "life's school of war"[68]—exploded into periodic military conflict throughout the seventh and sixth centuries. Just as Sparta had its Messene, and Rome its Carthage, Athens had Aegina. And like them, only *after* this great conflict had been resolved, in victory, could Athens undertake any broader political program in the region. Such a program, as Nietzsche tells us, was both a sign of her own tremendous cultural endowment, and at the same time the beginning of her political end.

The conflict was a very long time in the deciding. It was punctuated and interrupted several times by influences (primarily Persian) from abroad. What happened then constitutes a fascinating chapter in the history of this part of the Mediterranean. When the Persians first came to Greece in 490 BCE, they were repulsed at Marathon by a vastly inferior Greek force comprised mainly of Athenian hoplites as well as a contingent of Plataeans. It was, of course, a land battle, and thus Aegina—the only sea-power strong enough to rival Athens at the time—played no part in it. Nor for that matter did Sparta, although we should have expected her to do so. Spartan troops arrived shortly *after* the decisive battle had already been fought—a real sticking-point for the Athenians some decades later.

Ten years later, when the Persians returned, things looked very different indeed. On the one hand, the threat was far more grave: Athens was abandoned and given up for lost; its Acropolis (as well as the neighboring sanctuary of Eleusis to the south) was burned to the ground. Defeat seemed imminent. Then the Persians were unexpectedly repulsed at sea in the bay of Salamis (480 BCE) and decisively defeated on land, again, at Plataea in the following year. A substantial majority of Xerxes' forces never made it home again.

One reason for these victories is that the Greeks did what they only rarely managed to do—to put aside their local quarrels and to present a united military front. Even here they did not do so across the board. Thebes, for one, cast her lot with Persia and lost her freedom when Persia lost the war. Aegina straddled the fence until the final hour.[69] She was not certain she wanted to fight on the side of an Athenian fleet with which she had herself been warring off and on for decades. At the last moment, she rose to the occasion and cast her lot with the united Greek fleet. And rise to the occasion she surely did. After Salamis, when the Greeks awarded a prize to the naval contingent which had best distinguished itself (a characteristic Greek competitive custom, which Nietzsche surely loved), Aegina took the first prize—much to the chagrin of Athens, which had to content itself with second place.

With the spoils and monies they won in this battle, the Aeginetans conceived an enormous temple complex to Aphaia, patron goddess of the island, whose mythical "relationship" to this particular spot seems to have been very old, yet whose history was rather obscure.[70] Suffice it to say that the temple celebrates an important *local deity*, who is at least arguably more important for being local than she is for being divine. In fact, another sea-nymph—Aegina herself—had become the bride of Zeus, bearing him a semidivine son by the name of Aiakos. His sons, the Aiakidai, were known throughout Greece—as symbols of a lost and heroic golden age—but always had a special favor for this island. First there was Peleus, who fathered Achilles, a son of even greater renown. Then there was Telamon, who is also best-known as the father of a son who surpassed him: of Ajax.

Now the Aiakidai had allegedly been seen at Salamis, coming to the aid of the Aeginetan fleet—another reason, if any were still needed, for dedicating the spoils of war in a temple to a *local* deity. But there is far more to this temple than pious thanksgiving. The temple is situated on one of the highest points of the island, boasting a stunning panoramic view of the bay and the mainland beyond. It would have been visible from almost anywhere in Athens on a clear day—the eyesore of the Piraeus, said Pericles. It surely was designed to antagonize the Athenians,[71] whose own temples lay in ashes and were not to be rebuilt (as the Parthenon we now know) for some forty years.

That later age was the age of Pericles, the great age of Athenian imperial expansion and self-congratulatory "democracy."[72] When this same Athens finally took off the boxing gloves in the Peloponnesian War, she forcibly removed all the male inhabitants of Aegina and sold them into slavery. These people were not resettled until after the thirty-year conflict had been resolved in the Spartans' favor, and the Spartans offered free-passage to any Aeginetan desiring a homecoming. We do not hear much of this awful event,[73] but we have a poet who speaks of it at length.

That poet is Pindar.[74] An aristocratic native of Thebes—Theba being the sister-nymph of Aegina—he knew what it was to be on the losing side in a war of this magnitude. He knew the embarrassment of backing the wrong tyranny. And he seems to have wandered very widely, relying upon his growing notoriety as a poet to win him homes abroad, before he finally settled down, after a fashion, on Aegina. Nearly a fourth of his extant Victory Odes (eleven out of forty-five) are composed for Aeginetans who were victorious in the panhellenic games, and this seems to have been no mean coincidence. His epinikians were presumably performed—when the performance took place on Aegina—at the Aiakeion, the shrine of Aiakos in the center of town, and the island's many local myths served as grist for his poetical mill in many an ode. In every sense, Aegina had become his spiritual and adoptive second home.

Now the curious imagery of his *Eighth Nemean Ode*[75] makes a sudden, fresher kind of sense. Pindar sings the suicide of Ajax, ancient kin of Aiakos—and of Aegina herself, since person and place are ever of a piece in Pindar. Ajax killed himself, we are told, for shame after losing the honor of Achilles' armor to Odysseus—that slippery spokesman for a newer political savvy and Realpolitik. While there is always a danger in simplifying complex poetic and mythic images, there is still a truth—an *artistic* truth, Nietzsche would be quick to remind us—in the claim that "Ajax is Aegina, and Odysseus is Athens." Or, if that seems too simplistic, then Ajax is a symbol for an older, aristocratic world which had been made to look ridiculously hollow at Sparta, and which was challenged now by the ideology of Athenian democracy.[76] That is why Pindar makes so much of the fact that a whole ethos died when Ajax (who is also Aegina) did. The Greek world was no longer a place hospitable to this older brand of heroic virtue, a world where deeds, not words alone, were the measure of the man.

> A man who was short on words
> but great of heart, now lies crushed
> in darkness, buried by bitter words.
> For the world gives first prize
> to the glittering lie . . . [77]

Ajax was the only genuinely aristocratic hero left when Achilles died—an aristocrat of the spirit, not a moneyed gentleman such as the next generation would produce in such nauseating, philistine abundance. When Odysseus, Agamemnon, and others jealously schemed to steal a prize rightfully his, they sought to cut Ajax down to a more human size—and decapitated themselves in the process.

> The Danaans favored Odysseus
> with secret votes. And Ajax
> stripped of the golden armor
> rolled thrashing
> in his own hot blood.[78]

The world has been a smaller place ever since, Pindar tells us, tied to the Procrustean sensibility of democratic ideals which Nietzsche, too, laughed to scorn.

The history of these two places—Athens and Aegina—is even more intertwined than that. When Lord Elgin and his assistants had finished carting most of the best Parthenon marbles off to England in 1811,[79] four younger men—but especially Elgin's architect, Charles R. Cockerell, who later published a copious journal of their travels[80]—opted for further archaeological work in Greece and Asia Minor, rather than an immediate return to England and Bavaria. They went first to Aegina.[81] They came immediately to the precinct of Aphaia. And no sooner had they sunk a shovel in the soil, then they began pulling whole statues out of the ground. It was a cache of complete statues, beautifully preserved, which put even the Elgin marbles to shame. In a comedy of errors even more extreme than the one Elgin himself was forced to play (he lost his shirt when the British government offered him only £35,000 for the entire collection, roughly one-half of the incredible cost of dismantling the marbles and transporting them to England), the Aegina marbles were sold to King Ludwig I of Bavaria at public auction. Ludwig was still smarting at the loss of the Elgin pieces, and may even have bribed the auctioneers, encouraging them to hold the auction on the island of Zante (latter-day Zakynthos) rather than Malta (where the sculptures themselves had been moved for safekeeping) before the French and British delegations had assembled there. Ludwig's representative, Johann Martin Wagner,[82] then purchased the entire Aegina collection for the paltry sum of £6,000.

These pedimental sculptures, depicting the two generations of Greek warriors—the generation of Peleus and Telamon, and the generation of their children, Achilles and Ajax—who went to Troy, are still housed in Munich, at the Glyptothek museum on the Königsplatz.[83] It is arguably the single most stunning Greek collection in the world. It is, moreover, a very different "Greece" from the one we have been taught to recognize. It is not Classical, although it is even more "quiet" and "still" than most of the pieces we have been schooled to expect of the Greeks. These heroes are slimmer—not so thickly muscled, and not so thoroughly *male*—than their Parthenon counterparts. Longer, leaner lines, a more elegant posture, stylized and vaguely ornamental, smiling even in death[84]—it is a whole different canon of beauty, a different *perspective,* an entirely different aesthetic (a word which derives, after all, from the Greek word for *feeling*). It is the portrait of a much older Greece—a non-Athenian and even *anti*-Athenian perspective.

It is also, I think, a Greece which Nietzsche intuited, although he lived too early to know or say very much about it. He *knew* that it must be there. Standing in the Glyptothek today, Nietzsche is still very much with us, asking a question which he will no longer allow us to put off. As with Rome before, so too now with Athens and Aegina: *which* classical antiquity do we want?

And even more disconcerting is Nietzsche's suggestion of history's ultimate irony: Athens lost the war, but captured the cultural consciousness of the world. Did the *wrong side* win? Does the wrong side *always* win?

VI

Nietzsche characteristically seized the bull by the horns early in his career, claiming to be the only true philologist, and thus implying that everyone else had fundamentally *mis*understood the Greeks. His reasons for saying so are disarmingly simple. Socrates and Plato are late, *décadent* by definition (his own very distinctive personal definition). The real essence of the Greek genius is to be found much earlier, and in places we have not been taught to expect it—in the tragedians, perhaps in the pre-Socratic philosophers, and on island oligarchies like Aegina.

It is a measure of Nietzsche's brutal honesty, and his mature critical powers, that he was forced to recognize this as a matter of perspectival *choice*. That
is to say, you pick the Greeks you want, and tell one relatively coherent story
on that basis. I choose the Greeks I want, and tell a very different story. There
is no negotiating between these stories, just as there is no accounting for personal tastes. All that we can ask of the story is that it be internally consistent,
that it possess a "unity of style." This last point seems overdrawn to me, since
everything I have tried to show up until now is meant *to defend* Nietzsche's
reading of Greece *against* the "bad Philology" of the competing readings of his
contemporaries. I will turn to other misreadings, like Alasdair MacIntyre's, in
chapters 2 and 3.

It is in this sense that Nietzsche's *philological* training underscores the
great turning point in his *philosophical* career. Until now, he has been arguing
that he and he alone understands and has appreciated the "true" Greece, intu-
itively so, in all of her splendid, even outrageous, preClassical antiquity. But
now, with his dawning sensitivity to aesthetic perspective, he feels compelled
to give over this claim. All that matters is that we tell a good story, and that we
tell it *well*. What needs to go, finally, is the concept of *truth*. There is no "true"
Greece; there are only perspectives on the past—his, and ours. While that idea
is clear enough, it does not follow that there are no philological lies. Yet Nietzsche suggests precisely this in his later writings.

This is surely cold comfort on a winter's night, but if Nietzsche's beliefs
are accepted—about life's school of war, the nature of academic and scholarly
knowledge, and the vindication of "the wrong side"—then the fact that the
small-minded classicists of his day rejected his perspective on the past where
they did not ignore it is an ironic confirmation of its importance. After all, the
wrong side always wins.

This final insight, one of Nietzsche's most intensive later convictions,[85]
leaves us sitting squarely on the fence. Put positively, it challenges. Viewed
negatively, it indicts . . . and leaves us in an eminently antimodern predicament,
either pining away for some lost age of *pre*modern wholeness, or else march-
ing triumphantly and fatalistically forward, like some curious cast of academic
lemmings, into *post*modernity. In the urgent antimodernism of the tragic posture, anxious to be anywhere but here, we retreat into a fantasy-past, or else trot
off knowingly to the *boudoir*, and the abyss.

What I want to suggest, at this stage, is that Nietzsche's insight, while fruitful and profound in the philological arena, was applied far too broadly elsewhere, in violation of his own better insights. A vitally important case in point
comes as late as 1888 in *The Antichrist*, where he offers a far more balanced
and honest assessment of the philological calling. Authors' intentions, or rather
the kinds of truths resident in texts, really *do* still matter. It is not just about

"telling a good story." Rather, the matter is *die Kunst, gut zu lesen,* "the art of reading well."

> Another mark of the theologian is his *incapacity for philology.* Under the rubric of 'Philology' should be understood, here in a very general sense, the art of reading well—of being able to read a fact *without* falsifying it through interpretation, *without* losing caution, patience, and subtlety in the desire for understanding.[86]

Our difficulty lies in the fact that the seeds for Nietzsche's eventual, and at times rather whining, antimodernism are sown in the fertile soil of some of the very best of his *un*modern philological observations. It seems to me that both elements—the Nietzschean promise and the Nietzschean excess—are well-illustrated by the subsequent history of the Aegina marbles, and their home in the Glyptothek. The history of this architectural complex provides an eloquent postscript to the story I am trying to tell, eloquent testimony to the cultural import of the tragic posture,[87] as I have defined it.

The Glyptothek, today, stands on the south side of an enormous quadrangle called the Königsplatz (see map 2), flanked to the east by the *Propyläen,* a massive neoClassical imitation of the portal on the Athenian Acropolis and facing the other major gallery, the *Staatliche Antikensammlungen* to the north. The Glyptothek was intended to house all of the major sculptures in the Bavarian collections, whereas the Antikensammlungen made a lovely home for pottery, jewelry, and other smaller artifacts. Taken together, the Königsplatz was envisioned by King Ludwig I as a neoClassical testimony to the power of nineteenth-century Bavarian Hellenism. Several years ago I was fortunate enough to have seen these collections again.[88] The Staatliche Antikensammlungen was, at that time, presenting a retrospective entitled *Der Königsplatz, 1812–1988.* It is that exhibit—its impressive display of archival photographs and drawings, as well as the excellent research guide compiled with the assistance of the Munich State-Archives—to which I am indebted for most of the history which I will review briefly here.

In the generation before the acquisition of the Aegina marbles, King Maximilian I Joseph (1756–1825)[89] had made Bavaria a kingdom to be reckoned with, one of the major political players in the region. His son, our Ludwig I (1786–1868), inherited a wealthy kingdom of considerable military preeminence. It was Ludwig who made Munich the cultural and civic center of a newly ascendant Bavaria, before his abdication in 1848 and the accession of his son, Maximilian II (1811–64). Regensburg had been the state capital before then; thus Ludwig initiated an extensive building program throughout Munich, to establish its civic preeminence, to set it in stone, and to make it illustrative of that

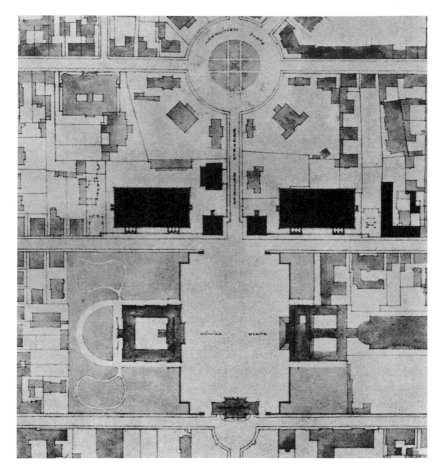

Map 2.   Plan of the Königsplatz and its surroundings after remodeling. The Glyptothek
is to the left. Black buildings to the west are all part of Hitler's new building programme
in the 1930's.

which the Bavarian *Reich* was capable of creating. It was all done in the grand
style—enormous open streets and parks, imposing neoClassical granite buildings, monumental gateways and propylaiae on the main thoroughfares into and
out of the city, but primarily along the central Maximilianstrasse. One of Ludwig's first monumental archways was dedicated to the Bavarian armed
forces—evidence of the fact that this king knew whence his power had originated and recognized, moreover, as per our previous discussion, whence the impetus for most preClassical and Classical building had come. All of these serve

Figure 6.   Paul Ludwig Troost's model of the completed Königsplatz, facing west circa 1935.

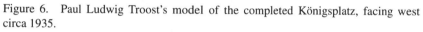

as testimonia to the crude linkage between philhellenism and military power which Nietzsche would later decry.

King Ludwig's favored architect was Franz Karl Leo von Klenze (1784–1864), who would be responsible for much that is neoClassical in Munich. When Ludwig I acquired the Aegina marbles in October of 1812, he envisioned the construction of an appropriate home for this remarkable acquisition. He and Klenze chose a site well to the north of the city proper, in an open marsh. That site is now our Königsplatz. Klenze conceived the Platz, as he conceived everything, on a massive scale: the Glyptothek was to be fronted, not by another museum, but by a neoClassical Apostle's Church—intended to marry two cultures and two worldviews in precisely the manner that Nietzsche later disallows. This plan was, interestingly enough, never realized. Ground was broken for the Glyptothek in 1816, the building was opened to the public in 1830, then fully dressed with pedimental sculptures in 1841.

Klenze had long desired to build his own version of the Athenian Propylaea, and that dream too was realized at this same time. The foundation for this massive portal was laid between 1848 and 1854—roughly overlapping construction of the Antikensammlungen—and the complex as a whole was completed in 1862. The Propyläen was itself illustratively decorated with relief sculpture depicting the Greek War for Independence from the Turks (Ludwig's younger son, Otho [1815–67], was made king of the foundling Greek republic

while still a minor in 1832, but was inconsistently popular and, after constitutional revolts and reforms in 1843, he was finally deposed in 1862).[90]

With the death of Maximilian II in 1864 and Ludwig I in 1868, developments at the Königsplatz came to a comparative standstill, save for the erection
of a monumental statue to Maximilian II in 1875. Maximilian's son, Ludwig II
(the so-called "mad Ludwig," 1845–86), was now on the throne and his architectural attentions were distracted by the erection of castles, the most famous
of which is the monstrosity called Neuchwanstein, in the Bavarian Alps. Ludwig was declared unfit to rule in 1886, and drowned himself three days later.
His reign oversaw an extended debate about the use of the Glyptothek's com-
panion-buildings. Many proposals were made: a memorial to fallen war dead
(we will be seeing much more of this idea in a moment); a hospital; the afore-
mentioned Apostle's Church; and even the Bavarian State Library. It was finally made the home for smaller Greek antiquities until 1898, when it was
transformed into the Gallery of the Munich Secession (through 1916). It then
became the New Bavarian State Gallery in 1919 and remained so until the out-
break of the Second World War.

So it is that, with the death of Ludwig I in 1868, the Königsplatz as he and
Klenze had envisioned it, was largely complete. An enormous, open arena to
the west, closed on the other three sides by massive neoclassical structures
to the south, to the north, and to the east—a home to the best Greek antiquity,
and a monument to the Greeks' newfound *modern* power—in the German-
speaking world. What remains to be told is the rather astonishing history of
what took place subsequently within this same enclosure, and for that we must
return to the sad fate of the Aegina marbles.

Ludwig had envisioned the Königsplatz as a home for this collection. They
were the initial motivation behind the entire building project. And they remained Ludwig's chief concern. It would probably be too simplistic to say that
these people were doing what everyone expected them to do, but there *does*
seem to have been an aesthetic canon in place, which determined what was to
be done with the Aegina marbles. So it was that Ludwig hired Berthel Thorvaldsen (1770–1844, a noted Danish sculptor then living among Charles Cockerell's circle in Rome, famous, among other things for a bust of Lord Byron),
who agreed to undertake the "restoration" of the Aeginetan collection. The Italian sculptor, Antonio Canova (1757–1822), also a part of Cockerell's Roman
circle, had refused Elgin's request similarly to "restore" the Parthenon Collection. What Thorvaldsen attempted in stone, I am arguing, many modernists
have done in philosophy and theology. This so-called "restoration" was, in fact,
an exercise in re-creation, of re-creating the past in one's own image, or rather,
according to one's contemporary—which is to say, "modern"—canons of good
taste. Thorvaldsen repaired chips and cracks, and—most shocking of all—re-

placed missing heads and limbs with his own work. In at least two cases, he opted for his own creations, even when the originals existed. *He simply preferred his own work.* When interviewed and asked specifically about this, about which pieces were original and which were his own, Thorvaldsen replied with characteristic bluntness and a hybristic disregard for the past that he could not see *any* meaningful difference. This is "bad philology," in Nietzsche's terms. Such was the state in which the Aegina marbles existed until twenty years ago, when the German government undertook a massive "de-restoration" project which really deserves the name.[91] Now, we can see what antiquity actually has to show us, rather than what a poorly trained nineteenth-century philhellene thought they should have shown—except in those cases where the alteration of carefully worked marble surfaces is irreparable. All of this is a gruesome record of the implicit dangers in reading our own modern (or antimodern) expectations back into the past.

I would like to move forward now to the end of the First World War. For a variety of reasons, Munich—and the Königsplatz, specifically—became an early focal point for the National Socialist Movement. Hitler's early career, in fact, could be read as an endless series of commutes between Berlin and Munich. There was an enormous demonstration held in the square on 28 July 1922, protesting against the imposition of a "false guilt" (*Schuldlüge,* and here the rhetoric of "lies" is telling) upon the German state. By 1924, plans had been drawn up for an enormous *Heldenplatz,* or "Hero's Square," an enclosed space dedicated to the memory of those who had fallen in defense of the Fatherland. The Königsplatz—with its explicit recollection of a much older, heroic age— was chosen as the logical site for such a memorial. In the rhetoric of the chief architect, in September of 1924, the link between premodern romanticism and antimodern disaffection is explicit:

> For the inner walls of the Platz sarcophagi were proposed, serving as a symbolic memorial for the Fatherland's countless martyrs—as well as symbols like palms, battle-scenes, and the like. The realization of this project here would be an even happier event, since in the past years the Königsplatz has developed into the practical political center of Munich. Its position, its size and scale, its overall arrangement—all combine to create the most suitable foundation on which to build a great patriotic movement.[92]

This plan was realized under Hitler who, working in conjunction with one of his favored architects, Paul Ludwig Troost,[93] envisioned the "completion" of the Königs-/Heldenplatz by closing off the west end (facing the adjacent Karolinienplatz) with a colossal group of no less than six neoClassical structures. Two enormous parliamentary buildings—rather antiseptic, if visually impressive at first glance—are less illustrative than the two proposed *Ehrentempeln,* or "temples of the heroes," which were meant to flank the western entrance to the square. In these open-air temples were to be reinterred a group of some sixteen fallen "martyrs" to the National Socialist cause who died in the failed *Putsch* of 1924 which landed Hitler in jail. Hitler had himself lived in Munich for a year during this same period, had directed the Party's business from here, had witnessed the deaths of his comrades, and planned one day to be buried alongside them here. He thought now to signalize his long-standing relationship to the city in a major building program which shared more with the Ludovician regime of which the Nazis were so critical than he cared to admit: same preClassical remains, same premodern nostalgia, same false identification of Germany with Greece, same imperial pretension.[94] In managing this project, the physical shape of the place was completely changed. Klenze had put the main road well beneath the level of the major buildings, at a depth of nearly four feet, in order to focus attention upon its three elevated, axial structures. Troost raised the entire Platz to the same level, covered it in granite, and by virtually fortifying the western end of the Platz, he reoriented the entire attention of the viewer away from the Glyptothek and Propyläen, and decisively westward toward the Ehrentempeln. There is a parable in this movement—from east to west—as I will argue in chapter 4. No longer a testament, however misguided and ill-informed, to Bavarian philhellenism, the Königsplatz was now fully a Heldenplatz—a testament to the overweening pretensions of the German Reich, a place in which the heroes were all German, and no longer shared anything with the Greeks at all.

Troost died prematurely on 21 January 1934,[95] thus failing to see the completion of his dream. But the place was completed with astonishing speed in 1936, at an approximate cost of some two and one-quarter million *Reichsmark.* When near completion, the following encomium was printed in the *Süddeutsche Monatshefte* for December 1935.

Paul Ludwig Troost, the Führer's greatest architect, has provided this fine memorial with the proper form—with a purity and a clarity which has nothing to do with the Classical nostalgia of the Ludovician epoch, but is founded rather on the independent and secure foundation of modern ideals and engineering. Through this he has achieved a rich cultural and symbolic image, a monumental image, an image which well characterizes the heroic path of a great political movement.

A cultural continuity and completeness now exists which did not exist here before. A real Platz has been created, a place which finally provides a secure foundation for the Greek temple buildings. So it is that now, for the first time, they stand proudly on the spot, and no longer appear to be accidental architectural bodies cast randomly about the place, as they did before.[96]

Classical Greek architectural and artistic forms have now found their proper place—testaments to the alleged "cultural continuity," an *antimodern* continuity, between things Classical and the overweening political-military designs of the German Reich. What Hitler did to the Königsplatz in 1936, he would do to mainland Greece, and even more dramatically to Crete, after 1941.[97]

It remains only to be said that most of these things did not survive the war, as little else in Munich did. The Aegina marbles, much as Thorvaldsen had remade them, were taken out of the Glyptothek for safekeeping. Every building on the Königsplatz was heavily damaged by Allied bombing, despite the Munichers' best efforts to disguise the place.[98] Most of the buildings, while all still standing, lacked roofs on Armistice Day.

The process of "denazification" (*Entnazifizierung*) began on the Königsplatz immediately in the following year. The Ehrentempeln were both dynamited in January of 1947, and the western end of the square was again opened. The Platz itself, still covered in granite, became an enormous parking lot in the late 1950s, until the "regreening" (*Wiederbergrünung*) of the place was initiated finally, after years of planning, in 1978. This project was only recently finished, in 1988, so that now the Königsplatz probably looks more as it did under Ludwig I than it has at any other time since his death.

VII

"What do these stones mean?" the children are expected to ask, after Joshua had collected them, giving them to Israel as a perpetual inheritance.[99] The question seems particularly germane to the Königsplatz today, both inside of the Glyptothek and outside of it. The same question seems to haunt all of Nietzsche's mature philological reflections. Ludwig I was, despite his many talents and insights, a product of his time, and thus the product of a sort of philhellenism which had been schooled on Winckelmann and, to a lesser degree, on Goethe.[100] He, and his Königsplatz, stand as eloquent testimonia to the implicit dangers of romanticizing the past, of finding what you want in it, of presuming to understand it better than the people who lived then could have done. In the name of an idea, he—or rather, Thorvaldsen—was actually willing *to destroy* the past, until the integrity of the stones themselves meant nothing at all. "Antiquity," Nietzsche tried to remind us, "speaks to us when it wants to, not when we do."

The "nazification" of the Königsplatz tells a related story. It speaks, as the National Socialist movement itself did, of the dangers implicit in antimodernism, especially a brand of antimodernism which wishes to leapfrog modernity on its way back to the past. Hitler came to power riding a groundswell of contemporary disaffection, and a crass rejection of all things "modern"—

Liberalism, democracy, Ludovician "nostalgia," and "decadence."[101] In the name of *that* idea, it becomes easy to ignore the past, to take from it only what you want—namely, the very military virtues which provide the standard by which to measure your own fall from grace, or better, from greatness. Bad Philology, again. Homer becomes merely a poet of the will to power, of the eternal seesaw of military contests,[102] rather than proof-positive that life's eternity is found in poetry and in music, rather than warfare. This Nietzsche himself said, briefly and passionately, but not for long. Having forgotten the message too well, a later philosophy would destroy—not the statues, which had become singularly irrelevant—but rather itself. The ironic parable of the Ehrentempeln, erected with remarkable speed and enthusiasm, only to be bombed by the Allies, then dynamited by those who originally built them, all within a single decade, tells its own tale.

I have spent more time here discussing the architecture of the Königsplatz than the Aeginetan sculptures themselves.[103] Goethe once referred to architecture as "petrified music."[104] Nietzsche, preferring the strains of poetry to the lyricism of stone, pressed this insight further, went so far even as to say that "without music, life would be an error."[105] Both claims are true enough, from the right perspective. Yet Nietzsche's later, antimodern polemics disallow the obvious point—a point which Nietzsche himself scores brilliantly against Wagner—that there is some music which is, not bad, but rather dangerous. That is the whole point of Nietzsche's "Case against Wagner," in which he repeats a single phrase to the point of monotony: "Wagnerian hangers-on pay a heavy price."[106]

> My greatest experience has been one of *recovery.* Wagner was simply one of my illnesses.
> Not that I want to be ungrateful for this illness. When I assert the proposition that Wagner is *harmful,* I will nonetheless assert that he is indispensable—for the philosopher. . . . Through Wagner modernity speaks its *most intimate* language. Modernity presents us with its good, with its evil, and has left all sense of shame far behind.[107]

Some music is clearly dangerous, however "fateful" it may be at the same time. So, too, is some architecture. It is a music which petrifies *us.* That was Goethe's point. That is Nietzsche's challenge, at least in the early period when he was working on these notes for *Wir Philologen*. In a sense, the great insight of Nietzsche's perspectivism also presents us with its most enduring problem. It is fine philology, but questionable philosophy.

If the people Nietzsche calls Romantics took the first step, then the National Socialists finished the job. The former romanticized the Greeks; the latter found in them an escape from modern times. It is this *anti*modernism which the Nietzsche of *Wir Philologen* will not allow. In his judgment, classical antiquity provides us, not with a long-lost utopia to which to return, but rather with a compelling and enduring model of greatness with which to wrestle. The Greeks, he says over and over again, are there for us to *surpass*. They call us, precisely, to *excellence*.

Nietzsche is at his insightful best when he is being unmodern. He trivialized his own perspective when he turned simpering and antimodern. The *Case of Wagner*, for all of its brilliance, is as clear a case of overstatement as one could hope to find. "Not a word I write is understood, . . . " Nietzsche concludes. "Things are bad everywhere. Decay (*Verfall*) is universal. The sickness goes deep."[108]

The sickness is not *that* deep. The wrong side does not always win. Nor is the wrong wide always "modern." Modernity is still capable of making its own kind of music, much of it far finer than anything the Nazis made. If we condemn ourselves to being "unmusical," if we tell ourselves that we have lost our bearings along with our ears, if we complain that we have grown "disenchanted" and "unlyrical"—as so many "moderns," from Max Weber onward have made a career of doing—then we ought not invoke the name of Nietzsche in defense of our despair. His philology will not come to the defense of our antimodernism. He was, at his best, singing a very different tune.

Notes

1. Alexander Nehemas has developed this point eloquently in his *Nietzsche: Life as Literature* (Cambridge, MA: Harvard University Press, 1985).

2. *The Case of Wagner,* epilogue. In every case, my citations are based on the German text found in Nietzsche's *Sämtliche Werke: Kritische Studienausgabe in 15 Bänden,* edited by Giorgio Colli and Mazzino Montinari (Berlin: Walter de Gruyter, 1967–77). So here, the citation is from volume VI, page 51 (VI.51).

3. For an interesting discussion of how Nietzsche's philosophical training led to this radical perspectivism, see Daniel L. Selden's "Classics and Contemporary Criticism," in *Arion, Third Series,* 1:1 (1990): 166–68.

4. Perhaps best and most succinctly dictated at *Beyond Good and Evil,* §4; *Sämtliche Werke,* V. 18.

5. I have been rarely privileged to enjoy what Nietzsche ever longed for—a community of colleagues who are friends as well as spiritual traveling companions. My graduate studies and my first simultaneous encounter with Nietzsche's thought, were indelibly marked by two friendships, the authors of whom are also authors of probing new interpretations of Nietzsche's thought.

The first of these is James J. Winchester's *Nietzsche's Aesthetic Turn: Reading Nietzsche after Heidegger, Deleuze and Derrida* (Albany: SUNY Press, 1994). My debts to Claude Pavur, now of Loyola University, will become apparent in subsequent notes.

6. For more on this dimension of Nietzsche's thought, and its importance to his intellectual development, I am indebted to countless conversations with Claude Pavur, whose unpublished dissertation at Emory University, "How One Lets Nietzsche Become Who He Is: Interpreting Nietzsche As a Humanist" (1990) lays out the issues persuasively.

7. See Walter Kaufmann, *Nietzsche: Philosopher, Psychologist, Antichrist,* 4th ed. (Princeton University Press, 1974), 24–30, and Alasdair MacIntyre; *Three Rival Versions of Moral Enquiry: Encyclopedia, Genealogy, Tradition* (South Bend, IN: University of Notre Dame Press, 1990), 33–35. For a fascinating contemporary portrait of Nietzsche in those years, see Sander L. Gilman's *Conversations With Nietzsche: A Life in the Words of His Contemporaries,* trans. David J. Parent (New York: Oxford University Press, 1987), 32–110.

8. See his 1874 essay, "History in the Service and Disservice of Life" for what Nietzsche himself considered one of his clearest explanations of this problem from this period.

9. This comes through most vividly in his pamphlet *The Case of Wagner,* composed in 1888. But see also *Wir Philologen* 5[98].

10. Nietzsche's most relevant comments on this point may be found in the later analysis of his "meditation" on Schopenhauer, in *Ecce Homo,* III.ii.§3. See also *Wir Philologen,* 5[21], 8[4].
For more on this complex relationship, see Martha Nussbaum, "The Transfigurations of Intoxication: Nietzsche, Schopenhauer, and Dionysus," *Arion, Third Series,* 1:2 (1991): 75–111.

11. This matter is complex. The reception of this first book actually was mixed. It seems to have been the only book which went into a second printing in his lifetime. Naturally, most of those who enjoyed *The Birth of Tragedy* and the *Untimely Meditations* could not make much sense of Nietzsche's later aphoristic writings, beginning with *Human, All-Too-Human.* See Sander L. Gilman; *Conversations with Nietzsche,* 33, 36, 54, 77–79.

12. Later, in his *Zarathustra,* Nietzsche had the following things to say, "On Scholars";
"This is the whole truth: I have moved out of the house of scholars, and I slammed the door behind me.
My soul sat hungry at their table too long; I am not, like them, trained to pursue knowledge like nut-cracking . . .
We are alien to each other and their virtues go against my taste even more than their falsity and loaded dice.
When I lived with them, I lived over them. That is why they got a grudge against me.

They did not want to hear how someone was living over their heads; so they put up wood, and soil, and filth between me and their heads." (*Sämtliche Werke*, IV. 160–62)

13. These essays, normally translated as "untimely meditations" or else "thoughts out of season" have been edited by William Arrowsmith under the title of *Unmodern Observations* (New Haven: Yale University Press, 1990), a translation which I consider absolutely appropriate, and to which I will return again shortly.

14. See, for instance, *Sämtliche Werke*, VII.699, 755 and VIII.188, 287–89.

15. These notes, comprising eight full or partial notebooks, may be found in the *Sämtliche Werke*, VIII.9–130.

16. *Wir Philologen*, 3[31]; *Sämtliche Werke*, VIII.23.

17. See my *Tragic Posture and Tragic Vision: Against the Modern Failure of Nerve* (New York: Continuum Press, 1994), 144–50.

18. *Wir Philologen*, 3[76]; *Sämtliche Werke*, VIII.38.

19. William Arrowsmith's presentation of this material nicely illustrates my point. He first offered a select translation of the notes for this essay, spiced with commentary from roughly contemporary and later works, in *Arion, First Series*, 2.1 (1963): 1–18; 2.2 (1963): 5–27; 2.4 (1963): 5–31. These selections gave what seems to me a rather false impression that the Philologist-as-*Übermensch* was Nietzsche's chief concern.

Arrowsmith later published these notes, and *only* these notes, in their entirety in *Arion, Second Series*, 1.2 (1974): 279–380. The complete text tells a very different story, one nicely captured in his later title "*unmodern* observations." Despite this fact, it is again the partial translation which appears in *Unmodern Observations* as "We Classicists," 307–87.

This raises the question, for me, of why Arrowsmith opted not to include *all* of the notes in his last translation, concluding as he does with the Fifth Notebook, and thereby ignoring what I consider to be two of the most sophisticated sections, from the Sixth and Seventh Notebooks.

Much of what I cite from *Wir Philologen* in this essay will thus be material available in only a single collection of Arrowsmith's translations, and that the most obscure of them all.

20. *Wir Philologen*, 5[142]; *Sämtliche Werke*, VIII.76. I have intentionally, if unhappily, opted not to use inclusive language in translating these notes, both because Nietzsche himself clearly would not have done so, but more importantly because the philologists he was describing were, at the time, all men.

21. See my *Tragic Posture and Tragic Vision*, 11–25.

22. *Wir Philologen*, 5[1]; *Sämtliche Werke*, VIII.41.

23. *Wir Philologen*, 5[115]; *Sämtliche Werke*, VIII.70. See also 5[121].

24. *Wir Philologen,* 5[88], 5[146], 5[180], 5[185], 5[195], 6[17], 6[21], 6[47].

25. *Wir Philologen,* 5[163]; *Sämtliche Werke,* VIII.86.

26. For a nice discussion of this idea, beginning with Nietzsche but moving well beyond him, see Walter Kaufmann's *Tragedy and Philosophy* (New York: Doubleday, 1968), §§34, 37–40, 48, 50.

27. *The Birth of Tragedy,* §9; *Sämtliche Werke,* I.64–71.

28. See for instance, Goethe's comments in the *Conversations with Eckermann,* translated by John Oxenford originally in 1850 and reprinted by the North Point Press in 1984: (1 May 1825), 90–91. Interestingly enough, Goethe is as highly critical of this prejudice as Nietzsche is.

29. See Martha C. Nussbaum, "The Transfigurations of Intoxication," 75–77.

30. A play which had been rediscovered and redone by Goethe—a man who did not share the scholarly disdain for happy endings—in 1787. See the English translation by Charles E. Passage (New York: Frederick Ungar Publishing Company, 1963).

31. *The Poetics* 1454a5–9.

32. *Wir Philologen,* 6[20]; *Sämtliche Werke,* VIII.105–6. The invocation of Pindar here is significant, and I return to him again shortly.

33. See my *Tragic Posture and Tragic Vision,* 87–99.

34. Although initially hesitant to do so, it is heartening to see Martha Nussbaum begin to take this eminently tragic idea seriously, as well as its profound rootedness in the classical thought-world. See *Love's Knowledge: Essays on Philosophy and Literature* (New York: Oxford University Press, 1990), 370, 375–76.

35. For an interesting, if highly unorthodox and far too critical, study of this broad topic of rediscovery, see Eliza M. Butler's *The Tyranny of Greece over Germany* (London: Cambridge University Press, 1935). This rediscovery, as she rightly notes, took an interesting turn when Heinrich Schliemann uncovered Troy, Mykenae, and Tiryns, thereby lending a greater archaeological concreteness to their picture of the past. See Schliemann's excavation reports, *Troy and Its Remains,* ed. Philip Smith (New York: Dover Publications, 1994).

36. *Contra* the genuine insights and sensitivities of cultural historians like Jacob Burkhardt, Nietzsche's friend and colleague at Basel, whose lectures Nietzsche himself attended, *Wir Philologen,* 5[58], 5[127]; *Sämtliche Werke,* VIII.56–57, 73.

37. *Wir Philologen,* 5[50]; *Sämtliche Werke,* VIII.54. He returned to this idea most notably in *Daybreak,* §§1, 36, 42, 44, 49, 102, 306, where he speaks repeatedly of the *pudenda origo,* the "dirty origins," of every cultural artifact.

38. *Wir Philologen* 3[74]; *Sämtliche Werke,* VIII.35.

39. *Wir Philologen* 7[7]; *Sämtliche Werke,* VIII.127. See also 3[4], 3[14], 3[16], 5[31], 5[45], 5[47], 5[50], 5[55], 5[57], 5[80], 5[87], 5[100–101], 5[126–27, 5[138], 5[156], 5[167], 6[11], 6[18], 6[42–43].

40. *Wir Philologen,* 3[16]; *Sämtliche Werke,* VIII.19.

41. *Wir Philologen,* 6[2]; *Sämtliche Werke,* VIII.97, emphasis mine. See also 3[18], 3[76], 5[20], 5[30], 5[46], 5[53], 5[111], 5[142], 5[189], 5[200].

42. This famous phrase—*edle Einhalt und stille Grosse*—was popularized by Winckelmann in his first book, *Gedänken Über die Nachahmung der griechischen Werke in der Malerei und Bildhauerkunst,* §79. He coined it in a discussion of the Laocöon group in Rome. "Why he should have chosen this particular group as an example of the very qualities it lacks," many have observed, 'is no easy question to answer" (E. M. Butler, *The Tyranny of Greece over Germany,* 47).

43. "Nothing," he says, "has preoccupied me more profoundly than the problem of decadence—I had reasons. Once one has developed a keen eye for the symptoms of decline, one understands morality too—one understands what is hiding under its most sacred names and value-judgments" (*The Case of Wagner,* preface; *Sämtliche Werke,* VI. 11–12).

44. Walter Kerr, *Tragedy and Comedy* (New York: Simon & Schuster, 1967) 36ff.

45. *Wir Philologen,* 5[130]; *Sämtliche Werke,* VIII.74.

46. *Wir Philologen,* 5[121]; *Sämtliche Werke,* VIII.72.

47. This *contra* Schopenhauer, *The World As Will And Representation,* trans. E. J. Payne (New York: Dover Publications, 1969), I.252–53. See also *Wir Philologen,* 5[21].

48. I mention here only the four most important passages, all of them rather late, whose importance for Nietzsche's larger project cannot be overestimated. They are: *Twilight of the Idols,* X.§5; *The Gay Science,* §370; *The Birth of Tragedy,* 1886 preface, §1; and *Ecce Homo,* III.i.§1. At the same time he was collecting his notes for *Wir Philologen,* he ventured a preliminary thesis for "Wagner in Bayreuth," §4.

49. Although these are presaged at *Wir Philologen,* 3[53] and 5[16]; *Sämtliche Werke,* VIII.28–29, 44.

50. *Wir Philologen,* 5[138], 5[148]; *Sämtliche Werke,* VIII.75, 79–80.

51. *Wir Philologen,* 3[76], 5[28], 6[18]; *Sämtliche Werke,* VIII.37–38, 47, 104–105.

52. *On the Genealogy of Morals,* I.§16. *Sämtliche Werke,* V.286.

53. *Wir Philologen,* 3[13]; *Sämtliche Werke,* VIII.18.

54. *Wir Philologen,* 5[136]; *Sämtliche Werke,* VIII.75.

55. *Wir Philologen,* 5[172]; *Sämtliche Werke,* VIII.90.

56. *Wir Philologen,* 3[13]; *Sämtliche Werke,* VIII.18. Admittedly, Nietzsche cannot resist the concluding barb that we are also suffering under the burden of that "funny sort of dishonesty which Christianity brings in train."

57. *Wir Philologen,* 5[47]; *Sämtliche Werke,* VIII.53. This is a point he had already made in *The Birth of Tragedy,* §18, and I will return to it in the fifth chapter.

58. *Wir Philologen,* 3[74], 3[76], 5[95], 5[99], 5[136], 5[150], 5[186], 5[195], 6[11].

59. *Wir Philologen,* 5[64]; *Sämtliche Werke,* VIII.59. And "how things are," Nietzsche is quick to add, are really quite miserable.

60. *Wir Philologen,* 5[65]; *Sämtliche Werke,* VIII.59.

61. *Wir Philologen,* 5[91]; *Sämtliche Werke,* VIII.64.

62. Nietzsche comments explicitly upon this theoretical and cultural philistinism in his essay on "David Strauss, the Confessor and the Writer," the first of his published *Unmodern Observations,* §§1–2.

63. For a fascinating description of Bernhard Förster's and Elisabeth Förster-Nietzsche's participation in the racist colonial experiment called "New Germany" in Paraguay, see Ben MacIntyre, *Forgotten Fatherland: The Search For Elisabeth Nietzsche* (New York: Farrar, Straus & Giroux, 1992).

64. *Wir Philologen,* 5[198]; *Sämtliche Werke,* VIII.96. See also 2[5], 5[9], 5[11], 5[14], 5[155], 6[47].
See also Strabo, *Geography* VII.7.§§1–3.

65. From *Nietzsche: Sämtliche Briefe, Kritische Studienausgabe in 8 Bänden* (Berlin: Walter de Gruyter, 1975), IV.23. Letter no. 239, dated 16 July 1872, emphasis mine. See also *Wir Philologen,* 6[17].

66. *Wir Philologen,* 6[43]; *Sämtliche Werke,* VIII.114. See also 3[4], 5[38], 5[39], 6[11], 6[42].

67. *Wir Philologen,* 3[70]; *Sämtliche Werke,* VIII.34.
It is fascinating that the same claim could be made *archaeologically* today. We are only now beginning to collect, and to study, and to learn about the *pre*Classical, Archaic style in Greek sculpture. The reasons for this are twofold. Until recently, we simply did not have enough material to work with, and there are some essential materials we will *never* possess. We have only *thirteen* bronze originals from the Archaic period, despite the apparent fact that this was the preferred medium in antiquity. And the Acropolis Museum in Athens pretty well defines our view of what this period had to offer in marble.
Nietzsche anticipated this state of affairs, and offers a radical explanation for it. While it is true that we do not have many non-Athenian materials, we have lived for so

long in the shadow of the Parthenon and the hegemony of the Classical Athenian moment that *we did not want to look anywhere else.* Perspective—in archaeology, as in aesthetics—is all.

68. *Twilight of the Idols,* I.§8; *Sämtliche Werke,* VI.60. The fundamental dictum of this school is that "what does not destroy me makes me stronger."

69. Herodotus, *The Histories* VIII.§83–94.

70. For one thing, she is known by many names. In Crete, she is *Britomartis,* or *Diktynna*—related to and later even equated with Artemis. Pausanias mentions a wooden statue of Britomartis at Olus in Crete (*Guide to Greece,* IX.40.§3), along with a wooden Athena at Knossos. Clearly there was great fluidity between local deities and the Olympian pantheon in the Aegean at this time.

In any case, Britomartis/Diktynna was a nymph daughter of Zeus, who fled Crete in order to avoid the amorous advances of King Minos. She arrived in Aegina, where she is known as *Aphaia,* and found refuge in a sanctuary of Artemis. That sanctuary was, tradition has it, marked by the construction of this temple.

71. One piece of artistic evidence to support this intentional antagonism recently caught my eye. One of the fallen figures from the Aegina pediment is contorted in a rather peculiar and unsatisfying position. He is normally pointed out as an example of lingering Archaic "primitivism." The sculptor wants to move out, to expand his figures fully in the round, but he is unable to bring it off. This, despite the fact that he seemed well able to do so in other pieces of the group.

In the Acropolis Museum at Athens, we have one figure, a fallen giant being killed by Athena, contorted in this same way (*see my appended photographs* at pages 36–37). Is it so difficult to imagine that this curious figure is actually *an intentional allusion* to the Archaic Athenian Parthenon, made by the Aeginetans and precisely intended to offend the Athenians, whose own temples had just been destroyed?

72. Aegina, like Thebes, was an oligarchy steeped in tradition and local myth. Pindar, for one, made much of these facts.

For an intriguing discussion of the issues I mean to raise here, see R. F. Tannenbaum; "Who Started the Peloponnesian War?" *Arion, Second Series,* 2.4 (1975): 533–46.

73. See Herodotus, *The Histories* V.§§84–90, VI.§§87–94; and Thucydides, *The Peloponnesian War* I.§§14, 41, 105–8, II.§27, and IV.§§56–57.

74. See William Mullen; "Pindar and Athens: A Reading in the Aeginetan Odes," *Arion, Second Series,* 1.3 (1974): 446–95.

Pindar is a difficult poet to appreciate, since the epinikian poetry for which he is our only representative is unlike anything we sing today. For an excellent introduction to this art-form, and the poet who excelled at it, see D. S. Carne-Ross' *Pindar* (New Haven: Yale University Press, 1985), particularly 66–68 on Aegina, and 184–89 on her political estate after the war.

75. Verses 23–34, translation mine. And not only this one. Pindar returns to Aeginetan politics repeatedly, nowhere more eloquently than in his *Eight Pythian.*

Good English translations of Pindar are as valuable as they are rare. Richmond Lattimore's *The Odes of Pindar* (Chicago: University of Chicago Press, 1947) is valuable for its great fidelity to the text, whereas Frank J. Nisetich's *Pindar's Victory Odes* (Baltimore: The Johns Hopkins University Press, 1980) is considerably freer and more poetic.

76. I am indebted to Herbert Golder for much of my understanding of this character, and of this poem. See his "Sophocles' *Ajax*: Beyond the Shadow of Time," *Arion, Third Series,* 1.1 (1990): especially 11–16.

77. Pindar, *Eighth Nemean Ode,* 41–44, translation mine. For the Greek text of Pindar's Odes, I am using the edition of Bruno Snell and Hervicus Maehler, *Pindari Carmina cum Fragmentis* (Leipzig: B. G. Teubner Verlagsgesellschaft, 1987), 127.

78. Pindar, *Eighth Nemean Ode,* 45–47, translation mine.

79. For a fascinating narrative of this and subsequent ventures, see Russell Chamberlin's *Loot! The Heritage of Plunder* (London: Thames and Hudson, 1983), 28–35.

80. *Travels in Southern Europe and the Levant, 1810–1817. The Journal of C. R. Cockerell,* edited by his son, Samuel Pepys Cockerell (London: Longmans, Green and Co., 1903).

81. See Cockerell's own reporting of these matters in *The Temples of Jupiter Panhellenius at Aegina and of Apollo Epicurius at Bassae Near Phigalia in Arcadia* (London: John Weale, 1860).

82. I am currently translating Wagner's report, which was immediately commissioned by Ludwig I. This fascinating text was edited and annotated by Friedrich Schelling, with the title *Bericht über die Aeginetischen Bildwerke im Besitz seiner königlichen Hoheit des Kronprinzen von Baiern* (Stuttgart und Tübingen: F. G. Gottaschen Buchhandlung, 1817). Nietzsche never mentions this text.

83. The site and its sculptures have since then generated an incredible bibliography. The sculptures may be seen in Dieter Ohly's *Die Aeginetan I: Die Marmorskulpturen des Tempels der Aphaia auf Aegina, Ein Katalog der Glyptothek* (München: Verlag C. H. Beck, 1976).

I have perhaps disingenuously sidestepped the complex issues of dating these sculptural groups—a third (and perhaps a fourth) of which was discovered during subsequent excavation under Ohly's direction—but it will be clear from everything I have argued to this point that I think a date *after* 480 BCE is absolutely essential to make sense of them.

For a survey of the arguments, see John Boardman, *Greek Sculpture: The Archaic Period* (London: Thames and Hudson, 1985), 156–57, figures 206.1–6; Brunilde S. Ridgeway, *The Archaic Style in Greek Sculpture* (Princeton: Princeton University Press, 1975) pages 40–83, 212–213, 308–311; and *The Severe Style in Greek Sculpture* (Princeton: Princeton University Press, 1970.) 13–17.

84. We have a single, tantalizing note in Nietzsche's *Nachlass:* "*The smile,* the expression of life, of these creatures of a day (even when they are dying, Aeginetans)" *Sämtliche Werke* VIII.536.

I have been unable to determine, despite considerable digging, whether Nietzsche himself ever visited the collection. It seems unlikely, since he never speaks of it. His correspondence makes clear that, during those times when he *did* travel to Munich, he never stayed long.

85. Nietzsche would even go so far as to apply it to the natural sciences, a later interest, and used the insight to devastating effect there. Turning the fundamental assumption of Darwinian biology on its ear, Nietzsche insists that "survival of the fittest" is an aesthetic assumption nowhere confirmed by the biological or spiritual facts. In fact, he argues, in our world the *mediocre,* not the fittest, survive.

> *Anti-Darwin:* The species do *not* grow in perfection: the weak will forever gain mastery over the strong—they are the great majority, and they are also more *clever.* . . . Darwin forgot the spirit (that is English!); *the weak have more spirit.* One must have spirit to get more—" (*Twilight of the Idols,* IX.§14; *Sämtliche Werke,* VI.120–21).

I will return to this idea in chapter 5.

86. *The Antichrist,* §52; *Sämtliche Werke,* VI.233.

87. For a fascinating example of the lingering temptation of applying the tragic posture to Nazi building projects, see Eric Michaud; "National Socialist Architecture as an Acceleration of Time," translated by Christopher Fox in *Critical Inquiry* 19.2 (1993): 220–33. As should be clear enough by now, I see the Nazi program as an attempt to retreat backward into a vague and idyllic Hellenism of their own creation, not to accelerate ahead into some inchoate future time.

88. I am delighted to record my fond debt to Julia Mahnke, then a student at the University of Munich, for being such a wonderful host, tour guide, and professor of modern German history during my too-brief stay in December of 1991.

89. I am including birthdates and dates of decease in the text. The dates of these kings' respective reigns are as follows:

Maximilian I (1806–1825)
Ludwig I (1825–1848)
Maximilian II (1848–1864)
Ludwig II (1864–1886).

Since Ludwig did not come to power until 1825, he acquired his sculptural collection while still the Crown Prince of Bavaria. For more on his artistic activities in this period, see Ludwig Müttl; *Ludwig I: König und Bauherr,* (München: Piper, 1987) 50–55.

90. See Vassilis Lambropoulos, *The Rise of Eurocentrism: Anatomy of Interpretation* (Princeton: Princeton University Press, 1993), 83–85.

91. For a critical summary of this project, see William J. Diebold, "The Politics of Derestoration: The Aegina Pediments and the German Confrontation With the Past" *Art Journal* Vol. 54, no. 2 (Summer 1995) 60–66. Diebold's sensitive criticism of the

"politics of derestoration" nonetheless underscores precisely the valves-relativism I ascribe to the later Nietzsche.

92. Hans Michael Herzog, *Der Königsplatz, 1812–1988,* 2nd ed. (Munich: Staatliche Antikensammlungen und Glyptothek, 1991), 38.

93. As Albert Speer notes in his remarkable memoir, *Inside the Third Reich,* trans. Richard and Clara Winston (New York: MacMillan, 1970), 79:

> It has been generally assumed that I was Hitler's chief architect, to whom all others were subordinate. This was not so. The architects for the replanning of Munich and Linz had similar powers between them. In the course of time Hitler consulted an ever-growing number of architects for special tasks. Before the war began, there must have been ten or twelve.

For more commentary on Troost, see 28–29, 39–43. On the classical style and Hitler's brand of Hellenism, see 62, 79–80, 96–97. On Speer's decisive trips—to Greece in May of 1935, and to Sicily and southern Italy in March of 1939—see 63–64, 146–48.

94. Speer, *Inside the Third Reich,* 67–69. On Speer's gradual realization that this, what he calls "our Empire style," was not Classical at all, but rather an art of imperial decadence, see 159–60, 315, and 529n5.

95. And Speer succeeded him, *Inside the Third Reich,* 49.

96. Herzog, *Der Königsplatz, 1812–1988,* 44–45.

97. See Mark Mazower, *Inside Hitler's Greece: The Experience of Occupation, 1941–1944* (New Haven: Yale University Press, 1993).

98. Herzog; *Der Königsplatz, 1812–1988,* 62–65.

99. Joshua 4:5–24.

100. For a lovely exploration of these successive German Hellenisms, see Simon Richter, *Laocöon's Body and the Aesthetics of Pain: Winckelmann, Lessing, Herder, Moritz, Goethe* (Detroit: Wayne State University Press, 1992).

101. On Hitler's anticosmopolitanism, see Speer, *Inside the Third Reich,* 14, 121. On his antimodernism, see 110.

102. See Nietzsche's early essay, "Homer's Contest," in *The Portable Nietzsche,* trans. Walter Kaufmann (New York: Penguin Books, 1954), 32–39, *Sämtliche Werke* I.783–792.

103. "Postmodernism," that ragbag phrase which is supposed by many to define "us" today, is perhaps most coherent as an architectural, not a philosophical, movement.
See David Harvey's remarkable exploration, *The Condition of Postmodernity: An Enquiry into the Origins of Cultural Change* (Oxford: Basil Blackwell, 1989). His commentary on fascist aesthetics is very much to the point: "It is instructive to note how

heavily fascism drew upon classical references (architecturally, politically, historically) and built mythological conceptions accordingly" (34–35).

104. Goethe; *Conversations with Eckermann* (23 March 1829), 246.

105. *Twilight of the Idols,* I.§33; *Sämtliche Werke,* VI.64.

106. *Sämtliche Werke,* VI.40–45.

107. *The Case of Wagner,* preface; *Sämtliche Werke,* VI.12.

108. *The Case of Wagner,* second postscript; *Sämtliche Werke,* VI.46.

Philosophical Texts

2

After the Polis?
On the Use and Abuse of Aristotle's Political Animal

Aristotelianism is *philosophically* the most powerful of pre-modern modes of moral thought. If a pre-modern view of morals and politics is to be vindicated against modernity, it will be in *something like* Aristotelian terms or not at all.
— Alasdair MacIntyre, *After Virtue*

In the last chapter we saw how Nietzsche's philosophical positions subtly changed, early to late, such that the same Hellenism which had made him so intriguingly *un*modern in the 1870s led him to a postured sort of *anti*modernism in the 1880s. In this chapter and then again in the next, I want to look at several texts which make ironically similar sorts of arguments—antimodern on the one hand, and anti-American on the other—and which ground these arguments similarly in the so-called classical tradition. That tradition in these two cases is primarily Aristotelian, and that already makes it a rather different sort of Hellenism from the one Nietzsche espoused. For what a variety of latter-day Aristotelians have found most compelling in Aristotle's philosophical views is his alleged prioritizing of the moral community over the self, the *polis* over the *psyche* (although it is, of course, one of the central claims of Plato's *Republic,* inherited by Aristotle, that the two terms mutually define one another and cannot be separated in any simple way). Nietzsche's Hellenism is a very different thing. For Nietzsche, as we saw, the classics are "classic" precisely insofar as they inspire us to competitive aspiration, that is, to the contemporary surpassing of Hellenic achievements. Nietzsche's fascination with the cultivation of individuality as an educational goal has been roundly criticized as erosively solipsistic, and thus as "modern" to the core. I wish to challenge that claim, in an attempt to defend Nietzsche's Hellenism against what I take to be a far more postured, however fashionable, contemporary Aristotelianism.

I

Aristotle is academically fashionable again. While few may be willing to go to the extreme Thomas Aquinas charted out by calling him "*the* Philosopher," there is no denying his sudden, new-found celebrity. This renascent Aristotelianism is part of a much larger academic fashion, in most cases (Martha Nussbaum is the interesting exception to which I will return periodically throughout this book)—namely, the devastating critique of Liberalism as a "sham tradition."[1] The argument, in a nutshell, is that contemporary Liberalism's radically individualistic premises have contributed to its own undoing. In such a world—devoid, as it is thought to be, of the moral *habits,* the *communitarian* sensibilities, the social *practices,* and the self-conscious participation in an ongoing conversation with a canonical body of *texts,* all of which, taken together, constitute a *tradition*—we lack the necessary cohesive threads which hold any healthy social fabric together. We are coming unravelled today. So runs the argument; so says the tragic posture.

Perhaps the most popular, and the most devastating, critic in this vein has been Alasdair MacIntyre. He begins his diagnoses of "modern times" with the presentation of several examples of insoluble moral conflict—debates about abortion, health care, and nuclear warfare[2]—and he argues that such conflicts "go all the way down" in a sham tradition such as Liberalism. We lack the moral grounding which only a real tradition can provide.[3] It is this sense of moral vertigo, this feeling that the ground is not really firm under our feet, as well as the complete absence of any common assumptions regarding the goals of the moral life which might moderate the stridency of contemporary moral debate, which constitutes our modernness . . . and our discontent. Liberalism, MacIntyre argues, reaches its zenith (it is also a death-knell) in Nietzsche's polemics,[4] as well as the "Nihilism, American Style"[5] which has been his chief legacy in the news, in the universities, and especially on television. Stanley Hauerwas, translating that same argument into Christian ethics, has said many of the same things about Liberalism and modern society.[6] He concludes that the Church is the only viable community today (at least it ought to be) with a clear sense of its mission and its goals in a world which is otherwise ethically fragmented and in moral disarray. The Church, as a society of loving and forgiving friends in a modern world which threatens to strip us of these very virtues, is the only viable *polis* in a world which has otherwise simply grown too large for us.[7] The image of a cosmopolis—a much larger, global community—is indeed "the hidden agenda of modernity."[8] Other people offer other communities as an antidote, other forms of *local* belonging. But these visions are consistently grounded in this same romantic nostalgia for the Greek *polis.* Both MacIntyre and Hauerwas offer Aristotle's moral philosophy, his portrait of what the development of the moral person really looks like, as an antidote to the twinned diseases of "Liberalism" and "modern times."

There is real power and creativity in this challenge. Even Robert Bellah and his co-authors, in an *academic* book which nonetheless enjoyed months on the *New York Times'* bestseller list, chose to entitle their diagnosis of modern North American society *Habits of the Heart*[9]—a phrase taken from Alexis de Tocqueville, who got it, in his turn, from Aristotle.[10] They do not refer to Aristotle much, and when they do, it is strictly to defend his claims about the importance of the middle class (a sociological component to his doctrine of "the mean") to the moral health of any polity.[11] Their argument, though less polemical on the face of it than Alasdair MacIntyre's,[12] is in its own way at least equally damning. They accuse persons in modern North America of being very nearly schizophrenic, attempting to draw upon the *communitarian* sensibilities of "biblical republicanism" and the radical *individualism* of the Liberal tradition at the same time. According to these authors, this unhappy marriage works only briefly, where it works at all, *since the citizen must be trained* into the history, the habits, the texts, and the civic virtues of the polity in which he or she finds herself if that tradition is to have articulacy and real meaning.

Failing to appreciate that fact sufficiently, most Americans have retreated into a relatively shallow and substanceless substitute for the locality of the *polis,* what the authors aptly call the "life-style enclave."[13] Such allegiances are founded, not on the bedrock of traditionalism and community, but rather on the "narcissism of similarity." Their contrast between this version of U.S. modernity and the myth of North American origins is dramatic.[14] The pioneer "who penetrates into the wilds of the New World with the Bible, an axe and some newspapers,"[15] de Tocqueville believed, was the proud possessor of more intellectual acumen and creativity than his counterparts in the best salons of Europe, a sort of life-style enclave, Parisian style. This was the virtue and the promise of the North American experiment in naturalism and pluralistic democracy. In addition to the Bible and the newspapers, these pioneers probably had some of the Greek and Roman classics as well, essential literature for any democratic polity.[16] And Shakespeare, always Shakespeare.[17] We, by contrast, are largely illiterate, culturally[18]—and the only books which find their way into our probing fingers these days probably come from the ever-growing Self-Help shelf of the local bookstore.

There is surely something to this challenge, although I tend as a general rule to be skeptical of the global, sweeping diagnoses of "sick cultures" and "sham traditions." This book is designed to call such modernist periodizations, and such myths of decadence, into question. Nietzsche was at his worst when he engaged in such antimodern polemics, as are most of those who, like MacIntyre, try to make him a key spokesperson for the modern predicament. In fact, it is Alasdair MacIntyre who insists that Nietzsche forces the issue for all of us—by drawing out the implicit assumptions of Liberalism, thereby demonstrating the bankruptcy of this sham tradition at the same time. In the modern age, MacIntyre insists, we are faced with a fundamental choice—"Nietzsche or Aristotle?"—and our cultural future hangs in the balance.[19] Either we go with Nietzsche down the path toward solipsistic self-assertion (and implicitly, to eventual madness), or we return, with Aristotle, to the happier, fonder fold of friends, community, and the traditional narratives which make up so much of who we are. Zarathustra or Socrates—the isolation of the mountaintop, or the fonder busy-ness of the marketplace.

II

I would like to offer the modest proposal that this is a gross simplification of Aristotle's (to say nothing of Nietzsche's) mature thought. The same Zarathustra who counsels going off to the mountaintop constantly returns, himself, unable to stay away for very long, unable to do without companionship, however inadequate or unsatisfying it may ultimately prove to be. Zarathustra demands more radical autonomy and individuality than we are capable of, and he knows it. He is merely a spokesperson for the *Übermensch,* playing John the Baptist to a way of life whose sandals he himself is unable to wear. We are "human, all-too-human"—this Nietzsche never tires of telling us—much too human for the demands of autonomy and unity of style his vision lays upon us. Yet still he writes, still he dreams, still he hopes. I want to suggest that Aristotle does much the same thing, that his moral vision embraces (perhaps in-habits is a better word) this same essential moral tension.

To make good that claim, let us look at a famous passage from the introduction to the *Politics,* a passage, says MacIntyre, "whose importance for the interpretation of everything Aristotle wrote about human life cannot be underrated [*sic*]."[20] This is the well-known passage in which Aristotle defines the human being as a "political animal," an animal which is, by definition and by nature, "meant to live in a *polis.*"

> From these considerations it is clear that the *polis* belongs to the class of things which exist by nature [*physei*], and that the human is by nature a political animal. Moreover, the apolitical person [*apolis*], whether he is so naturally [*physin*] or else by accident [*tychēn*], is either an idiot or something more than human [*kreittōn ē anthrōpon*].[21]

So far so good, and this is normally as far as people go with this text. To fail to recognize *the natural human fact* of our socialness, and to live in accordance with that natural fact, is to be condemned to the life either of a beast or an angel. MacIntyre uses this passage, I think, to write off Nietzsche's concept of the *Übermensch*—that paradigmatic "apolitical person"—as belonging "in the pages of a philosophical bestiary rather than in serious discussion."[22] He is a beast, MacIntyre suggests, not an angel. Surely Nietzsche's views *are* intentionally overdrawn, especially later in his career. Yet his *educational* vision, his profound communion with Greek thought, as well as the "unmodern observations" which set the stage for so much of his mature philosophy, cannot be so easily dismissed. I developed these in some detail in the last chapter. MacIntyre dismisses Nietzsche's vision because he claims that Nietzsche has misunderstood the constitutive role of community and narrative tradition in the formation of every human life.[23] Martha Nussbaum has shown, additionally, how essential it is to understand that Aristotle's project was a deliberate attempt to articulate the habits, skills, and social practices requisite for becoming fully human—not more and not less.[24] Here again is the Aristotle we customarily meet, the man of "the mean,"[25] who does nothing excessively or deficiently, who avoids the Scylla of bestiality and the Charybdis of angelism, a man of extraordinary balance, moderation, and philosophical discernment.

Martha Nussbaum has made the important point that this is neither an automatic nor a superficial task for Aristotle.[26] Rather, Aristotle says quite explicitly that "there are many ways to miss the mark [*hamartanein*],[27] and only one way to shoot straight. The one is easy and the other difficult—easy, I mean, to miss the target, and difficult to hit it."[28] That has important implications for my argument. It is too simplistic to say that Aristotle has set up two extremes (what are traditionally called 'vices')—that of angelism and *beastliness*—and that he is trying to articulate a mediating position, a humanizing portrait of the "political animal" in between them. Aristotle freely admits that some vices are more vicious than others,[29] just as the choice between Scylla and Charybdis must occasionally be made (Odysseus made it, after all). Neither angelism nor beastliness is "moderate" in any clear sense, but angelism clearly has something to be said in its defense which *beastliness* does not have. Not only is angelism clearly preferable; in some cases it is even *mandated.*

Aristotle is after the much more difficult point of view which admits that we live with a foot in each of two very different worlds, both of which lay a claim on us. Practical wisdom comes from being able to embody both. Living forever between the mountaintop and the marketplace, the solution is not "the mean"—what MacIntyre and Hauerwas threaten to make of the *polis,* it seems to me—but rather some richer experience of human being—the Greeks called in *sōphrosunē*—which grants the existence of both aspects in the fashioning of a human life. *Both* angel *and* beast, not some vague entity "in between" the two.

Aristotle is content to be human, we are usually taught, neither animal nor angel, and his entire moral project is an attempt to articulate that constellation of skills which make us, precisely, human, rather than angelic or bestial. Several factors begin to complicate this superficially simple story. First is the discussion of the *polis* which *directly* precedes this famous comment in the *Politics,* and which suggests that a fairly radical brand of individualism is actually the *goal* of the *polis.*[30] Aristotle is trying to prove that political community, the *polis,* is the "natural" state for human beings. He assumes that if the goal of the *polis* is both natural (*physin*) and final (*telos*), then it is the best (*beltiston*) means toward this eminently human end. What then, is the final end of a human life, for Aristotle? It is interesting that, in this discussion, he mentions neither life, nor liberty, nor the pursuit of happiness.[31] Rather, he mentions *self-sufficiency* (*autarkeia*). It is textually unclear which of two feminine nouns this adjective modifies: the *polis* itself must be materially self-sufficient, as the *psyche* who inhabits this city must also be. I strongly suspect that both senses are intended, and my reading here assumes that they are. I find it interesting that Aquinas takes the passage primarily in the personal, not the political, sense.[32]

In the sentence which *immediately precedes* the passage we have just been reading, Aristotle concludes: *ē d'autarkeia kai telos kai beltiston;* "Self-sufficiency is both the end and the best."[33] Lacking the Hebraic concern for the Sabbath, but raised on this eminently Greek interest in politics, Aristotle concludes that the *polis* was made for men, not men for the *polis.*[34] It begins to look as if the *polis* is a necessary *means* which will eventually be outgrown if it does its job well enough. The community is the arena designed to nurture individual human flourishing. And that raises serious problems for an "Aristotelian" criticism of Liberalism which, in its best moments, attempts to do the very same thing.

There is still more. For, having said that much positively, Aristotle concludes his frank discussion of the *polis* with an elliptical remark which seems to need more explanation and attention than it normally receives.

> This apolitical man [who is either an idiot or angel] is like the man of whom Homer wrote in denunciation
>
> > "Friendless, lawless [*athemistos*] and homeless is he"
>
> The man who is such by nature has a passion for war; he is like an isolated piece in a game of draughts.[35]

Here we seem to see Aristotle undercut the very thing he has just been arguing for, namely, individual self-sufficiency. To stand alone, he now suggests, is to doom oneself to the short life of a punchdrunk Achilles, indifferent to the suffering of enemies and friends alike. Now, the passage from Homer (presumably Aristotle's audience would have known this much better than we do) comes in the remarkable and pivotal ninth book of the *Iliad,* when Agamemnon is forced to admit his mistake and sends an embassy to Achilles, begging him to return. I will return to this scene, and will spend a good deal of time reading it, in the sixth chapter. The observation is made by Nestor, the Greeks' wordiest senior statesman, to Agamemnon, as a sort of pep-talk to the king who is even then swallowing his pride by making Achilles an offer he thinks it impossible to refuse (Achilles actually *does* refuse it, and therein lies the tale). He intends to be describing Achilles for the king's benefit, as a barbarian, an animal, who revels in cold conflict for conflict's sake. When he refers to him as "friendless" and "homeless," he is certainly on the mark. But he misses the mark when he calls him "lawless" (*athemistos*). He makes clear only that he has failed to understand Achilles, and what now motivates the man. Achilles has moved decisively outside of the heroic mores which define his fellows—there is the *real* "sham tradition," as I will argue in the next chapter, and then again in the last—but his disobedience is unarguably "civil," and astonishingly "articulate." He moves away from friends and the hearth, but he does all this in the name of what is right (*themis*).

This mention of the law, of *themis,* takes us to the heart of the moral dilemma.[36] A law can be legal, and still be unjust. Moreover, as Bob Dylan would remind any would-be disobedient, "to live outside the law/ you must be honest." It is absolutely crucial to understand that Achilles would have objected to Nestor's caricature precisely because he thinks that he is being eminently "civil" and "lawful" and "just." That is precisely his problem. He would surely have replied to Nestor that this conflict he has stirred up among the Greeks— cold though it be—is all done in the name of *themis,* the intuitive moral appeal to "unwritten laws" which must be vaguely intelligible to us, however inchoate the intuition may also be. These are the kinds of things many tragic heroes and heroines go to their graves defending. So Achilles' disobedience is hardly uncivil, hardly "lawless." So important is it to him that he considers it worth placing himself apart, like an isolated piece in a game of draughts, knowing full well that he may die for his intransigence, his insistence upon staying there so long.[37] It remains only to notice that Homer presents Achilles as "paradigmatic, not perverse" in so doing. Put even more strongly, "all heroes feel pretty much about themselves as he does. In short, the *Iliad* tells us very forcefully that social institutions are no consolation for individual deprivation."[38]

So it is that we have come full circle in this difficult and only superficially simple definition from the *Politics.* At the outset, we are told that self-sufficiency is the goal of political association. In conclusion, we are presented with a deliberately distorted Homeric image of an apolitical beast whose only vocation seems to be the waging of indiscriminate war—cold conflict among his own people, and a good deal warmer when it crosses over to the other side. The image ironically serves, in the context of the *Iliad* itself, as a way of *vindicating* Achilles' transcendence of the superficial values by which he is surrounded, the sham tradition of heroic values in which he is suffocating. Two images of radical autonomy, self-sufficiency, and heroic defiance, all sandwiching this oblique middling definition of humanity as "the political animal." We seem to stand in need of some further help in understanding this.

III

Help is available, it seems to me, in a fascinating and equally oblique passage which comes near the conclusion of Aristotle's *Nicomachean Ethics.* Alasdair MacIntyre goes so far as to say that the *Politics* and the *Ethics,* taken together, constituted an essential ingredient of the Western philosophical tradition (a tradition which gave birth, among other things, to the very Liberalism he criticizes so roundly). Presumably then (and in spite of the fact that the *Politics* contains some nightmarish convictions decidedly absent from the *Ethics*), we must read the works together.[39] I would like to pay some attention to this passage, which precedes Aristotle's concluding discussion of the contemplative life, in the last chapter of the *Nicomachean Ethics.* It is introduced with this same identical phrase—on being "more than human," *kreittōn ē kat' anthrōpon*—which concluded our passage from the *Politics:*

> However such a life would be *more than human.* A man who lived it would do so not insofar as he is human, but rather because there is something in him which is divine [*theion*]. . . . We ought not heed those who advise us to have human [*anthrōpina*] thoughts, since we are only human, and mortal [*thnēta*] thoughts, since we are mortal. Rather, we should endeavor to become immortal, doing everything in our power to live according to the highest which is in us, for though it seems small in size, in power and in value it far surpasses everything else. One might even regard it as everyone's true self [*hekastos*], since it is the ruling and better part.[40]

A difficult, and really quite stunning passage, unlike most of what we have been taught to expect from Aristotle. So different does it sound, say, from the sober counsel to become what we are—something *human,* neither more nor less— that Martha Nussbaum has argued the passage cannot really belong here at all. In a reading of Aristotle which is heavily indebted to Nietzsche,[41] and which on the whole I think serves as an admirable corrective to some of MacIntyre's more outlandish claims (as I hope to show in the next chapter), Nussbaum explicitly deletes this passage from the *Nicomachean Ethics*.[42] She does so because she feels, perhaps rightly, that it "has strong affinities with the Platonism of the middle dialogues," and is "oddly out of step with the view of value that we have been finding in the ethical works."[43] That is to say, *Plato,* not Aristotle, wanted to focus upon the divine element within us, that aspect of the human soul which armors it against the slings and arrows of outrageous fortune. In a moral world shot through with fragility, Aristotle cannot (like his mentor) counsel a retreat into the inner sanctum of the immortal soul. Aristotle's genius, in Nussbaum's judgment, lay in his deliberate placement of fragility at the very heart of the moral life, unwilling as he was to try to find the firmer, semidivine soil Plato gardened in. A flower is beautiful, Aristotle suggests, *because* it is fragile, not because of the soil in which it is rooted. Thus, while Nussbaum freely admits that Aristotle may have written the passage in question, she insists that he did so as an attempt to wrestle with the Platonic legacy and the challenge it represented to his own mature views. He never thought to include it in his concluding discussion of the moral life. A later scribe mistakenly inserted this passage into the text at this point, "a not unusual phenomenon in the corpus,"[44] she concludes.

I am always skeptical of the attempt to excise a passage from a classical text on the philosophical grounds that it seems not to "fit;" only *philological* arguments should be mounted against a passage's authenticity, and even then the job can rarely be done with certainty. "A properly emended author," Nietzsche quipped, "*does not count for much*."[45] Here, the rationale behind deleting a genuine Aristotelian passage seems to be simply that it does not square with Nussbaum's own interpretation of Aristotle's views. Aristotle's human, all-too-human, moral philosophy *seems* to give way here to an inconsistent Platonic striving after divinity.

We are in a peculiar situation. MacIntyre would not like the passage in question because it moves too quickly beyond our tradition-bound narrative selves in the name of some elusive divinity ("the true self") we are meant to possess. Nussbaum does not like it because it vitiates her plea for a human (all-too-human?) and fragile (all-too-fragile?) account of the moral life.

Yet the passage is thoroughly in line with Aristotle's mature arguments. This is how Aquinas understood it. Aquinas' discussion of the ultimate end of the contemplative life devotes most of its time, appropriately enough, to the concept of *leisure* (the Greek term is *scholē,* a critical reminder for "scholars," then as now). There are three things which one "constantly assigns to the happy person: self-sufficiency, leisureliness, and freedom from labor," he notes. Leisure, in fact, "is a special property of happiness, the ultimate end."[46] Aquinas emphasizes this point because the claim *seems* to undercut what Aristotle has been saying up until now—namely, that the moral life is a life of political *activity.* So Aristotle has argued. But, as Aquinas shows us with lovely clarity, the *practical* virtues of *political* affairs are set over against the *theoretical* virtues of pure contemplation. Politics, to say it again, is a *penultimate* moral concern. It seems that Aquinas is reading Aristotle on his own terms far more than MacIntyre or Nussbaum on this point, each of whom has a hidden agenda which disinclines them to this passage.

By contrast, Aristotle (and Aquinas) has no problem making something important of the divine within us, what he calls our "true self," a self which is not quite so vulnerable to the outrages of fortune, as Nussbaum would have it. He even has a word for it: *megalopsychia,* or greatness of spirit (often translated as "magnanimity").[47] It is an idea which undercuts many of the things both MacIntyre and Nussbaum say about Aristotle's moral psychology. Against MacIntyre, here we find an Aristotelian man who stands at a considerable distance from the narrative traditions, duties, and virtues of his fellows. He stands alone, singularly aloof, far above most of his lesser compatriots.[48] Against Nussbaum, here we meet an Aristotle whose moral psychology refuses to accept the *centrality* of fortune and moral accident. While there is no denying a moral place to ill-fortune or disaster, "the highest thing which is in us" cannot be deformed by such occurrences.[49] *Megalopsychia* is defined by a generosity in the bestowing of gifts, but a cautious hesitancy in accepting them. *Megalopsychia* stands at a considerable remove from human concourse, admitting at best a sort of penultimacy to human society, reserving its ultimate commitments for the privately contemplative, inner life. Finally, and most centrally, *megalopsychia* moves restlessly and eternally between the mountaintop and the marketplace. It was Nietzsche who perhaps best captured this high-spiritedness (and lent it a gaiety it had not had before) in his portrait of the *Übermensch.* I cannot agree with MacIntyre, that Nietzsche borrowed the word from Aristotle, but mutilated the idea.[50] Rather, I think that MacIntyre is wrong to present Aristotle and Nietzsche as antipodes.

By reading the passage from the *Politics* on the "political animal" in conjunction with this concluding passage in the *Ethics* where the same phrase about being "more than human" appears, it becomes clearer what Aristotle has in mind, I think. He knows that fortune and accident lay waste many of our labors. He knows that we are all situated, located in a *polis,* and a circle of friends, and a body of traditions—virtues and practices, epics and poetry. But he also knows that each of us stands alone—for so we are born and so we die— and he knows that "tradition" is not a sufficient armor against such loneliness, that social institutions are no consolation for individual deprivation. The *polis* is not an end in itself. Self-sufficiency is. The *polis* has an essential penultimacy about it. His is a very bracing human vision, borrowing the best, it seems to me, from *both* Plato *and* the poets.

IV

Let me illustrate what I think Aristotle had in mind with an analogy. It is actually Alasdair MacIntyre's analogy, but I will use it to make a point rather different from the one he wants. In his account of "the virtues at Athens," MacIntyre tells a story which, by his own admission, moves "from Sophocles to Aristotle."[51] As such, it is a story in which Plato is emphatically absent.[52] In any case, as Martha Nussbaum has made abundantly clear, Aristotle is heir to the epic and tragic world we have been at some pains to describe. In the moral domain, he accepts the range of issues much as Plato and the tragedians had defined them. His fundamental moral concerns continue to be Plato's: Can virtue be taught? If so, then how is it taught?[53] We meet this question very early in Plato's career.[54] There, as in much of his early work, Plato's solution involves the conviction that "virtue is itself knowledge [*phronēsis*]."[55] By definition, then, virtue *can* be taught, and, once it has been learned, the educated soul will not and can not do the evil.

Plato's dissatisfaction with this moral account—the seeds of it are sown already *in* the *Meno*—derives from the simple observation that practical experience belies these philosophical facts. Plato's enduring dilemma is the one presented by the fact of *moral failure*. Allegedly rational moral agents *do* choose the evil, all the time. And in thinking this problem through, Plato was inspired to develop a far more sophisticated moral psychology, particularly in the *Phaedrus* and the *Republic,*[56] where he endeavors to explain that moral fragility which seems to be our common lot. He does so by providing us with a moral psychology by dividing the soul into three distinct parts—which is to say, he explains moral failure *by describing the soul as divided against itself.*

Aristotle, as in so many areas, never moved far from his master here, no matter how much he may later have emphasized their differences.[57] His *Nicomachean Ethics* presupposes, it seems to me, a tripartite soul which is remarkably similar to the one Plato conjectured, in general shape if not in every particular.[58] In saying this, I am not making the naïve claim that the two thinkers are simply "the same." Great thinkers seldom if ever take up one anothers' ideas without altering them. But the alterations are seldom as determinative as their originators want to believe them to be. So too here—Aristotle agrees with Plato as to the nature of the relevant moral *questions*. And the relevant question at this juncture is one which we have had occasion to ask already: Can the moral agent be considered *rational* without first being habituated into a moral *tradition?*

Now, MacIntyre, anti-Enlightenment critic that he is, claims that Kant was the first thinker to deny this systematically (I think he is quite wrong about that—wrong that Kant was the first to say so, and wrong that he said so in such dramatic terms), whereas Aristotle had been emphatic about the *necessity* of moral education (*paideia*) in the process of the formation of rational, moral selves. Certainly he was, but Aristotle remains far more interested in the development of human *rationality* than he is in the articulation of *tradition* for its own sake.[59] My point, again, is that MacIntyre, by emphasizing *some* of the Aristotelian account but not *all* of it, subtly alters the focus of these texts. The end of the *polis* is *autarkeia,* self-sufficiency. Traditions have a *penultimacy* about them, for Aristotle and for Plato and for Nietzsche alike. Penultimacy does not imply unimportance. But it also does not imply ultimacy.

What, then, are the chief components of a moral *psyche?* Rather than spin out the specifics of what Plato and Aristotle say, I should like to present the scheme which emerges from what both thinkers said, taken together. In doing this, I hope to illuminate something implicit in MacIntyre's account which is well borne out by his analogy on moral education. Taken together then, what do Plato's and Aristotle's moral psychology look like?

The first "part of the soul," the *animal* part (is this the self which *needs* the *polis?* is that why we are, at the first, political *animals?*), pursues pleasure, pure and simple. The second, the *social* self, pursues pleasure as well, but these are pleasures which the society has defined and constructed for us. That is to say, pursuing a virtuous life, much like playing a game and unlike merely eating well, is a pleasurable activity because the society has helped to define it as pleasurable. We know the virtues when we are first told, and then taught, what they are. This, quite naturally, is that portion of the account which MacIntyre emphasizes, for moral *narratives* and *traditions* are what instruct us in this way. Nonetheless, the *rational* self—that elusive, possibly immortal, third part of the human soul—becomes *contemplative* about the moral life, probably for the first time. It has inherited, says Aristotle, "the that" [*to hoti*][60] of morality, but it seeks the rationale, "the because" [*to dioti*].[61] It seeks to understand *why* what has been defined as moral is moral *in fact.* And to do this, it must be shown how these virtues coincide most appropriately with the universal natural ends (*teloi*) of a universal, which is to say *rational,* human nature.

MacIntyre's example for illustrating this moral psychology is that of a small child learning to play chess.[62] It relies on his notion of something which he calls a "practice."[63] At the outset, the child is rewarded with candy for playing the game; attention is thus directed to *external goods,* goods which are not at all intrinsic to the practice of the game. This child is pursuing pleasure, in the guise of candy, and nothing else. That this cannot be the end of the matter for

Aristotle is clear. "Amusement," he reminds us, "is *not* the object with a view to which the young should be educated."[64] After a time, the child may be sufficiently habituated into the game, and along the way may have developed skills sufficient to appreciate the game as an end in itself. No longer pursuing the crass pleasures of candy, he or she now recognizes the socially defined *internal goods* of chess. And our children are now capable, at last, of playing social games for their own complex and highly specific rewards.

Yet there is a third stage on this youngster's moral horizon, the stage with which Aristotle was chiefly concerned, it seems to me, yet which MacIntyre has seemed reluctant to address at all until recently. There comes a time, with critical self-reflection, when the little girl or boy, now presumably a mature man or woman, will reflect upon what makes chess an intrinsically worthwhile pursuit. Why do we play *this* game rather than some other, and why do we no longer enjoy certain games which thrilled us as children? Tic-tac-toe eventually *gives way* to chess. This is but another version of Bentham's old question about the respective virtues of poetry and pushpin. Aristotle is completely willing to make such hierarchical value judgments, as is MacIntyre, although for different reasons. "Tic-tac-toe is not an example of a practice in this sense, nor is throwing a football with skill," MacIntyre observes, "but the game of football is, and so is chess."[65] What Aristotle likes about such pursuits is their implicit rationality, the fact that they engender contemplative skills which can be advanced with age and repetition. MacIntyre likes their socialness.[66] Where Aristotle emphasizes the structure of the games we play, MacIntyre emphasizes the fact that we are all playing together.[67] There is a world of moral difference in these analyses.[68]

What is clear, and needs to be stressed at this juncture, is that Aristotle's position is clearly indebted to Plato's formulation of the problem. And he concludes his psychological observations with precisely the claim that gave Plato such endless theoretical trouble: that the truly rational moral agent would never choose to do the evil—since he or she simply has no reason any longer to do so.[69] Once again the moral life, when properly ordered, has something determinate, and very nearly automatic, about it. By beginning our narrative in a certain way, we destine it to a certain sort of ending. That this continues to be the attractiveness (and the naïveté) of the Aristotelian position for MacIntyre becomes even clearer in his more recent work. MacIntyre's earlier example of a child learning to play chess has given way to that of a hockey player[70] who, in the final seconds of a game, automatically (and very nearly by instinct) passes the puck to a teammate with a better chance of scoring. Here again, it is the certainty and uniformity of role-playing in a well-ordered moral community which MacIntyre wants, not the process—with all of its attendant difficulties and risks and ambiguities—of practical rational deliberation and moral development. His children, in a sense, never grow up, which is to say, they never become particular moral individuals.

V

We could say a number of things by way of concluding this discussion. I would like to mention several things, in passing, as suggestions worthy of further reflection. This book is, in large measure, an attempt to reflect further upon them. Academic orthodoxies are always worth questioning, and they always die hard. I think the contemporary "rediscovery" of Aristotle stands badly in need of critical examination. Not that Aristotle is unimportant, but we ought at least to ask ourselves *what* we consider so important about him. For me, Aristotle is neither a brilliant creative thinker (Plato was that), nor is he so one-dimensional as MacIntyre has made him out to be. *He is enormously important as a summarian of the received classical wisdom.* In MacIntyre's own terms, he is an encyclopaedist.[71] That is how Nietzsche understood him, and Nietzsche remains one of the most creative classicists and philological interpreters of the past century. There is far more sophisticated probing into the nature of tragic drama in *The Birth of Tragedy* than there is in Aristotle's formalistic reflections from the *Poetics*. Nietzsche's perception of Aristotle's place merits considerable attention, considerably more than it usually receives:

> The desire for some sort of certainty in Aesthetics led to the worship of Aristotle. I believe it will gradually be proved that he understood nothing about art, and that what we marvel about in him is simply the echo of clever Athenian chatter.[72]

In our rediscovery (and revaluation) of Aristotle's moral philosophy, we seem to have arrived at a critical *educational* question. *Whose* Aristotle do we prefer, and *how* shall we teach him? Is his portrait of the moral life as instinctual as MacIntyre's hockey-players make it seem? MacIntyre's insistence that the real moral question in our day must be "Nietzsche or Aristotle?" is too simplistic by far. Nietzsche and Aristotle, as I have tried to suggest briefly here, share much in their reflections upon self-sufficiency, and upon the *penultimacy* of the *polis* and its traditions. As a tentative working definition for the purposes of this essay, I would like to suggest that Liberalism is itself not overtly hostile to tradition—that is what the tragic posture makes of it—but rather critically ambivalent about tradition. *Liberalism teaches the* penultimacy *of the polis,* the importance, but also the simultaneous inadequacy, of traditional moral training. It does so in the name of cultivating *individual* excellences. Liberalism thus also maintains some distinction, however problematic, between *personal* issues (which do not change so very much across the accidents of place and time), and *political* issues which address matters of more essential differences, ones which we try to come together to sort out legislatively. The educational ideal is, whether we like the word or not, directed toward a more private kind of aesthetics.

I think MacIntyre's question might be better put as "Aristotle or [our] Aristotelianism?" A related question, then, is Nietzsche's: Why do we continue to return to the Greeks? Where does their enduring cultural power come from? And why are they worth such careful (and constant) scholarly attention?

I cannot agree with MacIntyre that we read Homer, or the poets, or Aristotle, in order to understand how their *pre*modern sense of community and tradition has given way to *our* "modern" discontents. Nor can I agree that the Greeks "just so happen" to be "our" beginning in a place called "the west." What we share in common with some eastern Mediterranean philosophers and poets who lived and wrote some twenty-five hundred years ago, or more, is unclear to me at first glance, apart from the assumption of the existence of something resembling what is traditionally called "human nature." I recognize how naïve a claim this must seem, given the current academic fashion of problematizing such concepts, but I also know of no better or more convincing philosophical and artistic alternative.[73] We do not read the Greeks chiefly to learn how to inhabit a tradition or to live in a *polis*. In point of fact, the Greeks themselves proved singularly incapable of doing either one very well. Their genius, as Nietzsche knew perhaps better than anyone, was *aesthetic,* not ethical. We study the Greeks to learn about ourselves. We study them because they present us with such a remarkable array of astonishing artistic (and political) personalities in such remarkable conjunction. Here again, it is Nietzsche who took the point.

> The Greeks are interesting and fantastically important, because they have such
> an incredible number of great individuals.
> How was that possible? *That* needs study.[74]

Nietzsche is amazed that so many great spirits could inhabit the same *polis* without ostracizing or killing one another (though they often did). Here were *Übermenschen* who seemed to manage the definitive human cycle, from mountaintop to marketplace, with unusual aplomb. Their "traditions" were but a step on the way toward that greatness of spirit and self-sufficiency which Aristotle went so far as to call the final end of the *polis*. The city-state, and her traditions, are all there for us, if not exactly to outgrow, then at least to find gradually incomplete.

The end of the matter is clear enough. For Aristotle, as for Nietzsche—and against most of those who are trying to "rehabilitate" Aristotle, somehow, for this antiliberal day and age—to live outside the *polis* was neither a beastly nor an angelic thing. It is rather the fine thing, the *human* thing, human in the fullest sense. It is where Achilles and Antigone—to say nothing of Socrates, curiously enough, and now Zarathustra—were all heading. If not exactly a human thing, as we customarily use that word, this movement appeals to the highest which is in us, and remains the highest calling of which we are capable. Movement "outside" and "beyond"—from marketplace to mountaintop, and back again—is an essential part of our moral destiny. Perhaps we are political animals. But that part of us which is not merely "animal" is not precisely at home in the *polis* either. Nietzsche is, here as elsewhere, both trenchant and inescapable: "To live alone one must be animal or god—so says Aristotle. There is yet a third case missing: one must be both—*a philosopher.*"[75] As is clearer now, I hope, it is precisely this "third case" which I mean to defend in this book.

At this point I am not so naïve as to assume that I have proven that Aristotle was an "individualist" in the way that most "modern" people are. All I hope to have accomplished at this point is a systematic putting of the question. If, by the end of this book, I have succeeded in sensitizing us to how slippery these modernist buzzwords really are—'individualism' and 'community,' 'tradition,' and 'modernity' most of all—then I will be satisfied. For now, all I want to highlight is what should be the fairly obvious point that there is a *penultimacy* about the *polis.* In the next chapter and then again in the last, I hope to nail this point down by demonstrating that "the individual" whom we are told is so distinctive a feature of our "modernity" is, in fact, already clearly in evidence in Homer. In order to make good that claim, however, I need to turn first to one of the most influential brands of antimodern, antiliberal Aristotelianism. That is Alasdair's MacIntyre's narrative account of our decline and fall—*into* "modernity."

Notes

1. See Alasdair MacIntyre, *Whose Justice? Which Rationality?* (South Bend, IN: University of Notre Dame Press, 1988), 326–48.

2. Alasdair MacIntyre, *After Virtue,* 2nd ed. (South Bend, IN: University of Notre Dame Press, 1984), 6–7.

3. Of course, the natural, and ultimately unanswerable, next question is, What constitutes a "real" tradition? For some attempt to answer that vexing question, see MacIntyre's *Three Rival Versions of Moral Enquiry: Encyclopedia, Genealogy, and Tradition* (South Bend, IN: The University of Notre Dame Press, 1990), 170–215.

4. MacIntyre goes so far as to call Nietzsche, not Aristotle, *"the* philosopher . . . *for the modern age"* (*After Virtue,* 114).

5. The term was coined by Allan Bloom in his astonishingly popular (astonishing because so much of what he had to tell us was terrible) *The Closing of the American Mind: How Higher Education Has Failed Democracy and Impoverished the Souls of Today's Students* (New York: Simon & Schuster, 1987), 139ff.

6. Indeed, one of the things Hauerwas most appreciates about Aristotle is that he cannot be made a "liberal," as he thinks Martha Nussbaum wants to do. See his "Can Aristotle Be a Liberal? Nussbaum on Luck," *Soundings* 72.4 (1989): 675–91.

7. These points are laid out most clearly in Stanley Hauerwas, *A Community of Character: Toward a Constructive Christian Social Ethic* (South Bend, IN: University of Notre Dame Press, 1981) and *The Peaceable Kingdom: A Primer in Christian Ethics* (South Bend, IN: University of Notre Dame Press, 1983).

8. Stephen Toulmin, *Cosmopolis: The Hidden Agenda of Modernity* (Chicago: University of Chicago Press, 1990), 67ff.

9. Robert Bellah, Richard Madsen, William Sullivan, Ann Swidler, and Stephen Tipton, *Habits of the Heart: Individualism and Commitment in American Life* (Berkeley: University of California Press, 1985).

10. Alexis de Tocqueville, *Democracy in America,* translated in two volumes by Henry Reeve (1840), revised by Francis Bowen (1862) and Philip Bradley (1945) (New York: Random House, Vintage Books, 1945), I.310.

11. Bellah et al., *Habits of the Heart,* ix, 119.

12. The book is deeply indebted, too indebted finally, I think, to MacIntyre's definition of "the problems," which commits them, in turn, to some form of his "solution." See *Habits of the Heart,* xii, 301–2.

13. Bellah et al., *Habits of the Heart,* 71–75.

14. For an important qualification of the dramatic overstatement which comes with telling our stories this way, and an important reservation about the desperate account of our modernness which we get in *Habits of the Heart,* see Jeffrey Stout, *Ethics After Babel: The Languages of Morals and Their Discontents* (Boston: Beacon Press, 1988), 191–96.

15. de Tocqueville, *Democracy in America* I.328–29.

16. *Ibid.,* II.65–67, against II.85.

17. *Ibid.,* II.62.

18. That idea has generated a seemingly endless bibliography since its popularization in 1987, and *another* interminable (academic) debate about what constitutes "the canon" of the Western tradition. Allan Bloom offered a sort of wake-up call to university educators in his *The Closing of the American Mind,* where he scored some strong points about what he considered "the fall" of the modern American university. Still and all, his postured narrative continues to participate in the problem, it seems to me—the postured assumption that we are living today in the great age of moral collapse. I find E. D. Hirsch's *Cultural Literacy: What Every American Needs to Know* (Boston: Houghton, Mifflin Company, 1987) a helpful corrective, for the *tone* with which he writes as well as the content of what he says. He reminds us, rightly I think, that there are certain things we all ought to know, certain things which a college education ought to presuppose, *and* that it is fairly easy to acquire this knowledge. Debating the *meaning*, not the *content*, of a "traditional" education is the interesting matter, and probably where we will always disagree, up to a point. Such disagreements can be reflective of the health, not the dis-ease, of a culture or a tradition.

No one person can "read it all," and the good news is that none of us need do so. We all appropriate, and embody, our fair share of it. Since that is the case, new things can be, and always are, added to the syllabi of any responsive "traditional" college course. To argue that "the Western tradition" needs to be excised is as overdrawn and nonsensical as the claim that it must be taught in every generation "the same as it ever was." That is a sham doctrine of tradition.

"The tradition" we are arguing so much about, as I will argue in the fourth and fifth chapters, is a many-splendored, often non-Western and decisively non-American thing, insofar as it has its roots in the ancient world of the eastern Mediterranean. It is as unmodern (not antimodern) as it is non-Western (not anti-Western). Moreover, these traditions are as accessible, as teachable, now as they ever have been. Our refusal to see or say that is, in my view, "where we are beginning to fail."

See also Alasdair MacIntyre, *Three Rival Versions of Moral Enquiry,* 228.

19. MacIntyre, *After Virtue,* 109–20.

20. MacIntyre, *Whose Justice? Which Rationality?,* 96–97.

21. Aristotle, *Politics,* 1253a1–4, translation mine. For the Greek text I am using W. D. Ross' *Aristotelis: Politica* (Oxford: Clarendon Press, 1957, 1988), 3.

The famous phrase, *politikon zōion,* or "political animal," makes it clear that Aristotle has the Greek city-state, the *polis,* in mind, and does not necessarily mean what we mean by 'political.' He means, quite simply, that humans are the kind of animal which "live in a civic association of some kind." Defining the *best* kind of civic association is the self-appointed task for the entire book.

22. MacIntyre, *After Virtue,* 22.

23. *Ibid.,* 118–19, 129.

24. Martha Nussbaum, *The Fragility of Goodness: Luck and Ethics in Greek Tragedy and Philosophy* (New York: Cambridge University Press, 1986), 420.

25. The so-called Mesotes Formula is described at *Nicomachean Ethics* 1109a20–1109b26.

"That moral excellence is a mean [*mesotēs*], that is, a mean [*mesotēs*] between two evils—one of excess and the other of deficiency—and that it is such as a sort of striving for the mean [*meson*] in feeling and in actions, is now clear enough," Aristotle concludes.

For the Greek text of the *Nicomachean Ethics* I am using H. Rackham's in the *Loeb Classical Library* (New York: G. P. Putnam's Sons, 1930).

26. Martha Nussbaum, *Love's Knowledge: Essays in Philosophy and Literature* (New York: The Oxford University Press, 1990), 378–79.

27. This word, a cognate of *hamartia* (the New Testament term for "sin") is consistently translated as "sin" in Thomas Aquinas' *Commentary on Aristotle's Nicomachean Ethics,* trans. C. I. Litzinger (Notre Dame, IN: Dumb Ox Books, 1993), 107.

28. The passage continues with the identical phrase about excess and deficiency: "So it is that excess and deficiency are evils, and that the mean [*mesotēs*] defines excellence." Aristotle *Nicomachean Ethics* 1106b28–35, translation mine.

29. See Aquinas' *Commentary on Aristotle's Nicomachean Ethics,* 123–26.

30. "For the *polis* is an organization, not a society, and 'political' is not synonymous with 'social'." Hannah Arendt, *The Human Condition* (Chicago: University of Chicago Press, 1958), 28–37.

31. I am aware that elsewhere, in the *Nicomachean Ethics,* he does invoke *eudaimonia* as the final end of a human life. I need only observe here that he did not necessarily mean what we mean by "happiness," a point that MacIntyre has made well. Still more importantly, for my argument, is that he does *not* say this here, precisely where we might well have expected him to do so.

See the remarkable essays by Thomas Nagel and J. L. Ackrill entitled "Aristotle on *Eudaimonia*" in Amelie O. Rorty's *Essays on Aristotle's Ethics* (Berkeley: University of California Press, 1980), 7–34.

32. Aquinas, *Commentary on Aristotle's Nicomachean Ethics,* 628.

33. Aristotle, *Politics* 1252b35.

34. See Janet Coleman, "MacIntyre and Aquinas," in John Horton and Susan Mendus, eds., *After MacIntyre: Critical Perspectives on the Work of Alasdair MacIntyre* (Notre Dame, IN: University of Notre Dame Press, 1994), esp. 82–87.

35. Aristotle, *Politics* 1253a5–7.

It is interesting that Aristotle only quotes the first half of this passage from *Iliad* IX. 63–64, which reads:

Friendless, lawless and homeless is he
who sows cold conflict among his own people.

The passage in the *Politics* then concludes with a fascinating observation of the uniqueness of human language:

> The reason why humanity is the political animal more than bees or any other humorless animal is clear enough. As the saying goes, "Nature does nothing in vain." And only humanity possesses speech [*logon*].

36. For a brief discussion of the importance of this notion of *themis* to Greek tragic and moral speculation, see my "The Tragic Posture in the Modern Age: An Essay on Tragedy—Classical, Christian and Modern," an unpublished dissertation, Emory University, 1990, 49–61.

37. This is all offered against MacIntyre's description of what is happening in heroic societies, where one's identity is precisely one's social role. I will show, I hope, what nonsense that makes of the *Iliad* in the next chapter, and then again in the last.

38. W. Thomas MacCary, *Childlike Achilles* (New York: Columbia University Press, 1982), 30.

39. Alasdair MacIntyre, *After Virtue,* 116–20, 148–50, 252; and *Whose Justice? Which Rationality?,* 102–203, 124–25, 209–10.

40. Aristotle, *Nicomachean Ethics* 1177b26–1178a3, translation mine.

41. Nussbaum, *The Fragility of Goodness,* 15n.

42. Ibid., 373–77. Yet she has returned to the issue, at the urging of Charles Taylor, in an essay entitled, appropriately enough, "Transcending Humanity," in *Love's Knowledge,* 365–91, especially 368–69. Even here, however, she counsels us—*against* Aristotle, it seems to me—to keep to mortal thoughts, never attempting to "transcend" them (388–89).

43. Nussbaum, *The Fragility of Goodness,* 375.

44. *Ibid.,* 377.

45. Nietzsche, *Wir Philologen,* 5[168]; *Sämtliche Werke,* VIII. 89.

46. Aquinas, *Commentary on Aristotle's Nicomachean Ethics,* 628.

47. Aristotle, *Nicomachean Ethics* 1123a34–1125a17.

48. *Nicomachean Ethics* 1124a20.

49. *Nicomachean Ethics* 1124a21–1124b9.

50. MacIntyre, *After Virtue,* 117. For a defense of Nietzsche's views as vaguely Aristotelian, see Walter Kaufmann, *Nietzsche: Philosopher, Psychologist, Antichrist* (Princeton: Princeton University Press, 1974), 382–85.

51. And that quite briefly, *After Virtue,* 145.

52. This criticism applies only to *After Virtue*. Plato is suddenly and surprisingly present in *Whose Justice? Which Rationality?*, 69–87, but even here he is granted no more prominence for moral reflection than, say, Thucydides.

53. For the discussion which follows, I am deeply indebted to Myles F. Burnyeat's "Aristotle on Learning to Be Good," which appears in Amelie O. Rorty's *Essays on Aristotle's Ethics*, 69–92.

54. *Meno*, 70a.

55. *Meno* 88d, although this knowledge is also claimed to be a gift, or a destiny, from the gods (*theiai moirai, Meno* 100b).

56. *Phaedrus* 246a–249d, and *Republic* 375a.

57. Werner Jaeger, in his *Aristotle: Fundamentals of the History of His Development* (Oxford: Clarendon Press, 1934) makes the really crucial observation that it is far more interesting to talk about the ways in which Plato and Aristotle are similar, than to move too quickly to the assumption that they stand at an infinite remove from one another. MacIntyre himself later admits as much (*Whose Justice? Which Rationality?*, 88–102), although he discusses Jaegar, oddly enough, as one of those scholars who perpetuated this myth of *difference* (94)!

58. See *Nicomachean Ethics* 1098b1–6, 1102a5–1103a10, and 1138b20–1139a18, 1143b17–1144a37]
R. D. Hicks, in his critical edition of *Aristotle's De Anima* (Amsterdam: Adolf M. Hakkert, Publisher, 1965), xxx–xxxvi, is quite explicit on this point: "We find nothing in Aristotle but the development in systematic form of the Platonic heritage . . . the differences between them count for little, however much Aristotle may exaggerate them." Similarly, Gerald F. Else argues that Aristotle's only real difference comes when he tries to argue that the 'animal' part of the soul is "not wholly out of touch with reason," as Plato seems to have suggested at *Republic* 439c–e. See *Aristotle's Poetics: The Argument* (Cambridge, MA: Harvard University Press, 1957), 434–35.

59. Janet Coleman, "MacIntyre and Aquinas," in Horton and Mendus, eds., *After MacIntyre*, 82.

60. *Nicomachean Ethics* 1095b1–7 and 1098b1–3. As "a first thing and a starting point," Aristotle notes, the 'that' of morality is not *entirely* susceptible to rational and causal explanation—a primitive version of MacIntyre's much more sophisticated emphasis upon the contingency of every starting point, which I will take up in the next chapter.
That is to say, we begin our stories arbitrarily . . . and they predetermine us to a certain sort of ending. This last point is important, almost a summary of my overall disagreement with MacIntyre's position. I find the beginnings of the moral life a little less arbitrary than MacIntyre does, and the ending decidedly less determinate.
The essential methodological statement of this, in Aristotle's work, appears at *Metaphysics* 981a29–30.

61. Aristotle, *Nicomachean Ethics* 1095b1–7, 1144b1–1145a11, and 1178a16–19.

62. MacIntyre, *After Virtue,* 188–90.

63. MacIntyre's definition of a 'practice' immediately precedes this discussion, at *After Virtue,* 187:

"By a 'practice' I am going to mean any coherent and complex form of socially established cooperative human activity through which goods internal to the form of activity are realized in the course of trying to achieve those standards of excellence which are appropriate to, and partially definitive of, that form of activity, with the result that human powers to achieve excellence, and human conceptions of the ends and goods involved, are systematically extended."

For an uneven analysis of MacIntyre's definition which nevertheless raises one essential question—*what are we to do about noxious or immoral social practices?*—see Elizabeth Frazer and Nicola Lacey "MacIntyre, Feminism, and the Concept of a Practice," in Horton and Mendus, eds., *After MacIntyre,* 265–82.

64. Aristotle, *Politics* 1339a29. See also *Whose Justice? Which Rationality?,* 110.

65. MacIntyre, *After Virtue,* 187.

66. See Martha Nussbaum's astute and highly critical review of *Whose Justice? Which Rationality?,* "Recoiling from Reason" in the *New York Review of Books* 36.19 (7 December 1989): 39.

67. See Philip Pettit, "Liberal/Communitarian: MacIntyre's Mesmeric Dichotomy," in Horton and Mendus, eds., *After MacIntyre,* 183–86.

68. Janet Coleman, "MacIntyre and Aquinas," in Horton and Mendus, eds., *After MacIntyre,* 66, 82–87.

69. Aristotle, *Nicomachean Ethics* 1152a6–8, and Burnyeat, "Aristotle on Learning to be Good," 88.

70. See *Whose Justice? Which Rationality?,* 140–41.

71. See MacIntyre's *Three Rival Versions of Moral Inquiry,* 14, 18–25, 33, where he outlines "the enduring effects of the encyclopaedists' conception of *the unity of enquiry*" (8). My disagreement with MacIntyre obviously derives from my fundamental agreement with Nietzsche's insight, namely, that Aristotle is an "encyclopedic" rather than a "traditional" thinker, firmly committed to "the unity of enquiry" as well as the *summary* quality of all philosophic thought. MacIntyre also states that "it is the mark of encyclopedia that the present stands in judgment upon the past, assigning to itself a sovereignty which allows it to approve that in the past which can be represented as a precursor of its own standards of judgment" (160). That seems to be *precisely* the conviction of Aristotle's *Metaphysics*.

72. Nietzsche; *Wir Philologen,* 5[13]; *Sämtliche Werke,* VIII.43.

73. See Martha Nussbaum, *Love's Knowledge,* 45, 95–96, 165–67, 220–29, and "Non-Relative Virtues: An Aristotelian Approach," *Midwest Studies in Philosophy* 13 (1988): 32–53, as well as my "Against Positions: Notes on the Relation Between Moral Vision and Moral Debate" *Soundings* 78.3/4 (1995) 501–518.

74. Nietzsche, *Wir Philologen,* 5[14]; *Sämtliche Werke,* VIII.43.

75. Nietzsche, *Twilight of the Idols,* "Maxims and Arrows," §3; *Sämtliche Werke,* VI.59.

3

After Virtue?
On Distorted Philosophical Narratives

> Hegel usually writes as if the Greek *polis* were more har-
> monious than in fact it was; he often ignores the existence
> of slaves. But then, so did Plato and Aristotle.
> —Alasdair MacIntyre, *A Short History of Ethics*

> What this brings out is that modern politics cannot be a
> matter of genuine moral consensus. And it is not. Modern
> politics is civil war carried out by other means. . . .
> My own conclusion is very clear. It is that on the one
> hand we still, in spite of the efforts of three centuries of
> moral philosophy and one of sociology, lack any coherent
> rationally defensible statement of a liberal individualist
> point of view; and that, on the other hand, the Aristotelian
> tradition can be restated in a way that restores intelligibility
> and rationality to our moral and social attitudes.
> —Alasdair MacIntyre, *After Virtue*

We sense that the question of *how to begin* is one of the most perplexing human questions—nowhere more so than in literary matters. We take pen in hand,
we sit down at our desk—perhaps we linger over a second cup of coffee—and
we *worry* about where, and how, to begin. When writing a letter, or a book, the
first sentence is often the hardest. Once you have set it down, then the rest theoretically follows much more naturally. It may even be that the best letters and
books begin in such a way that leads us clearly and inexorably to their end.
"Well begun, half done," in the words of an ancient Greek proverb of which
Aristotle was particularly fond.

Many think that this question—*the question of beginnings*—is one of the
defining questions of the so-called modern age. When Descartes set out to

doubt everything systematically, and to see what was left when he had done so, he was setting an agenda for a great deal of subsequent thought which called itself "modern." He was underscoring how difficult it is to begin. And he was implicitly suggesting that there is only one proper way to begin. By beginning with the inescapable fact of human consciousness, he believed, Descartes arrived at the only appropriate philosophical conclusions. We are heir to his first claim about the difficulty of beginning, I think, although we have in most cases dispensed with the second claim. As we shall see, Hegel did not dispense with it. Indeed, he had an intriguing view of the status of the second claim, which I will examine in some detail here.

I

Alasdair MacIntyre begins with this Cartesian insight, but radicalizes it by emphasizing the *arbitrariness* which this beginning always has about it.[1] In doing so he leaves Descartes behind, and moves further down the road to "modernity," in the direction of Hegel.[2] MacIntyre means to emphasize what he *thinks* he sees at issue in this Hegelian doctrine, yet he seems to me to miss the subtle irony of Hegel's thought.[3] It is one of Hegel's most interesting claims—it is actually the vision which animates his entire philosophical program—that this apparently arbitrary beginning will gradually be recognized for the necessity it always was. We do not "merely" begin; we gradually come to realize, through philosophical reflection, that we began much as we *needed* to begin.

MacIntyre's point is less subtle than this. Our beginnings *are* always only assertions. We all make them with our eventual ends pretty clearly in view. We assume the things which will allow us to get where we want to go, in order to tell ourselves the story we want to hear.[4] *There is, finally, no essential difference between narratives and philosophical arguments.*[5] That is to say, where we begin inexorably conditions where we can go. The beginning lends a peculiar destiny to our destinations.

By emphasizing the sheer *contingency* of the starting point in every narrative and/or philosophical tradition, MacIntyre is out to accomplish several things. First, he wants to articulate a very different perspective on the Greeks, who represent *our* starting point in "the west." MacIntyre wants to tell a very different—anti-Cartesian and non-Hegelian—story about the (arbitrary) rise *and* (modern) *fall* of the west.[6] The Greeks are where the west *just so happens* to begin.[7] And the extraordinary age of Greek letters itself *just so happens* to begin with Homer. Thus Homer, while he has in large measure destined us, is not a destiny as such. It could all have been very different, had the Muse elected to sing it differently to begin with. We never get back to any *necessary* beginnings or first principles. There is no necessity, only narrative. "Because every such rational tradition begins from the contingency and positivity of some set of established beliefs," MacIntyre tells us, "the rationality of tradition is inescapably anti-Cartesian."[8] One of the *leitmotifs* of this book—it derives chiefly from Hegel's Aesthetic lectures, and constitutes the real heart of my disagreement with MacIntyre's overall narrative arguments—is that Homer and the tragedians are classic for one very excellent reason: their poetry represents a subtle and vaguely "necessary" beginning to the story we tell about human consciousness and human socialness.

As with the beginning, so too with the end. MacIntyre insists that the contingency of our origins also makes a sheer contingency of our ending point. He means to disqualify any sort of Hegelian narrative closure, any story-telling (such as we get in Hegel's *Phenomenology*) which culminates in a form of knowledge which is believed to be 'Absolute.'[9] "No one at any stage," MacIntyre cautions, "can ever rule out the future possibility of their present beliefs and judgments being shown to be inadequate."[10] I suspect that this word of caution is underscored because MacIntyre's recent intellectual program is precisely designed to alert "Liberals" to the fact that this has happened to them, here and now, in the "modern" age.[11]

In his hugely influential *After Virtue*, MacIntyre chooses to begin with what he himself admits is "a disquieting suggestion." It is *intended* to be "disquieting." His whole *narrative* is designed to be "disquieting." It is, in essence, his own apocalypse, his own picture of the end—*our* end, in the era of Liberal modernity.

The circularity of this argument is important: he begins with an ending, a disquieting end which is, oddly enough, not quite so arbitrary as he alleges. MacIntyre's whole argument insists that it was *necessary*. His narrative shows us a broken moral world, shattered and in disarray. He describes a fictive world in which books have been burned, an entire culture systematically (though not entirely) erased, the very language we use hopelessly muddled, ripped out of a context in which it once made sense.[12] We can make sense no longer, he claims, in this moral world, *after* Babel.[13]

MacIntyre's parting image is as arresting as the first. He concludes this massive and hugely influential diagnosis of our modernity by insisting that "the ideology of modern bureaucratic individualism" has failed, for three full centuries, to give any rational account of itself. "Modernity"—we hear this same claim put countless times in countless different ways—is "inarticulate." And he believes that the Greek tradition—as it was summarized in the moral and political philosophy of Aristotle, that great encyclopaedist of received Greek wisdom—can be reconstituted in such a manner as to restore order and coherence to our moral languages. Living after Babel, and Eden, we can nonetheless restore a certain vision of the Classical Greek *polis*.

Ironically enough, our own age is, MacIntyre insists, spiritual kin to Rome (not Greece) in *her* last days, with the only difference being that, this time, "the barbarians are not waiting beyond the frontiers; they have already been governing us for quite some time."[14] We need to retreat from empire to forms of local community, from Rome in her last days to Greece in her political heyday. We are waiting, he thinks, for "a new and doubtless very different St. Benedict"—presumably, a man who will provide the new rules, the new table of virtues, which may yet restore articulacy and civility to social lives which are, even now, in the process of coming all undone. In fact, "it is our lack of consciousness of this that constitutes part of our predicament." Traditions, it would seem, have to be self-conscious to be "articulate."[15]

In a certain sense, this book begins and ends with MacIntyre's diagnoses, especially to the degree that they echo the claims of the later Nietzsche. This is so because I view him as eloquently representative of a contemporary academic fashion—something I have called "the tragic posture"[16]—something which I earnestly hope is nothing more than a passing fashion and not a reflection of the fact that the barbarians really *are* here to stay. My own view begins with a frustration which derives, in its turn, from a suspicion: that the enduring significance of Greece, and of her poetic-tragic legacy in particular, has been decisively undermined by this contemporary posture—which wants to view our age as "tragic," an epoch of irrecoverable losses, the collapse of faith and the failure of reason. Tragedy, a Greek word and an eminently Greek idea, does not necessarily connote catastrophe—a point which bears considerable reflection, if the Greeks' enduring legacy is to be properly assessed.[17] This age of ours—despite what we tell ourselves, despite what our culture-despisers claim—lays no special claim to doubt or disarray. It is not, as MacIntyre would have it, that we are unconscious of our predicament; the predicament is not nearly so severe, and certainly not so unique, as he has made it out to be. 'Modern' need not be, and probably should not be, a proper noun.

We may take one further step. MacIntyre's interest in narrative *has* convinced me that any tragic construal of the "modern" age is thoroughly bound up in an often unstated account of the past. That is to say, if one grants MacIntyre's assumptions about the elusive necessity of narrative beginnings, then it is all-to-easy to believe in an equally fictive narrative ending. It is also easy to become convinced that this end is imminent. The beginning may be half of everything, but as Hegel reminds us, particularly in his aesthetic writings, all beginnings are not equally arbitrary. There is a subtle necessity about beginning in certain ways.

The Greeks are our beginning; and Homer is the literary and cultural beginning of what we know now as "Greece." There is, moreover, something about Homer which makes him a uniquely suitable starting point in my judgment. Unlike MacIntyre, I do not see beginnings and endings as equally arbitrary. Rather, I see Homer as a uniquely appropriate beginning for us, a beginning with no real end in sight.

The *Iliad* is, after all, a surprisingly "modern" story—in MacIntyre's terms—a story about what it is to feel alien in the world, about what it is to question the values of one's society, as well as to leave behind the friends who continue to live and die by those values. It is the painful story of individual detachment and maturation. It is a story about the *penultimacy* of the *polis*. Achilles' predicament is astonishingly recognizable. Hegel is explicit about something which MacIntyre denies—namely, that in Homer we are privy to a remarkably "modern" voice, a voice which is at the same time a very old one, a voice which articulates perplexities and problems we must recognize as very like our own. Sometimes, says Hegel, "we get the beginning and perfection all at once."[18] That is an antidecadent insight if ever there were one.

> The nostalgic tradition runs from Rousseau through Marx to Levi-Strauss. The *Iliad*, however, and then Hegel and Freud, and now Derrida and Foucault, correct their false yearning, for they reveal that without struggle there is no definition. Our individuality exists only as a function of our suspension of disbelief in the values our society has formed for us and the models it has erected for our emulation. . . . Achilles realizes this and tries to tell the horror of it, but we refuse to listen if we are humanists, and if we are nostalgic socialists we say that individuality is a perverse concept determined by the capitalist system. As critics of the *Iliad*, however, we should admit that the struggle is always already there.[19]

In Homer, we find a text which is infinitely richer than, and resists equation with, other heroic epics—an equation which MacIntyre insists upon, with profound consequences as we shall shortly see. In Homer, the beginning is a uniquely appropriate one, remarkably contemporary and illuminating. It is neither simply nor arbitrarily what it is. I will go so far in this essay as to consider the *Iliad*, a little outrageously, "timeless."[20]

As I say, MacIntyre's views will not allow this. He insists that the present—"modernity," which is also an ending—is all bound up in a fictive beginning which is now lost. *That* is the story he wants to tell. Our losses make sense only in the purer light of what some Golden Age allegedly possessed.[21] This uncanny nostalgia reads Homer as the childlike portrait-painter of a lost world, an heroic world where comrades-in-arms agreed about most of the important things in life, and were capable of participating in tasks which were genuinely common. It is almost as though the *Iliad* were no longer a poem about a war, where the two chief Greek protagonists cannot agree about the distribution of spoils or, so it finally appears, about anything at all. Real agreement, in Achilles' case, is reserved for one of the enemy.

The great advantage of a Hegelian critical perspective is that it negates nostalgia. It allows the critic to focus on an object which has historical locus, and to admire it, without being absorbed by it. From [most all] other perspectives, authenticity is a lost reality that can only be approximated in the decadent critical present.[22]

MacIntyre's beginning, his Homer, is a very different thing from Hegel's (and from Nietzsche's as well). This difference is determinative. Our allegedly "modern" losses ring true only if we believe what MacIntyre alleges about some idealized heroic past. *The narrative end is always tied to some myth of origin.* This is why the Greeks become definitive in a book about our many "afterwords" (and afterthoughts). A teleology always implies an archaeology. Or, since this word has a peculiar resonance after Foucault, a teleology needs a narrative—a decidedly arbitrary and romantic beginning, and a really rather desperate end. MacIntyre himself insists on this *necessity* of narrative.[23] It is nothing less than the nature of his narrative—the way he begins (with the Greeks) and the way he ends (with us)—to which I am objecting.

II

MacIntyre himself underscores how essential this narrative structure is. At the outset, he outlines his project for the entire story of *After Virtue*—a sort of philosophical-narrative plotline—which is comprised, not surprisingly, of two distinct but intimately related tasks: his beginning and his end.[24] First, he wants to articulate "the specific character of the modern age" (chs. 3–9); then he wishes to "identify and describe the lost morality of the past" (chs. 10–13). Only at that point will he be prepared to offer a restatement of the Aristotelian tradition of the virtues (chs. 14–16) which will be able to defend itself against rival accounts more in accord with the "Liberal" and "emotivist" sham-traditions of modernity (ch. 17). We need to pay careful attention to these two intimately related tasks: a pessimistic interpretation of the present, and an idealized (read: distorted) portrait of the past.[25] Taken together, they constitute MacIntyre's tragic posture. As I have said several times now, his myth of western origins is intimately tied to his account of the modern end—that linkage is the first law of coherent narrative construction. My objection, therefore, cuts to the very heart of his entire project: If MacIntyre is wrong about his Homer, as I would like to suggest that he is, then his arguments about our "modern" predicaments are, to say the least, highly suspect.

The cultural unity of the Greeks, MacIntyre argues, has given way to the moral incoherence of "modern" times. Note the choice of genre: It is a classical morality play, a decline and fall. The moral Paradise (of Homeric Greece) has given way to the Fall (industrial revolution and bourgeois society) and we are now living in the prelude to Apocalypse (Liberal modernity). MacIntyre's nostalgia is embedded in an argument which says, quite simply, "then they had it, and now we don't."[26] That is a problem in two directions, past and present, Homeric and modern. My objection is, simply put, that "they *never* had it," at least not in MacIntyre's idyllic terms. Even if he does not invoke tragic language explicitly at this point, as George Steiner does,[27] MacIntyre *does* seem wedded to the modernist prejudice for unhappy endings which perhaps best characterizes the tragic posture. That point will become crucial toward the end of this chapter. It is tied to the way he (mis)reads his Homer.

This is a posture, so I am arguing, which is as misleading as it is pernicious. It serves either as counsel to wallow in our times, or else simply to reject them out of hand. We end up as culture-despisers, or fatalists—tragic posturers and apocalypticists. If we begin unmodernly, then we end in antimodern despair. We saw this same movement in Nietzsche's intellectual career.

MacIntyre seems to insist that "modernity is itself the problem." We would do well to turn this question around. "What times have *not* been 'the problem'?" Where was it *ever* any different? Apocalypticism, while it waxes and wanes in human society, is surely never absent, and *that* is the critical fact which we are in danger of overlooking today at the end of our millennium. Frank Kermode has pointed out how postured, and how very *academic*, this apocalypticism tends to be:

> This assertion [that we are living in the great age of crisis], upon which a multitude of important books is founded, is nowadays no more surprising than the opinion that the earth is round. There seems to me to be some danger in this situation, if only because such a myth, uncritically accepted, tends like prophecy to shape a future to confirm it. . . . Even the scholar who studies crisis as a recurrent, if not perpetual, historical phenomenon, tends to single out ours as the major instance.[28]

MacIntyre's cultural diagnostics, his conviction that we are living *after* "virtue," seem emblematic of this highly academic posture. We need to be on guard against it, I think, particularly when we import these modernist assumptions back into our reading of Homer. MacIntyre, like countless other moderns, has told himself this story of dissolution and despair for so long that he, and many of us with him, have begun finally to believe it. We have *habituated* ourselves into a sort of antimodern disgust.

My disagreement will be, I hope, systematic and wide-ranging. It will be paradigmatic for the disagreements in every chapter to follow. First and foremost, I am calling his reading of the past into question, specifically the Greek tradition we find in Homer and the tragic poets. I agree with Aristotle that there is substantial agreement between epic and tragedy (a point which Hegel seemed to deny on historical grounds, but granted in aesthetic practice). I emphatically disagree with MacIntyre that there is no such thing as thinking apart from a social setting, no rationality which is tradition-independent. The *Iliad*, and the tragedies too, insofar as they are what Simone Weil called them—"the loveliest of spiritual mirrors"—tell precisely the story which MacIntyre claims we today are the first to tell ourselves with such desperate intensity: the story of moral uncertainty, inarticulacy, and the gradual detachment from the mores of the community in which we find ourselves. In fact, Achilles is but the first of a never-ending cast of heroes—Antigone is another one, and Ajax is a third—who find that the search for self-definition pushes them inexorably outside of the social order and the cold comfort which is all their friends' truisms have to offer. The *Iliad* may be the first (it is by no means the last) adventure in human self-discovery.[29] Homer *already* preaches the penultimacy of the *polis*.

More, perhaps, than any other contemporary thinker, Alasdair MacIntyre has helped me to see that "modernity" is indeed what is at issue in these disparate debates. His characterization of "the modern age" as uniquely chaotic and confused lies behind his entire argument, even his reading of the *Iliad*, and is precisely what I mean to call into question. 'Modern' finally becomes one more weapon in a lexicon of philosophical abuse, just like 'cosmopolitan' and 'liberal' and 'bourgeois.'[30] Ours is an age of moral apocalypse, MacIntyre claims. And yet, to my mind, Homer depicts a moral world already astonishingly close to us, as I hope to demonstrate here and then again in the last chapter.

Despite the intensity of the manner in which he writes, and despite the apocalypticism of his imagery, there remains a curious ambivalence which lies at the heart of MacIntyre's troubling diagnoses. I still do not know how "troubling" MacIntyre means to be, nor how "troubled" he means us to be, by way of response. How interminable are the conflicts of our own day? How recoverable is the past?[31] *Which* past does he want? Homer's heroic society? Plato's Athens? A medieval university or monastery?[32] Those who found *After Virtue* most compelling, it seems to me, have been by and large our contemporary culture-despisers—those *anti*modernists who read in our own conflicts symptoms of an advanced state of moral decay. They are by and large the same ones who find MacIntyre's less apocalyptic, later work unsatisfying.

Their liturgy is well known. We no longer agree about anything. We no longer share enough in common even to understand what it is about which we are disagreeing. We are locked inside the iron cages of our own private worlds, where *my* interests never take *yours*, to say nothing of *ours*, into account. We are individualists run rampant. MacIntyre calls this Emotivism; I call it a posture.

III

Before moving on to Homer, let me briefly rehearse MacIntyre's argument in more detail. We in the west are heir, he says, however unwittingly *and however contingently,* to the thought world of the Greeks. Their moral and philosophical language largely shaped our own, and for this very reason ironically continues to do so.[33] The "modern" world, however, has inherited only fragmentary bits and pieces of a once-coherent Greek moral vocabulary, and the communal sensitivity which made sense of it, such that our own moral languages are less the moral Esperanto we would like them to be, more akin to the gibberish spoken *after* Babel.

What, then, did this integrated moral vocabulary, and its implicit worldview, look like? It insists, first and foremost, as we saw in the last chapter, that humanity is meant for community, for the *polis.* We are all "political animals." To be human is to exist always-already in community with others. MacIntyre takes the peculiarly modern interest in the social construction of human selves and insists that it is neither peculiar nor modern—it was, so it appears, the chief tenet of the Greek account of the virtues.[34] Yet this view is absolutely dependent upon MacIntyre's narrative beginning—namely, a highly idiosyncratic reading of the *Iliad.* The *community* defines what is good and what is virtuous and what is moral. The human "individual" is educated and habituated into this community of virtue with its attendant roles and duties. To be a good citizen is to be well-schooled into the virtues of the community. To fail to be so educated, or to reject the schooling, is by definition to be less than human, to be a person without a country or narrative community, to be thoroughly "apolitical." As I pointed out in the last chapter, that is not necessarily a beastly thing. It is, in some important respects, our moral destiny. It can be a fine thing, the *human* thing. In the post-Enlightenment world of moral philosophy, and now "after Nietzsche," MacIntyre wants to say that each and every one of us have been doomed to live in moral exile—unless we can get back home, to Ithaca.

MacIntyre suggests that the heroic societies portrayed in Homer as well as in a variety of other epic poems *had* such a coherent account of the virtues. There was no critical (read: "individualist") vantage-point to which one might climb, and in moving decisively "outside," to assess the moral merits of such a world. It was *impossible* for the Homeric hero to be 'apolitical'.[35] This heroic moral order was subject to dissolution and critical decay in the fifth century BCE, MacIntyre tells us, and the tragedies reflect something of this turbulence.[36] But Aristotle, as René Girard reminds us, "is above and beyond the crisis of tragedy. . . . That is why he is so great, *and so one-sided in his greatness.*"[37] MacIntyre, in one sense, could not help but agree. Yet his reasons for doing so are very different—narrative, not necessity. MacIntyre finds Aristotle fascinating because he writes *as if* this coherent moral world, and the virtues that are commensurate with it, were still accessible in his own day.[38] Aristotle knew that he was living "after virtue"—that is why he writes so much about friendship, where the virtues of civility and duty can still play a major, if somewhat more private, role—but he manages to write his political and ethical studies *as if* this heroic world of the virtues were still intact.[39] To assume that Aristotle's moral philosophy is grounded in such a willing suspension of moral disbelief is as oversimple (though not entirely without substance), on my view, as MacIntyre's reading of the *Iliad*.

In moving beyond MacIntyre, and more authentically "back to the Greeks" than his own account will allow, I would like to offer an alternative reading of what the Greeks were about. At the outset of his argument, MacIntyre quotes the Greek proverb—"Call no man happy until he is dead"[40]—and uses this as a proof-text for his claim that every human life, at least as the Greeks understood it, is thoroughly teleological in character. Every human life takes the shape of a certain kind of story. And dramatic plots have endings, events toward which everything moves. No human life is properly evaluated until it has achieved its final end, just as no play makes complete sense until the curtain has been drawn down. We need to know how things *end*. Now, this all sounds fine until we recognize that it makes nonsense of Herodotus. This was not the point of the proverb at all. Rather, the point of the proverb is to highlight the *fragility* of human life, and of every human virtue.

The publication of MacIntyre's studies happily coincided with that of Martha Nussbaum's *The Fragility of Goodness*,[41] a text to which I have already had occasion to refer. Nussbaum provides a refreshingly different picture of what the Greeks were about, a very different reading of their enduring significance.[42] Perhaps the differences, as well as what is at stake in these differences, might best be made by concentrating on these twinned notions of happiness (which, as we saw, is an extremely complex concept for Aristotle) and of death (which is the ultimate fragility in an embodied life, and the only *ending* with which the Greeks were consistently concerned).

The proverb—"Call no man happy until he is dead"—was originally reported by Herodotus, as I say.[43] And the story in which it appears admirably illustrates the very kind of fragility which Nussbaum is talking about. Teleology does not figure here. Humanity is not growing *toward* some alleged natural or social end; rather, as we age, we grow *away* from the possibility of calamity. With our death, there comes an end to the suffering which the gods can impose upon us. Tradition has it that Solon, after giving Athens its new code of laws, left the city for a decade, during which time he traveled the length and breadth of the known world. Herodotus chooses to focus upon his visit with Croesus, the king of Lydia and, at the time, the wealthiest man in the world. His wealth is carefully contrasted with Herodotus' sober and rather chastened concept of happiness. Seeking cheap praise after inviting Solon to tour the royal Lydian coffers, Croesus asks Solon "Who is the happiest man you have ever seen?" Solon's terse reply:

> My lord, Tellus the Athenian. . . . In the first place, he hailed from a good city and he had sons who were noble in every way [*kaloi k'agathoi*], and he lived to see all of his children bear children in their turn, all of them grown straight and tall. Secondly, while his life had gone well, at least by our standards, its ending [*teleutē*] was its most brilliant part. When war erupted between the Athenians and their neighbors in Eleusis, Tellus came to the Athenian defense, routed the enemy, and died even more nobly than he had lived. The Athenians awarded him a state burial where he fell, and honored him greatly.[44]

Croesus is predictably nonplussed and, a bit miffed, he seeks at least "the second prize." This he does not get, and it is here that Solon's playful irony turns serious. For the next story he tells is the well-known myth of Cleobis and Biton, two dutiful youths who yoked themselves to an ox-cart in order to take their mother to a distant festival, in honor of the goddess Hera. Here they won the accolades of both mothers and men (the phrase "they were greatly honored" is repeated here), and in honor of her sons' actions, the mother prayed for "whatsoever is best for the gods to give to mortal man." The two youths fell asleep in the temple and never awoke: "a heaven-sent proof of how much better it is to be dead than alive," says Solon.[45]

After hearing this story, Croesus can contain himself no longer. He rather pointedly asks Solon about *his own* happiness. Solon's reply deserves to be heard at some length:

> Croesus, it is clear to me that Heaven [*to theion*] is jealous, and turbulent, yet you have asked me about human affairs. In the long coil of time, there are many things to see which we would wish not to see, and many things to suffer. . . . Clearly, Croesus, *life is a chancy thing*. In my eyes you seem wealthy enough and you rule over many people. But as for the question you put to me, I cannot answer it until such time as I am persuaded that you have died [*teleutēsanta*] well. The very wealthy are no happier than others, unless Fortune ordains a good end [*teleutēsai*] to life as well as the possession of many things. . . . Now if such a one ends life well, then that man is the very one you seek. He it is who may be called happy. *But until he dies [teleutēse], reserve judgment. Until then, call him lucky, not happy.* It is necessary *to look to the end [skopeein teleutēn]* of every matter, before one disembarks.[46]

Now this phrase—"look to the end" (telos horān)—is the very thing to which Aristotle himself alludes,[47] and it is surely this discussion which MacIntyre has in mind.⁴⁸ For, in his discussion of the role which fortune plays in the constitution of the moral life, Aristotle is unwilling to admit as much fragility into it as Solon would seem to have done. "Fortunes [*tais tychais*] do not determine whether we fare well or ill, but are, as we said, merely an accessory to human life; activities in conformity with virtue [*aretēn*] constitute happiness [*eudaimonias*]."⁴⁹

Still, fortune and fragility *are* undeniably the focus of Herodotus' attention. Croesus dismisses Solon peremptorily, considering him something of a fool. Yet "after Solon was gone, a great *nemesis* fell upon Croesus, and one may guess that it was because he thought he was of all mankind the most blessed."⁵⁰ Actually, a whole series of calamities befall Croesus and his kingdom. The final insult comes after his consultation with the Delphic oracle, where he inquires about the advisability of a military engagement against Cyrus of Persia. Croesus is told only that, if he presses this conflict, he will destroy a mighty empire. Like Oedipus before him, Croesus presses on toward the fulfillment of a cryptic destiny, strives to uncover the hidden meaning of ambiguous words, only to bring about his own destruction in the process. "So the Persians held Sardis and made Croesus their prisoner."

> Fourteen years he had reigned and fourteen days been besieged, and he had indeed fulfilled the oracle, in that he had destroyed a mighty empire—his own.⁵¹

As he is about to be burned at the stake, Croesus recalls Solon's "divine words," and realizes—too late—that they, too, were destined for him. Everything is uncertain—the richest man in the world today may yet die a pauper tomorrow, or something even worse.⁵²

Fragility, *not* Teleology—the moral implications of that misreading are legion. Herein lies the essence of the corrective which Nussbaum offers to the somewhat one-sided and emphatically antimodern readings which are the hallmark of MacIntyre's method. Nussbaum attempts to show how Aristotle is concerned with *both* teleology *and* fragility, and her correctives bear close scrutiny. Once she has flagged several critical ideas—fragility, chance (*tychē*), mortality (*thanatos*), and destiny (*moira*)—it is impossible to read an Archaic or Classical text without being impressed anew by their centrality. Concern for these very questions prompted Herodotus to undertake his "Researches," as he himself confesses at the outset. Thucydides, who differs from Herodotus in so much else, shares this mingled fascination and horror before the utter happenstance of our political lives.⁵³ The tragedies also are rife with this concern for Necessity (*Anankē*), "that set of unalterable, unmanageable facts which we call the human condition," and which represent "the crucial center of Greek tragedy."⁵⁴

And the tragedians are, in their turn, building upon the canonical insights of Homer, our first singer of such strange and troubling tales. No matter how far back in time one cares to travel, the Greek genius expresses itself best in this subtle portrayal of the fragility and multiplicity of our moral universe.

Let us return again, then, to MacIntyre's narrative, and to a brief rehearsal of MacIntyre's lapsarian argument. It is a story with three turning points, the kind of contingency he foregrounds. Homeric society had this coherent account of the heroic social virtues; it degenerated in the fifth century BCE; Aristotle is so fascinating precisely because he writes *as if* this moral homogeneity still exists. There is no better way to argue against this posture than simply to read the *Iliad.*

IV

"Sing, goddess, the wrath of Achilles . . . "

This, the opening half-line of the *Iliad,* makes several points which serve to qualify MacIntyre's rather extraordinary claims about the nature of heroic societies. In a world which is allegedly devoid of human personality—where 'character' connotes the narrative roles we inhabit, and very little else—one character achieves prominence from the very start. This is a hero, with a name, and with a wholly distinct personality. He could *never* be mistaken for anyone else. He is Achilles. And he is angry. Angry about what? In a word, he is angry about the very thing which MacIntyre claims he never could be angry about. For "morality and social structure," MacIntyre insists

> are in fact one and the same thing in heroic society. There is only one set of social bonds. Morality as something distinct does not yet exist. Evaluative questions *are* questions of social fact.

And again:

> There is indeed in the vocabulary available to Homer's characters no way for them to view their own culture and society *as if from the outside.*

And yet again:

> There is thus the sharpest of contrasts between the emotivist self of modernity and the self of the heroic age. The self of the heroic age lacks precisely that characteristic which we have already seen that some modern moral philosophers take to be an essential characteristic of human selfhood: *the capacity to detach oneself from any particular standpoint or point of view and to view it*

from the outside. In heroic society there is no 'outside' except that of the
stranger. A man who tried to withdraw himself from his given position in
heroic society would be engaged in the enterprise of trying to make himself
disappear.[55]

MacIntyre's argument here participates in the one-sided misreading of Aristotle on the political animal, to which I referred in the last chapter. He is worried,
to use Aristotle's own image, about being left alone, like an isolated piece in a
game of draughts. What he fails to see is that the entire *Iliad*—and we must say
the same thing for the *Odyssey*—takes place "outside," before the walls of a
foreign city, or else in distant cities and islands where vague moral claims may
still be intelligibly and meaningfully made. Still, it is the *wrath* of Achilles
which has our attention here. He is angry about the heroic code, that sham-
tradition of sham-duties which his world has imposed upon him, yet which cannot make adequate sense of his inner life. He has himself moved decisively, and
permanently, "outside." There is no going back—not for him, and not for us.

Given MacIntyre's distressingly shallow portrait of heroic society, I fail to
see what this epic poem could possibly be about.[56] For the *Iliad* is nothing if
not the story of Achilles' gradual detachment from the mores and the worldview which surround him. "Homer sings the tradition," to be sure, "but he also
sings Achilles."[57] The tradition is an aristocratic one where those with the
wealth are those who can excel in public debate and on the battlefield. The
Homeric ideal is to be a doer of deeds and a speaker of words. In the verbal
arena, armed now only with his intellect (and his words), Achilles gives over
the battlefield, saying things no hero, according to MacIntyre, should be able
to say. He says them in that same pivotal moment to which Aristotle alluded, in
the ninth book of the *Iliad*: "my life, once lost, can never be given back to me,
and nothing is worth my life."[58] Achilles will go on to argue that he would rather
live a long life as a farming slave than the short life of "virtue" to which he
seems destined. Again, the point is deceptively simple: Achilles' wrath lies at
the very heart of the poem, a wrath which turns out to derive from his rejection
of the very moral world into which his society has educated him. He has been
habituated, but not homogenized. There is a *penultimacy* about the *polis*.

Now this wrath—or, less strongly, this moral turbulence—is hardly
Achilles' alone. The sole spectacle which Homer never tires of showing us is
the inner debate,[59] in which each of the heroes before Troy debates whether to
stay and fight—as their moral schooling tells them to do—or to turn and bolt—
as their hearts so often insist.

The strange nostalgia for a completely integrated society, which so dominates
the thinking of such seemingly disparate commentators on the *Iliad* as Red-

field and Havelock [we should add MacIntyre to this list], should be mentioned. . . . It must be said about [their] readings that they contradict the poem's own focus, which is on Achilles' refusal to live within the heroic code. Furthermore, the *Iliad* presents Achilles as paradigmatic rather than perverse.[60]

The *Iliad* hammers home the very insight which must overthrow MacIntyre's assertion that there is no individual, critical standpoint apart from the *polis*, the idea that there is no "outside" to which the Homeric hero may retreat. Where MacIntyre tells us that 'the self' in heroic societies is "a social creation, not an individual one,"[61] Homer sings a very different tale indeed. Already in the *Iliad*, what we find is that the individual is left to internalize the social rules, or else not to do so. Now, it is true that in almost every case the heroes of the *Iliad* choose to stay, and fight, and very often to die before the gates of Troy. But it is surely telling that in at least two cases—and these by far the most important—they do not. Achilles, in refusing to fight and in rejecting everything his society tells him is worth fighting for, is the focal point of this entire tragedy. Apart from the tragic conflict lodged within his soul there would be no *Iliad*. Homer tells us this much in his opening line. Then, too, there is Hector, who faces Achilles upon his return to the field in book xxii, cannot stand before him, but turns and bolts at the last moment—in what is surely one of the most pregnant and enduring scenes in the poem.

There is food for wonder here, in that the oldest western poem known to us already speaks of the individual as the moral court of last resort, the *non plus ultra* even and especially in such a "traditional" society. Such individualism, however "situated," is neither so "emotive" nor "bureaucratic" nor "modern" as is often alleged. This is an important distinction. It may seem at times that I am speaking too broadly of "the individual," and that, in so doing, I have failed to understand one of the chief tenets of MacIntyre's whole program. For MacIntyre wants to argue that the modern bureaucratic individual is something new under the sun, a creation of the Liberal bourgeois cultural order in western Europe over the past two hundred years. I think, and hope, that I *have* understood MacIntyre's argument; I simply do not find it convincing. It is asserted rather than argued—his beginning is frankly a little *too* arbitrary, although it does make for a most compelling story.

What, then, are the alleged characteristics of this "modern" individual? MacIntyre devotes a great deal of attention to this question, but for our purposes, two points suffice. In the first place, there is the question of severance, of *detachment*, from "tradition" and the *polis*. There is a deep philosophical question here as we saw in the last chapter: may one become truly "rational" without *first* being habituated into the customs and mores of a "traditional" society? According to MacIntyre, Aristotle answered this question emphatically in the negative; Kant represents the real turning point to the world of individualistic modernity because he said "yes" for the first time.

It seems to me—that this oversimplifies *both* philosophies. Aristotle was not so strictly "traditional," nor was Kant's "individual" such a free-floating, traditionless entity. But that point is less important than the point—to which MacIntyre constantly returns—that the results of this alleged Cartesian/Kantian detachment from a traditional framework have been an unparalleled conceptual disaster. It had never been done before, MacIntyre claims, at least not in this fashion. The point it, as always, narratively overdrawn. An individual is *always* "situated," always located in a particular place, a particular time, a particular "tradition." But no individual remains strictly "traditional." The process of *detachment,* whereby the individual criticizes the very customs and convictions which comprise that tradition, is no "modern" problem. There is a *penultimacy* about the *polis,* as there has always been. Achilles already speaks eloquently about this, and does so in terms which MacIntyre would be forced to call "modern," if he had the ears to hear it and the eyes to look.

The second characteristic of the allegedly "modern" individual, according to MacIntyre, is related to this first. It concerns the *standards* to which Achilles appeals in the course of his own moral detachment. Such appeals, in the modern situation, are always couched in the solipsistic terms of "what I want." This is the brand of Emotivism which is MacIntyre's chief (and quite apt) concern.

> "I want it to be the case that such and such," as we noticed [previously] cannot function as the expression of a good reason for action within Hume's scheme any more than within Aristotle's. The emergence of a type of practical reasoning in which this kind of expression can be the initiating premise of a practical argument marked a moment of post-Humean cultural change, one corresponding to that involved in coming to understand the arenas of public choice not as places of debate . . . but as places where bargaining between individuals, each with their own preferences, is conducted. . . .
>
> What I am claiming is that [this claim and its social context] defined a new social and cultural artefact, "the individual."[62]

Clearly, MacIntyre wants to argue that our modern forms of "I want" mean something very different, that this modern "individual" who calls him- or herself "I" is something new under the sun. We are all products of the capitalist marketplace, he says, and when we think about moral conflict, we think in terms of competitive trading, of exchanges between "individuals" who "want." In the market, tradition and tragedy have no real place.[63] I remain unconvinced that all we worry about in the marketplace is wanting; we all assume the existence of moral structures even where we do not articulate this explicitly.[64] This is more antimodern cant.

And, in any event, there is nothing novel in all this wanting. This appeal—to "what I want"—already plays the pivotal role in *Homer's* picture of practical reasoning. We simply cannot understand the underlying conflict between Achilles and Agamemnon—nor how complete is Achilles' break with the heroic world—if we do not recognize how Achilles argues and exactly what it is that he "wants." He wants, to say it plainly, a different world. He wants—and the very language he uses clearly indicates that he is trying to find a way to say it—*another* kind of justice . . . *not* the heroic doctrine of loving your friends and hurting your enemies, but something which recognizes that every individual in the *Iliad* is, finally, "a brother in the same distress."[65] What he wants forces him to the "outside." What he wants is *justice,* neither heroically nor traditionally defined. And that idea, as we saw briefly in the last chapter and will see again in the last, is expressed by a Greek word, *themis.*

V

Homer is relevant to my disagreement with MacIntyre in another way as well. I am very much concerned with who gets to interpret him. MacIntyre has been somewhat reticent about entering the complex debate about interpretive communities—as Stanley Hauerwas has done so emphatically (and rather one-sidedly, I will suggest in the fourth chapter)—I suspect because he realizes that "we" who interpret Homer are a good deal more diverse and more cosmopolitan than his vision of the *polis* would allow. Homer is a common human inheritance. He was neither "white" nor "western," yet he is now a canonical part of the "western" Euro-American tradition.

Homer nevertheless presents us with an opportunity to ask MacIntyre's question again, "Nietzsche or Aristotle?" As I said in the last chapter, if what we are concerned to do is to explore the meaning of epic and of tragedy, then our choice is relatively clear. "The *Poetics* is not the best starting-point for an understanding of Greek tragedy," says R. P. Winnington-Ingram, "not Aristotle, but Homer."[66] This the early Nietzsche knew well. MacIntyre, by contrast, begins and ends with Aristotle, and seems to accept Aristotle's rather formal definitions as canonical.[67] Halfway through *After Virtue,* as he undertakes the telling of his story all over again, "from the beginning," MacIntyre returns to Greece, that is, to Homer. He brackets the historical question of how accurate Homer's picture of that bygone heroic age really was. What is important for MacIntyre's thesis—recall that this is also what remains significant about Aristotle—is that Homer writes *as if* this world really once existed, that his understanding of the values of heroic society formed "a necessary part of the understanding of classical society and its successors."[68] That is to say, Homer's is the fiction that every western society—even our own, in MacIntyre's distorted philosophical narrative—endlessly retells itself.[69] Call it Ithaca, call it Eden, we are all looking for the Paradise we have lost.

What, we may well ask, best characterized this heroic age, MacIntyre's version of the lost Homeric Eden, the age *before* Babel? We have asked this question before, and have already gone some way toward answering it, I hope. It is already clear how far MacIntyre's critique of individualism, as a uniquely "modern" and "bureaucratic" artifact, stands from the tragedy of Achilles and Hector which Homer tells. Achilles is already a paradigm for Hegel's "unhappy consciousness," a paradigm for each and every one of us. Yet MacIntyre says far more than this about Homer and heroic society. He isolates *courage* as a characteristic heroic virtue and as, in all likelihood, *the* definitive virtue in Homeric society.[70] MacIntyre goes on to say that the virtue of courage enjoys a unique relationship to three other critical heroic notions: friendship, fate, and death. Courage implies dependability and the constancy of character upon which one may rely in a crisis, hence its centrality to the Homeric conception of friendship, where all friendships exist between men who are warriors, first and last. One reason that Achilles and Patroclus can drink so deeply at the well of their friendship is that they are so completely and steadfastly present to one another, that they are so constant and so brave. Moreover, in this fragile, warring world, it is apparent that courage is necessary to keep one from going mad. In the face of the inevitability of misfortune and the probability of violent death—only Odysseus and Menelaus, after all, of all the Greek heroes at Troy, ever makes it home again (and it takes Odysseus a decade)—courage acquires a centrality among the virtues which may seem foreign, and even strange, to us.

This sudden focus upon the concept of fragility should attract our notice. Courage is always courage, MacIntyre says, in the face of *inevitable* defeat. That is *his* definition of "tragic" heroism. And epics are extended discussions of little more than fate.

> The man therefore who does as he ought moves steadily toward his fate and his death. It is defeat and not victory that lies at the end. To understand this is itself a virtue; it is a necessary part of courage to understand this.[71]

MacIntyre accepts the Aristotelian dictum, the similarity of tragedy and epic, but he draws a different lesson from it. He argues that both genres—epic and tragedy—embody a sort of *fatalism* where inexorable fate and inevitable defeat are the only certainties. Defeat, not victory, and the inevitability of death— these are the only authentically "tragic" categories MacIntyre allows. It is a curious sort of teleology, involving a peculiar taste for unhappy endings. A depressing pall of melancholy dominates the world of the epic hero, painting it over in a gloomy caste of grey. Heroic narratives end badly—be sure to note, just as we moderns are ending badly, here and now. It seems to me that this highly idiosyncratic reading of Greek literature, and MacIntyre's desperate account of the modern age, are of a piece. Both are animated by a bitterness which is borne on the wings of a bad teleology, this fixation upon (unhappy) endings.

Such a view misses all the richness and nuance of Homer. This fixation upon fate and finality would make better sense if Herodotus had concluded with Croesus' death, or if Homer had ended his *Iliad* with the portrayal of Achilles' death. But neither writer does this. Homer does something else, something wholly unexpected and infinitely more satisfying. He concludes his poem with an image of enemies reconciled, and the *peaceful* burial of Hector, the single greatest enemy of the Greeks. The final note is one of profound reconciliation, not despair. I suspect that MacIntyre misses this, or at the very least fails to say it, for the very simple, but infinitely telling, reason that he considers Homer one among a larger number of writers who may be loosely called "heroic." Homer's is hardly a unique voice. Specifically, MacIntyre equates Homer's narrative world with the world portrayed by the Icelandic sagas of the thirteenth century CE as well as the Irish sagas of the twelfth.[72] This collapsing of essential distinctions has characterized MacIntyre's reading of the Greeks up to this point; in this section it is determinative.

For Icelandic saga is unlike any other literature known to us in the quality of its bitterness, the exquisite despair with which it views the world.

> The gods know that a day will come when they will be destroyed. Sometime they will meet their enemies and go down beneath them to defeat and death. The cause the forces of good are fighting to defend against the forces of evil is hopeless. Nonetheless, the gods will fight for it to the end. Necessarily, the same is true of humanity. If the gods are finally helpless before evil, men and women must be more so. . . . In the last battle between good and evil, they will fight on the side of the gods and die with them. [This is] as somber a conception as the mind of man has ever given birth to. The only sustaining support possible for the human spirit, the one pure unsullied good men can hope to attain is heroism; and heroism depends on lost causes.[73]

Asgard is a grim and forbidding place, "surely as strange a heaven as ever conceived by poets." When the poets do conceive it, it is cast in shadow, a darkness which derives from the fateful foreknowledge of inevitable disaster. This is a heaven dominated by the oppressive anticipation of *Ragnarök,* the "twilight of the gods," which Nietzsche popularized in his later period, when he too had adopted an antimodern posture.[74]

These gods know, as do all the heroes who fight and die beside them, that death and defeat are the only destiny, grim resistance the only heroic duty.

Grimness—how many Nordic names contain this word?—and a profound melancholy lie at the heart of this "heroic" *ēthos*.[75] Life is a story which must end badly; this simple fact alone qualifies it as 'tragic'.[76] A mournful weight hangs over the heads of these heroes even at their most triumphant, a melancholy impressionism which is a world away from the brighter colors of Homer.

The simple reason for this is that Homer was not a fatalist, as the Norse mythographers most assuredly were. Here is the reason why Nietzsche finally rejected Schopenhauer's philosophy, in the name of his own, gayer moral science. It was tragedy—Homeric and Sophoclean alike—which taught him this.[77] Here again, a crucial distinction has been papered over, with philosophical consequences which are profound. One simply may not speak of the *Iliad* and *Njal's Saga* in a single breath, as MacIntyre wants to do.[78] "Fate will take its own course," Njal says, and that is the end of the matter.[79] And these words are placed in the mouth of a hero who is prescient, who, like Prometheus, possesses second sight and knows his destiny. Yet Njal does *not* know, as Prometheus does, that one day he will be vindicated and delivered, in triumph; he knows only that he and all his family will one day be murdered in their home.

By reading a Nordic fatalism back into texts which had already moved far beyond this (although written nearly two thousand years earlier), MacIntyre has done more than misread Homer; he has also tipped his own elusive tragic hand. For MacIntyre *does* have—like Hegel and Nietzsche—a subtly normative conception of what constitutes a tragedy. But his norms are very different than Homer's or Sophocles'. The tragic hero lives in a world where inevitable defeat lies at the end. Heroism resides in lost causes, pure and simple. Tragedy involves the unhappy choice "between wrong and wrong," and we need simply to have "the strength to resist false solutions."

> What philosophy has to tell [the physician] is precisely why [he] cannot hope for solutions. For a philosopher to try to go beyond this would be for him to misunderstand either the present situation or the scope and limits of his discipline. A philosopher offering positive moral advice in this situation would be a comic character introduced into a tragedy. Imagine Socrates introducing himself with advice for Antigone or Creon, or Plato trying to counsel Philoctetes, Neoptolemus and Odysseus.[80]

MacIntyre's imagery is at once suggestive and deeply misleading. It seems to me that Socrates (like Hegel)[81] precisely *did* intend to give advice to characters such as Antigone and Creon—and believed moreover that we are all like them, to one degree or another, in our crises and confusions. It is one of my chief interests in this essay to demonstrate the manner in which a philosopher can make a career out of reading a tragedy or epic, such as the *Iliad*. And in this reading, one's perception of the present is profoundly affected. To define tragedy as

MacIntyre has defined it is, as I say, to read a profoundly Nordic pessimism, hence a *teleology,* back into a very different Greek view of the world. Greek tragedy in the classical period was profoundly uninterested in how things end, something which obsessed the Icelandic saga-writers, and continues to fascinate the apocalyptically minded among us. We have traded a Teutonic for a Hellenic *ésprit.*

By contrast, Homer and the tragedians are no pessimists. The issue of fatalism is determinative in several other respects as well. The most obvious, and the most important, of these is the simple fact that there remains a world of emotional distance between Homer and Icelandic saga, as I have said. Hegel sensed this well—Hegel, who, in a discussion of epic poetry where he could wax so eloquently over Homer, dispenses of Norse mythology with scarcely a second thought: "I must confess that I have little taste for the savagery and the dark confusion of such tales."[82] The Norse heroes are trapped in a world they did not make, moving decisively only in the direction of what Fate has decreed for them—inevitable defeat, and certain death.

Not so Homer. It is as though, to use another of Nietzsche's images, light had suddenly burst into an oppressive, fatalistic darkness.[83] Homer's is a world where every hero's act, and every hero's destiny, is uniquely his own; no destiny is every simply handed down from on high. The classicists have invented a term for this characteristic Homeric device: double determinism. It is a simple idea, yet absolutely essential for understanding the Homeric worldview. Simply put, the gods cannot ever *create* a hero. They can, in fact, do little more than reinforce the natural excellences of the man or woman who was born already half a hero. A courageous fighter will be made even more daring. Such is the case, archetypically, of Diomedes in book vi of the *Iliad.* The feet of a supremely swift runner will be lightened, made even swifter, as are Achilles' in book xxii. A man or woman's natural beauty will be, in certain moments, made even more surpassing and irresistible. One thinks here of Helen and Hector and Odysseus. But in no case do the gods create out of whole cloth. They work in a medium which already possesses an intrinsic and natural worth. That medium is decidedly individual.

The point is a simple one. I mean merely to note that Homer is in no way a fatalist, at least not in the traditional Nordic sense of this term. Homer's determinism is much more sophisticated, much more complex. It leaves room for an astonishing degree of individuality—astonishing, when we come to the *Iliad* after reading MacIntyre's description of the poem. And the *Iliad,* as I have said many times, is not "just another heroic epic." Our beginning is not quite so arbitrary as all that. Hegel sensed the power and contemporaneity of Homer, and spoke of it with peculiar eloquence and urgency. His reflections on double determinism provide a marked contrast to MacIntyre's Homer:

Certainly in Homer the gods often rush to the aid of particular heroes, but they appear invariably only as the universal side of what the man is and does as an individual for himself and at a moment when he is exerting the full force of his heroism toward that end. Otherwise, in giving the Greeks full help, the gods need not have refrained from slaying all the Trojans at once. Homer, in his description of the main fighting, focuses on the combat of individuals.[84]

In Homer already—so far is he from being a fatalist—we are privy to a picture of what the world looks like when gods and people engage in *common* projects. To make Homer over in Icelandic dress, to make a virtue of fatalism, as MacIntyre has done, has a damning final implication: it creates the very beginning which dooms us, narratively, to our allegedly "modern" end.

VI

Now, admittedly, MacIntyre has abundant reasons for emphasizing these penultimate virtues of "community" and "tradition"—everything, in short, which he places under the umbrella of the *polis*. It is precisely this aspect of our selves which have received largely negative description in the "modern" age. He has a real point here. Existential philosophy made a career out of placing the radically free human individual over against the "inauthentic" human collective, what Heidegger termed 'the They'.[85] Their misreading of Aristotle is as one-sided as MacIntyre's. If MacIntyre tries to anchor us, with Socrates, firmly in the marketplace, in the *polis,* then Nietzsche weights anchor in search of more "open seas," tries finally to make us "apolitical" and places us, with Zarathustra, on the mountaintop, alone. The fact of the matter is a little less dramatic than that. Human life is a constant ebb and flow of society and solitude, friendship and isolation. We live in both spheres, entirely at home in neither.

In one of the most fruitful and important discussions of *After Virtue* (chapter 15, where he is attempting to present his own *re*vision of "a tradition of the virtues"), MacIntyre makes a number of claims which take us rather far from his antimodern polemics. Suddenly, a "tradition"—so far is it from being a seamless sacred canopy as he had seemed to say it was in his Homeric discussions—is nothing more than a forum for debate and even rather divisive moral conflict.

When a tradition is in good order, it is always partially constituted by an argument about the goods the pursuit of which gives to that tradition its particular point and purpose. . . . Traditions, when vital, embody continuities of conflict. . . . A living tradition, then, is an historically extended, socially embodied argument, and an argument precisely in part about the goods which constitute that tradition.[86]

Such an account of "tradition," while certainly truer to life, does death to the polemics which fuel the fires of MacIntyre's antimodernism. That is, as I have said, the great and probably insoluble tension in his work—whether to be un-modern or antimodern. He wrestles with it still. And we will return to this same tension throughout this book. In a nutshell, *After Virtue* is grounded in an iron-ically Nietzschean premise: that "traditions" are monolithic, uniform, and when healthy, find themselves necessarily engaged in *conflict . . .* with other "rival" traditions.[87] Cultural *syntheses* are the great illusion, and always have some-thing dishonest about them. Four years later, MacIntyre is far less polemical, and now discusses the phenomenon of cultural syntheses at some length. I can only assert my belief here that this represents a *profound* rejection of the chief premise of *After Virtue,* and signals to us that MacIntyre is now involved in a very different task. He himself senses this, asking himself the next logical ques-tion: "What then sustains and strengthens traditions? What weakens and de-stroys them?"[88] His answer will not surprise us: "the exercise or lack of exercise of the relevant virtues."[89] And one of the chief virtues at stake here—MacIntyre insists on this point—is *"the virtue of having an adequate sense of the tradi-tion to which one belongs."*[90]

We find ourselves again on difficult and complex ground. The real issue lying behind this account is some vision, however ill-defined, of civil disobe-dience, of the individual's ability to climb "outside" of a moral community. For our disobedience, detachment, and critique to be substantive, it must reflect a deep and abiding understanding of the canons of our own day—a living sense of "tradition." Only this will guarantee that it be civil, and not the chaotic mish-mash of emotivist rant which characterizes so much "modern" disobedience, MacIntyre feels, "after Nietzsche." I have some sympathy with MacIntyre's di-agnosis of what he calls Emotivist culture, particularly in its therapeutic mani-festations.[91] But I disagree with *the historical narrative* which he is convinced explains it all, as well as the extent of his posturing antimodernism. MacIntyre assumes that Achilles' disobedience—if, in fact, he ever really disobeyed—must have been profoundly "civil." Yet Achilles' objections are absolutely fun-damental, and cut to the very heart of the virtues and values of the society in which he can no longer live. His break with the heroic tradition is absolutely fundamental, and is made—not in the name of "tradition," which is precisely what he means to reject—but in the name of himself, his desires, and the value of his own life. Once the historical narrative which MacIntyre is telling goes, then the postured pessimism about our "modernness" needs to go as well. This posture is not even Aristotelian. There is no ultimacy to "political" matters. For Aristotle, such social habituation is merely a step along the way to full rational and moral development. He gives his lectures on ethics to people who, it is presumed, have been properly habituated into the "that" of Attic morality, that is, who all largely agree on what is good, and virtuous, and true.[92] They already knew "the that." Aristotle is attempting to articulate the rational "because"— an explanation of why these virtues and goods are virtuous and good *in fact.*

This is a matter of some importance; it concerns our very understanding of what Greece was all about. MacIntyre—and he is hardly alone in this—seems to feel that the Greeks were supremely *moral* thinkers, much along the lines of the Hebrew prophets. I wonder, still. With Hegel and Nietzsche, I have come to see Greece's most lasting legacy in her *tragic* and *erotic,* not her ethical, literature. Harmonizing and organizing these disparate interests is indeed a fitting task for philosophical enquiry.

It is perfectly apparent that MacIntyre believes the real force behind Aristotle's *Nicomachean Ethics* lies in his sensitivity to our social existence, the communal ideal of the *polis.* It is this which can help correct the deformed and erosive individualism of modern times. Nietzsche's Hellenism in the 1870s helps to show that this is a scholarly assumption—a prejudice, in fact—which may well be romantic and wrong. Such a concise and unambiguous statement cannot fail to qualify the way one reads Aristotle's discussion of the "necessity" of political association, unless one is predisposed—as MacIntyre seems to be— to see individualism solely as a problem, and a rather "modern" one at that.

For all the criticisms which have focused upon MacIntyre's work in the past decade, few have taken this essential point. MacIntyre's argument hangs or falls according to the accuracy of his historical narrative, its beginning and its end. We are living in the midst of a great crisis, he tells us—the crisis of Liberal individualism—and I am going to narrate for you how this all came about. But the *substance* of this historical narrative—*a reading of the Greek past from Homer to Aristotle*—has never been seriously questioned. For MacIntyre, as we have seen, what the Greeks had most essentially was *community.* The *polis* becomes, in his writings, that long-lost cultural and social ideal, the idyll which animates his whole project.[93] The sectarian ideal of small face-to-face communities of civility and virtue is the underlying myth of Greece which he endlessly recapitulates. It is, in every crucial respect, a myth.

At one level, it is a myth which the Greeks told to themselves: the *polis* was to be that ideal social unity, not too small and not too large, but just the right size.[94] Yet it is more than this. It has become a myth we moderns construct: the myth of the *polis,* the fiction of a homogeneous and seamless narrative community which all Greeks shared in common. There simply never was such a thing.[95] "After all 'public' is only a word," Nietzsche reminds us. "It has no homogeneity, nor is it a consistent quantity."[96] It is the *smallness* of MacIntyre's world, the strictness of the boundaries which he seeks to impose, as well as the highly questionable movement—from Homer to Aristotle, from Troy to Iceland, then back again—which I find most distressing and distorting about his story. Far from being any sort of solution, MacIntyre's highly sentimental re-working of the Aristotelian *polis,* lies at the heart of the modernist dilemma. It is grounded in a deeply romantic portrait of the past—his narrative beginning—and an equally specious brand of antimodernism—his apocalyptic version of the end.

These are the cornerstones of the tragic posture. And they seem to sell nowhere quite so well as in that other great marketplace of Golden Age anti-modernism, the nostalgic world of a narrowly *scriptural* religiosity. Antimod-ernism, coupled now with a Hellenism which posits the past as a Golden Age, is a poisonous political or philosophical combination, as we saw in chapter 1. I will now offer a possible explanation of the fact that, whereas many philoso-phers read MacIntyre quite appreciatively, a number of contemporary theolo-gians positively venerate him. To that explanation I turn next.

Notes

1. MacIntyre thinks that Aquinas, rather than Aristotle, was the first really sys-tematic thinker to found his system upon this insight. That is why, MacIntyre says, Aquinas *begins* the *Summa Theologica* with a dispute, rather than with an assertion. I expect that Hegel was actually the one who made this insight the cornerstone of a sys-tem. His *Logic* "begins" as follows:

> And yet we must make a beginning: and a beginning, as primary and underived, makes an assumption, or rather is an assumption. It seems as if it were impossible to make a beginning at all. (Hegel, *The Science of Logic,* §1, trans. William Wallace [The Oxford University Press, 1975], 3.)

The trick—and it remains the really fascinating thing about Hegel for me—is that by the time we get to *the end* of the story, we discover that *the beginning* was not quite so arbitrary as we had originally thought. That is absolutely determinative for the way Hegel reads Homer, the tragedians, and "the Greeks." For more on this, see my *Tragic Posture and Tragic Vision: Against the Modern Failure of Nerve* (New York: Contin-uum Press, 1994), 87–99.

2. I am indebted to Stephen Toulmin's *Cosmopolis: The Hidden Agenda of Moder-nity* (University of Chicago Press, 1990) for making clearer to me how central the as-sumption that Descartes represents the beginning of "modernity" really is for anyone who, like MacIntyre, wishes to be critical of modernity's "hidden agenda." Toulmin demonstrates convincingly that "modernity" is not one thing, but several related things, and that there really are noble intellectual insights which ought to be preserved—from both Montaigne and Descartes, as well as their more modern heirs.

3. For a provocative and sophisticated analysis of the unstated (and incomplete) Hegelianism in MacIntyre's philosophical diagnoses, see Gordon Graham, "Mac-

Intyre's Fusion of History and Philosophy," in John Horton and Susan Mendus, eds., *After MacIntyre: Critical Perspectives on the Work of Alasdair MacIntyre* (Notre Dame, IN: University of Notre Dame Press, 1994), 161–75. MacIntyre himself edited a volume on Hegel, *Hegel: A Collection of Critical Essays* (South Bend, IN: University of Notre Dame Press, 1972).

For more on method, see Martha Nussbaum's *Love's Knowledge: Essays on Philosophy and Literature* (The Oxford University Press, 1990), 24–25.

4. See MacIntyre, *After Virtue*, 2nd ed. (South Bend, IN: University of Notre Dame Press, 1984), 212–15, as well as *Whose Justice? Which Rationality?* (South Bend, IN: University of Notre Dame Press, 1988), 360–61. The idea enjoys a long and proud history, however, as we see in *Republic* 377b and *Nicomachean Ethics* 1098b6.

5. MacIntyre, *After Virtue*, 265–72. For MacIntyre's criticisms of others' *selective* historical narratives, see his withering attack on Herbert Marcuse in *Herbert Marcuse: An Exposition and a Polemic* (New York: Viking Press, 1970), 15.

For my defense of the difference, the *moral* difference, between narratives and philosophical arguments, see "Of Coins and Carnage: Rhetorical Violence and the Macedonian Question," *Soundings* 77.3/4 (1994): 350–57.

6. As will be clearer in Chapter 5, I have great sympathy with the view that "the rise of the west" is a rather contingent historical fact. But this entire book is designed to exhibit my reservations about the modernist claims of a contemporary "fall."

7. Naturally enough, such narratives distort in important ways. The Greeks are not "western" in any simple sense. See Vassilis Lambropoulos, *The Rise of Eurocentrism: Anatomy of Interpretation* (Princeton: Princeton University Press, 1993) and my review, "On Being Greek or Jewish in the Modern Moment," *Diaspora* 3.2 (1994): 199–220.

8. MacIntyre, *Whose Justice? Which Rationality?*, 360.

9. See his "A Partial Response To My Critics," in Horton and Mendus, eds., *After MacIntyre*, 295.

10. MacIntyre, *Whose Justice? Which Rationality?*, 361.

11. Louis Dupré, *Passage to Modernity: An Essay in the Hermeneutics of Nature and Culture* (New Haven: Yale University Press, 1993), 6.

12. MacIntyre, *After Virtue*, 1–5.

13. If his thesis were right, one could only wonder how we would be aware of it. Here is where MacIntyre's criticism of Marcuse is again quite telling:

> The central oddity of *One-Dimensional Man* is perhaps that it should have been written at all. For if its thesis were true, then we should have to ask how the book came to have been written and we would certainly have to inquire whether it would find any readers. Or rather, to the extent that the book does find readers, to that extent Marcuse's

thesis does not hold. (*Herbert Marcuse: An Exposition and a Polemic*, 70. See also 72–77.)

See also MacIntyre; "A Partial Reply to My Critics," in Horton and Mendus, eds., *After MacIntyre*, 283.

14. *After Virtue*, 263. Subsequent quotations in this paragraph are from the same passage. It is important to note how similar the diagnostic imagery here is to Nietzsche (particularly in *On the Genealogy of Morals*, III.§27), where he predicts the advent of "new barbarians" who will overrun a rapidly collapsing Christian world. The irony here is that MacIntyre claims to be offering the only coherent *alternative* to Nietzsche's apocalyptic moral philosophy. Yet MacIntyre's account is every bit as apocalyptic.

15. MacIntyre, *Whose Justice? Which Rationality?*, 326.

16. See my *Tragic Posture and Tragic Vision*, 11–25.

17. For a brief presentation of some of the philosophical implications of this idea, see my "Mark's Tragic Vision: Gethsemane," *Religion and Literature* 24.3 (1992): 1–25.

18. *Hegel: On the Arts*, translated and abridged by Henry Paolucci (New York: Frederick Ungar Publishing Company, 1979), 122.
See also Nietzsche's *Wir Philologen*, 6[17]; *Sämtliche Werke* VIII.104. "Among the Greeks," he observes, "it is much more the case that *an older form is the higher*, i.e., with *Dithyramb* and *Tragedy*."
Nietzsche has been, with Hegel, one of the most important sources in developing my primary thesis: *that a romanticized portrait of the Greek past is fueled by scholars' contemporary discontent.* The world's greatest pessimists, Nietzsche notes, can muster up optimism only for a world completely out of sight.

19. W. Thomas MacCary, *Childlike Achilles* (New York: Columbia University Press, 1982), 33–34. This remarkable book, like Martha Nussbaum's work, is an exemplary performance of what I would also like to be doing, namely, to bring modern philosophers into dialogue with the past.

20. I am arguing, with MacCary, that this is an Hegelian insight, that is to say, that the *Iliad* is the paradigm for Hegel's understanding of the evolution in human consciousness. It might be countered that this "stage"—of epic poetry—is a strictly *historical* one for Hegel. And so it is, up to a point. But it is more than this.
Hegel's *Phenomenology of Spirit* attempts to chart out *two* dialectical processes: the development of the individual consciousness, in the first half; the historical development of collective consciousness, or *Geist*, in the second. I find the second half of the *Phenomenology* somewhat obscure and overdrawn. Hegel becomes frankly *obsessed* with history. In his clearer moments, Hegel recalls that "sometimes we get the beginning and perfection all at once." In that same vein, the things which Hegel says about human consciousness—in light of the *Iliad*—seem incredibly probing to me. I do not

read Achilles' conflicts as a strictly *historical* moment—as MacIntyre and the vast majority of modernist interpreters do—but rather, with MacCary, as a *moral* moment which all of us will vaguely recognize as our own.

21. *After Virtue*, 121. See also George Steiner's *In Bluebeard's Castle: Some Notes Toward the Redefinition of Culture* (New Haven: Yale University Press, 1971), 1–9.

22. W. Thomas MacCary, *Childlike Achilles*, 241.

23. MacIntyre, *After Virtue*, 205ff.

24. *Ibid.*, 22.

25. Jeffrey Stout, in his *Ethics After Babel: The Languages of Morals and Their Discontents* (Boston: Beacon Press, 1988), 220–42, presents an interesting criticism of MacIntyre precisely because he emphasizes what I have not. He is worried about MacIntyre's postured account of the "modern" and "liberal" situation, whereas I am worried about his account of the past. These two tasks *are* doubtless related, but given the linkage of beginning and end in any story, especially MacIntyre's, it seems to me that we need to tackle the first task first, namely, his problematic reading of the Greek tradition.

26. I am indebted to Jon P. Gunnemann for this insight. In his "Human Rights and Modernity: The Truth of the Fiction of Individual Rights," *Journal of Religious Ethics* 16.1 (1988): 162, he is specifically addressing claims which MacIntyre made at the Emory University Human Rights Symposium in May 1983, as well as in *After Virtue*, 69. See also Jeffrey Stout, *Ethics after Babel*, 191–219.

27. Particularly in *The Death of Tragedy* (New York: Hill and Wang, 1961). For an excellent rebuttal of Steiner's thesis, see Walter Kerr, *Tragedy and Comedy* (New York: Simon & Shuster, 1967), 13–79.

28. Frank Kermode, *The Sense of An Ending* (New York: Oxford University Press, 1966), 94–98. See also George Steiner, *In Bluebeard's Castle*, 3–4, and *Real Presences* (Chicago: University of Chicago Press, 1989), 87–93.

29. MacCary, *Childlike Achilles*, 249–50.

30. "I have already noticed," MacIntyre remarks, "Marcuse's diagnosis of the ills that have befallen language in advanced societies. One of these ills he does not note: it is the taste for pretentious nostrums described in inflated language which induces excitement rather than thought. To this corruption of language Marcuse's prose has made a major contribution." MacIntyre, *Herbert Marcuse: An Exposition and a Polemic*, 97.

31. *After Virtue*, 4–5, 263. See also *Three Rival Versions of Moral Enquiry: Encyclopedia, Genealogy, Tradition* (South Bend, IN: University of Notre Dame Press, 1990), 165–69, where he suggests that the collapse of "traditional" Thomist thought in the face of the challenge brought by Duns Scotus, was later overturned—and "tradition" reestablished—"*by what is either pure historical contingency, or divine providence*" (163). Such claims seem to me to beg the essential causal questions.

32. That MacIntyre's position *has* changed on this score is clear in both *Whose Justice? Which Rationality?*, x, and "A Partial Reply to My Critics," in Horton and Mendus, eds., *After MacIntyre*, 291–94.

33. *After Virtue*, 117–20. See also *Whose Justice? Which Rationality?*, 360–61, 372.

34. For a more balanced presentation of a similar idea, but without the polemic and without the apocalypticism, see Werner Jaegar's masterful *Paideia: The Ideals of Greek Culture,* trans. Gilbert Highet (New York: Oxford University Press, 1939, 1945), ix–xxix.

35. And yet Charles Segal, in his *Tragedy and Civilization* (Cambridge, MA: Harvard University Press, 1981), chapter 1, note 23, observes that this concern for 'apolicity' is a distinctively Sophoclean dramatic device, reflecting Sophocles' keen interest in the only superficial and tenuous order imposed by what we call 'civilization.'
The term *apoptolis* appears three times in his extant work (*Oedipus Tyrranus* 1000, *Trachiniae* 647, and *Oedipus at Colonus* 207) while the term *apolis* also appears three times (*Antigone* 370, *Philoctetes* 1018, and *Oedipus at Colonus* 1357).

36. For a fascinating discussion of the real dynamics of this critical historical debate, see Martha Nussbaum, "Aristophanes and Socrates on Learning Practical Wisdom," *Yale Classical Studies* 26 (1976): 43–97.

37. René Girard, *Violence and the Sacred*, trans. Patrick Gregory (Baltimore: The Johns Hopkins University Press, 1972, 1977), 292, emphasis mine.

38. For more on the imagery of "as if" thinking, see MacIntyre, *Three Rival Versions of Moral Enquiry*, 171.

39. MacIntyre, *After Virtue*, 147–48, 159.

40. *Ibid.,* 34. This is Aristotle (*Nicomachean Ethics* 1100a10) quoting Herodotus (*The Histories* I.32). It is less clear that Aristotle "got Herodotus wrong" than it is that he is trying to use Herodotus for a different purpose. MacIntyre, by contrast, seems to me simply to have misread the text.

41. Martha Nussbaum, *The Fragility of Goodness: Luck and Ethics in Greek Tragedy and Philosophy* (New York: Cambridge University Press, 1986). For MacIntyre's own comments upon Nussbaum's work, see *Whose Justice? Which Rationality?*, 165, 187ff.

42. For Nussbaum's support of my comparison here, see her "Reply," *Soundings* 72.4 (1989): 741.

43. In his *Histories* I.30–33. The recent publication of a new translation by David Grene (Chicago: University of Chicago Press, 1987) marks a real event in the world of Herodotus scholarship, and will, I hope, get people to reading again this most engaging personality of the classical world. In all cases here, I have consulted Grene's translation

as well as the earlier edition of Aubrey de Sélincourt (New York: Penguin Books, 1954, 1983), where I have not opted for my own.

44. *The Histories* I.30, translation mine.

45. *The Histories* I.31, Sélincourt translation.

46. *The Histories* I.32, translation and emphasis mine.

47. *Nicomachean Ethics* 1100a10–1100b11. I have everywhere consulted the Greek text of Aristotle's *Ethics*, as given in Loeb Classical Library edited and translated by H. Rackham (Cambridge, MA: Harvard University Press, 1975), 46–51. In this case also, Aquinas' *Commentary on Aristotle's Nicomachean Ethics*, trans. C. I. Litzinger (Notre Dame, IN: Dumb Ox Books, 1993), 59–62, confirms my reading *against* Mac-Intyre's hypothesis.

48. Yet he misses the engaging word-play which allows Herodotus to refer back and forth between the end (*telos*) of a matter, and the final "end," which is death (*teleutē*). Failing to notice or to account for this leads to the central problem of this misreading.
See Aristotle's *Metaphysics* 1021b28–30 for more on this.

49. *Nicomachean Ethics* 1100b7–10. It is interesting that this conclusion really undercuts the force of Martha Nussbaum's assertion, namely, that Aristotle is trying to reintroduce the centrality of the concept of fragility after Plato had so emphatically driven it to the periphery in his own moral philosophy. I suspect that this point is tied to her deletion of the concluding passage from the *Ethics*, as I noted in the last chapter.

50. *The Histories* I.34, Grene translation.

51. *The Histories* I.86, Grene translation.

52. Croesus is not killed, however. Cyrus hears him muttering to himself, asks him what he is going on about, and is so moved by the tale that he releases him. That crucial fact—that the apparent end is never *necessarily* the end—is a point of considerable importance, as we shall see shortly.

53. A. Lowell Edmunds, *Chance and Intelligence in Thucydides* (Cambridge, MA: Harvard University Press, 1974).

54. William Arrowsmith, "The Criticism of Greek Tragedy," *Tulane Drama Review* 3.3 (1959): 40–43, 55.

55. MacIntyre, *After Virtue*, 123–26, emphasis mine.

56. It is nothing short of bizarre that MacIntyre should write about the *Iliad* this way, given his awareness of the remarkable essay by Simone Weil, "The *Iliad*, or, The Poem of Force." In it, Weil insists that Homer is the first great antiwar (*and* antiheroic) poet in the West. MacIntyre edited this essay, with Stanley Hauerwas, in their collection

of essays entitled *Revisions: Changing Perspectives in Moral Philosophy* (South Bend, IN: University of Notre Dame Press, 1983).

57. MacCary, *Childlike Achilles*, 41.

58. *Iliad* IX.307–429, 607–19. I will be reading this scene in some detail in the last chapter.

59. See, for example, *Iliad* V.251–73; VI.440–65; VII.92–102, 123–60, 206–18; XI.401–20; XII.307–28; XXII.95–130.

60. MacCary, *Childlike Achilles*, 29–30, emendation mine.

61. MacIntyre, *After Virtue*, 129.

62. MacIntyre, *Whose Justice? Which Rationality?*, 338–39. See also *After Virtue*, ch. 2, on "The Emotivist Context," especially 11–12.
    In *Three Rival Versions of Moral Enquiry*, MacIntyre suggests that this "individual" with his or her crisis in personal identity, can only emerge "in the aftermath of some tradition" (199). I will return to this specious imagery—one more in a never-ending series of "afterwords"—in the last chapter. Traditions rarely die; they evolve and change. That is all.

63. For a stunning discussion of the relationship between the Market and the Theater, see Jean-Christophe Agnew, *Worlds Apart: The Market and the Theater in Anglo-American Thought, 1550–1750* (Cambridge University Press, 1986).

64. Michael Walzer, *Spheres of Justice: A Defense of Pluralism and Equality* (New York: Basic Books, 1983), 95 –128.

65. Simone Weil, "l'Iliade, ou, Le Poème de la Force," in *La Source Greque* (Paris: Editions Gallimard, 1953), 26.

66. R. P. Winnington–Ingram, *Sophocles: An Introduction* (New York: Oxford University Press, 1981), 324n49.

67. See Alasdair MacIntyre, *Against the Self-Images of the Age: Essays on Ideology and Philosophy* (South Bend, IN: University of Notre Dame Press, 1978), 70–71.

68. MacIntyre, *After Virtue*, 121.

69. *Ibid.*, 130.

70. He returns to this idea in *Whose Justice? Which Rationality?*, 40–41.
    For an alternative, and less "political," analysis of this virtue, see my "The Virtue of Courage: Changing Conceptions for Changing Times" (forthcoming).

71. MacIntyre, *After Virtue*, 124.

72. *Ibid.*, 121, 128.

73. Edith Hamilton, *Mythology* (New York: The New American Library, 1940, 1942), 300. See also H. R. Ellis Davidson, *Gods and Myths of Northern Europe* (New York: Penguin Books, 1964), 213–14.

74. For the portrait of *Ragnarök,* I am using *The Prose Edda of Snorri Sturluson,* trans. Jean I. Young (Berkeley: University of California Press, 1954), 86–90. While this prose piece is relatively late—Snorri himself was born in 1179 CE and was murdered in Iceland in 1241 CE—it preserves material which is much, much older, specifically here from a poem called "The Sybil's Vision." Moreover, while the Edda was conceived some 200 years after Iceland's official conversion to Christianity, it possesses very little trace of this later spirituality (save in Snorri's postscript), further testimony to the antiquity of its sources.

See also Davidson, *Gods and Myths of Northern Europe,* 35–38, 202–10.

75. If this is implicitly MacIntyre's view, it is George Steiner's even more explicitly. See *In Bluebeard's Castle,* 139–41, on the "heroism" of lost causes.

76. Here again, compare Steiner, *The Death of Tragedy,* 8–10, with Kerr, *Tragedy and Comedy,* 36.

77. See Martha Nussbaum's essay "The Transfigurations of Intoxication: Nietzsche, Schopenhauer, and Dionysus," *Arion, Third Series,* 1.2 (1990): 75–111.

78. MacIntyre, *After Virtue,* 128. Nietzsche, it should be noted, did much the same thing (and just as speciously) in the epilogue to *The Case of Wagner.*

Finally, it should be noted that this denial of a Nordic brand of pessimism to the tragedies represents my one serious criticism of Martha Nussbaum's work. See my "Martha Nussbaum: On Tragedy and the Modern Ethos," *Soundings* 72.4 (1989): 201–17, and *The Fragility of Goodness,* 78–79 for her defense of Schopenhauer.

79. *Njal's Saga,* trans. Magnus Magnusson and Hermann Pálsson (New York: Penguin Books, 1960), 250. See also pp. 49, 65, 91, 110, 146, 156, 227, 233, 243–50, 332, for the *leitmotif* of fatality which runs throughout the Saga. See also Davidson, *Gods and Myths of Northern Europe,* 217–18.

80. MacIntyre, "How Virtues Become Vices: Values, Medicine and Social Context," in *Evaluation and Explanation in the Biomedical Sciences,* ed. H. T. Engelhardt and S. Spicher (Dordrecht: D. Reidel Publishing Company, 1975), 97–121, here 110–11. It is surely worth noting the objections raised by Samuel Gorovitz in his response to MacIntyre's paper, since they accord so fully with my own.

"The sense of tragedy can be overdrawn. Virtue does not lie in saintliness any more than knowledge lies in certainty. . . . No period of human life has been devoid of tragedy; none, I'm sure, ever will be. Human life is always tragic, and false solutions should always be resisted. So, too, should false despair." (120–1)

81. Ruprecht, *Tragic Posture and Tragic Vision,* 71–79.

82. Paolucci, *Hegel: On the Arts,* 156–57.

83. Nietzsche, *The Birth of Tragedy,* §9.

84. Paolucci, *Hegel: On the Arts,* 31. See Bruno Snell, who is himself a convicted Hegelian classicist, in *The Discovery of Geist: The Greek Origins of European Thought,* trans. T. G. Rosenmeyer (Oxford: Basil Blackwell, 1953), 29.
Finally, see MacCary, *Childlike Achilles,* 231–33, where he argues that the gods, in this regard, function "rather like Kant's *noumena,* i.e., human reason's projection of unknowable essences."

85. MacIntyre, *After Virtue,* 32, 205, 214.

86. *Ibid.,* 222. See also *Whose Justice? Which Rationality?,* 12.

87. Ruprecht, *Tragic Posture and Tragic Vision,* 137–44, 242–47.

88. MacIntyre, *After Virtue,* 222.

89. *Ibid.,* 223.

90. *Ibid.,* emphasis mine.

91. See also George Steiner, *In Bluebeard's Castle,* 82.

92. See *Whose Justice? Which Rationality?,* 110, 124. This is the aspect of Aristotle's moral philosophy I tried to underscore in the last chapter. See also Myles F. Burnyeat, "Aristotle on Learning to Be Good," in Amelie O. Rorty, ed., *Essays on Aristotle's Ethics* (Berkeley: University of California Press, 1980), 81.

93. This is stated most succinctly in *Whose Justice? Which Rationality?,* 140–41, but it is the operative assumption behind everything he writes. See the conclusion of *After Virtue,* 263.

94. Aristotle, *Politics,* 1326b2–20.

95. See Martha Nussbaum, "Recoiling from Reason," 41.

96. Nietzsche, *The Birth of Tragedy,* §11; *Sämtliche Werke,* I.79.

Religious Texts

4

After Christendom?
On Distorted Theological Narratives

Menenius:	I shall tell you
	A pretty tale: it may be you have heard it
	But, since it serves my purpose, I will venture
	To scale 't a little more.
2nd Citizen:	Well, I'll hear it, sir; yet you must not
	think to fob off our disgrace with a tale . . .
	—Shakespeare, *Coriolanus* I.i

The work of Stanley Hauerwas in Christian ethics has become curiously popular; he is by far the most widely read ethicist currently working in North America. I say that this is "curious" for much the same reason that I consider Alasdair MacIntyre's popularity curious: it is curious because so much of what these men have to tell us about ourselves is so uniformly negative. In both cases, we see the attempt to articulate a decidedly unmodern view of the moral life degenerating into the posture of antimodernism. As we shall see, Hauerwas' antimodernism is actually the by-product of a far subtler opposition—namely his anti-Americanism. This *failed* experiment in pluralistic, Liberal democracy, in his judgment, is what makes the political vision of the Church newly viable and attractive. We live *after* Christendom, which is to say, *after* the presumption of calling ourselves "a Christian nation."

Hauerwas and MacIntyre have been friends and co-workers for a long time; they are now colleagues at the same educational institution. Their reformative programs draw deeply on one another, although MacIntyre has been less forthcoming than Hauerwas has been about this. Both ground their premodern view of the moral life in Aristotle. Both call for a return to a tradition of the virtues. Both argue for the centrality of narrative in the formation of moral character and moral lives. And, as I will demonstrate here, both submit to the tragic posture, precisely insofar as their antimodernism is grounded in a curious brand of nostalgia which is, in its turn, part of a much grander narrative *which begins with the premodern Greek world.*

I

The funny thing about stories, as I have tried to suggest, is the way they have of beginning and ending in their own special way, the way they have of establishing narrative boundaries which are unbridgeable, the way they have of creating a self-contained narrative world. Narratives are very much *un*like rational arguments[1]—which tend to be a little open-ended, aporetic, and are rarely ever finished. Narratives end—when and where we want them to. And the way they end is profoundly dependent upon the way we have chosen to begin them. Any playwright worth her quill or fountain-pen will tell you that the main characters need to be sketched indelibly in the opening scene. Shakespeare was a master at this, as he was a master at so many things. That is to say, at the beginning, we have already destined our characters and our stories to a certain sort of end. There is always a certain artistic *contrivance* about it all, something artificial, if not deliberately misleading.[2] Nietzsche characterized this, as I showed in the first chapter, as the artistic "love of lies,"[3] those "necessary fictions" we need in order to create an articulate human character and coherent human meaning.[4] Alasdair MacIntyre's incisive criticism of our modernness also depends upon a narrative, a narrative of decline and fall in which we have lost touch with our rootedness in local community and its traditions, living now *after* the *polis* and thus *after* virtue.

Stanley Hauerwas takes these insights further still, but arguing that *narratives actually constitute human selves,* that there is really no "self" prior to its spiritual formation (shouldn't we rather say "indoctrination"?) by a set of socially constructed narratives. The story has an epistemological priority over the self.[5] Hauerwas is going further than those who argue that the "self" emerges only *after* the acquisition of language. There isn't even a "self," Hauerwas says, until there is a relatively coherent story or set of stories which provides it with a narrative frame of reference.[6] Thinking that there is is a modern prejudice, tied to our overvaluation of the concept of individuality. In fact, we are not really "rational" apart from the stories which define what "rationality" is for us. There is no such thing as universal human reason, because there is no such thing as a universal human narrative. Assuming that there is was the Enlightenment's great ("encyclopaedic") error, and continues to be Liberalism's greatest self-deception. The relevant moral questions become, on this view, much narrower: "Whose stories are (part of) me?" and "which rationality do I want?"[7]

In some important ways, Stanley Hauerwas, America's most eloquent theological antimodernist—which also, I think, dooms him to some form of the postured apocalypticism of most intellectual antimodernism—has only recently become explicit about the story he really means to tell, the story he *wants* to tell. He has always called his narratives 'Christian.' But Hauerwas has begun to see another dimension to all this talk of teleology, why the notion of the end is so important and all-embracing in his and in MacIntyre's thought. A narrative is neater and cleaner than actual lived experience because of the way it wraps things up at the end. Part of being a Christian, *a narratively formed Christian,* is precisely this commitment to "the end." Teleology and eschatology go hand in hand. "Christians hope not on 'the processes of history',," Hauerwas cautions, "but on the God Whom we believe has *already determined the end of history* in the Cross and resurrection of Jesus Christ."[8] To be a Christian is to believe in "the script." In a rather psychedelic brand of postmodern Calvinism, Hauerwas argues that the self has been "scripted," and that the end is scripturally ordained. "It is written" has a force and authority in Hauerwas' theology which it has had in no other theology for quite some time, probably not since Luther. The problem is, in my judgment, that this narrative ending is so intimately bound to its beginning. There is a necessary *circularity* about narrative. One must begin a certain way if one wishes to end it all as Hauerwas and MacIntyre both wish to do, in this day and age.

The simplistic survey of this story he now calls 'Christendom'[9] lacks the very local color, the nuance, and the "thickness"[10] he accuses most modern stories of erasing. It is only a story, in the end, not history at all—just as MacIntyre's narrative was. It is painfully apparent that the term, and the story— 'Christian' and 'Christendom'—have become labels with which he baptizes his own virulent brand of anti-American antimodernism. Christianness is a weapon he uses against the "Liberal," "Enlightenment," and "modern" traditions he hates. Such a specious narrative—once again, in the genre of decline and fall—begs all the hard questions, even in his own terms: "Whose story? Which gospel?"

Hauerwas' resurrection of that dubious western doctrine—"outside the Church, no salvation"[11]—is meant to make this same point. *The community itself* provides us with a set of overarching narratives, witnessing to "the gospel" and to the real presence of God in history. That community which so witnesses is neither global nor modern. It cannot be. This is one of Hauerwas' surest and most insistent convictions. It is traditional, premodern. It is the Church, the only viable *polis* in the modern world. As he has insisted so many times, the Church does not *have* a social ethic; it *is* a social ethic.[12] Without such a set of stories which the community provides, our lives and our selves are in danger of coming unravelled. That disarray, that fragmentation, that "inarticulacy"[13]—these things, taken together, constitute this, "the modern age."

Therein lies the tale, *Hauerwas'* oft-told tale. The story he wants to tell, it seems to me, has two chief assumptions. They are his narrative beginnings. First, is the argument he takes from MacIntyre, that Liberalism is a bankrupt tradition, a *sham* tradition, that it lacks the moral resources to make sense of a whole range of modern problems because it lacks a set of coherent stories (as well as the coherent morals such stories are supposed to have). Modernity, post-Enlightenment modernity that is, wants to tell the story of the whole world—and that is a story which simply can't be told. The scope is too grand, the picture loses focus and blurs around the edges. A good play is about two or three hours long (of course, so is a good gospel, like Mark's).[14] Shakespeare was painfully aware of that fact. Longer than that and the audience gets restless. That was one of the many reasons Nietzsche could not abide Wagner—for his hubristic eight-hour epics which placed such unreasonable demands on players and audiences alike. We need to be more particular and more focused in our story-telling. So it is that Hauerwas' own unhappily schizophrenic[15] life—as a Christian theologian in a secular university—is labelled "a Babylonian captivity of theology by the Enlightenment university."[16] It is, like so much else in Hauerwas' corpus, a stunning image which upon further reflection is seen to be a falsifying analogy. Unlike the Babylonians, no one is holding Hauerwas anywhere. In fact, the tradition of modern Liberalism came as a sort of new Cyrus, announcing to each and every religious community that it could now come *out* of exile, could in fact go home and be left in peace. One is not in exile, if one is free to leave. Those Jews who elected to stay in Babylon after Cyrus' edict (and there were many) were assimilated, no longer exiles at all. It is not at all clear to me why—if Hauerwas really believed what he was saying (as storytellers sometimes do not)—he would not simply leave the modern university, and be more at peace. He suggests that he remains because this is his Christian duty, to witness to an idolatrous and universalizing state.[17] I assume that it is also because Hauerwas knows that there is an *inescapability* about certain Enlightenment values, to say nothing of their embodiment in our major universities. Liberalism's rather benign "empire" is one with which our own latter-day religious communities, even the most sectarian, must deal. That is surely the fundamentalist dilemma, as we shall see more clearly in the next chapter.

Hauerwas uses Aristotle—and 'uses' is the right word here—and the communitarian sensibility he thinks he finds there, to make better sense of our modern moral perplexity. Aristotle, he believes, articulates a *pre*modern moral vision over against the corrosive standards of Enlightenment universalism, *our* modernity.[18] I have been extremely critical of this perspective for a variety of reasons. It is grounded in a muddled and highly romantic picture of the *polis,* as I pointed out in chapter 2. Furthermore, it relies upon a caricature, a straw-argument which he and MacIntyre both call 'modern,' a word which has not, to my knowledge, been adequately defined by anyone. It makes an equally specious caricature of Liberalism as the milktoast belief in radical autonomy, pure tolerance, *and nothing more.* Taken together, Liberalism and modernity become the twinned source of problems which are actually part and parcel of that glorious and exasperating experience of trying to live together in an always-already, uncannily pluralistic, yet integrated, global community. That is the problem—which is at least as old as the *Iliad*—endemic to any attempt to inhabit something, however inchoate, which we call a "tradition." Such criticisms are tied to a frankly simplistic account of Aristotle's moral psychology which emphasizes its socialness and its "political"[19] nature to the total exclusion of the profound individualism and solitariness of the (often contemplative) *megalopsychos*. In a word, Hauerwas has overgeneralized Aristotle, and Liberalism, *and* thus our "modernity" itself. It is a compelling narrative, but like most drama, it depends upon caricature at least as much as it does on character.

Now, in one of his most recent books,[20] Hauerwas says something which is much more interesting, although it interests me not precisely for the reasons he intended. He says that we are living "After Christendom," that the Christian era is now somehow past. That idea resonates strongly with MacIntyre's apocalyptic antimodernism, the image with which *his* cultural symptomatology began.[21] MacIntyre asked us to envision a world in which books have been burnt (by whom?) and a whole mode of discourse has been jumbled and confused where it has not been jettisoned outright. What we have left are bits and pieces, words mostly, of a moral vocabulary which has been detached from a whole way of life (and its context, in the scriptorium) in which it once made sense. That world no longer exists. Because of that, we are all merely sloganeering in the modern age—"living amid fragments," Hauerwas calls it[22]—using bits and pieces of a language (and a set of stories) which once made sense and make sense no longer. Premodern articulacy has given way to postmodern nonsense.

Translate that image into a North American Protestant church on Sunday morning, and you have a pretty good idea of why Hauerwas is so distressed. More sloganeering, more parroting of empty phrases from the Bible quoted out of context by people who lack the *awareness* of context—*where* these stories come from, *when* they were written, in *what language, why* they are placed here in an overarching narrative of martyrdom and resurrection.[23] Whether in a nominally Christian culture, or in this self-congratulatory "Christian nation" of ours, or else in the pews, Christians have lost touch with the kinds of smaller, *anti-wordly* communities in which their stories originated, and in which they once made sense. That, as I will try to show in a moment, defines *the normative status of "the Early Church."* Hauerwas' narrative, the lens through which he wants to view our modernness, is a rather simple, and to my mind rather simplistic, one. That is not necessarily a problem. *Most* great art has something profoundly simple about it. Shakespeare certainly does. Hebraic character-sketches certainly do. Some fictions probably *are* necessary, and their necessity is tied to their simplicity. But then, other narratives are simply, well, *simple*—and I am afraid that Hauerwas' narrative has become precisely that.

II

Hauerwas' story has four crucial moments, four narrative turning points. It really is—his own protests notwithstanding, for now[24]—a fairly simple and nostalgic narrative of decline and fall. Any storied account as indebted as Hauerwas' is to Alasdair MacIntyre's narrative could hardly be otherwise. What we see is a profoundly romanticized period of "the Early Church"—Hauerwas' narrative beginning—whose representative character-types[25] are the evangelist and the martyr (I will turn to them in more detail in a moment). This gives way to the "Constantinian Revolution," the alliance with worldly power, and the great dawn of "Christendom" (how he can ignore the gulf which separates Rome from Constantinople is a key problem with this distorting narrative, it seems to me, a "schism" which Constantine helped create in the very act of building Rome a *second* capital on the Bosporus).

That dream dies, as it was doomed to die, through Schism. The "Lutheran heresy," as Hauerwas is increasingly inclined to view it,[26] seems to me less profound than the Great Schism of 1054 CE. Luther's "schism" is part of an argument among western European clerics. The debate between Eastern and Western Christendoms went far deeper than that, and existed arguably "from the beginning."

But let that lie. Luther is one of the first "modern" men, in *this* story's unfolding. Ironically, he serves much the same purpose in Nietzsche's antimodern narrative, although Nietzsche dislikes him for a very different, a virulently "anti-Christian," reason. Hauerwas dislikes him for strictly "antimodern" reasons. Luther represents a new, and infinitely worse, beginning for Christendom. He made Christianity a matter of the heart, by badly *mis*reading Paul and Augustine, Hauerwas thinks. Luther (or rather, the Lutherans who came after him) radically individualized the faith in the process of misreading them this way. We each stand alone before God, to work out our salvation in fear and trembling.[27] Luther was wrong about everything, Hauerwas insists: wrong in the way he conceived of salvation;[28] wrong in the way he conceived of the individual;[29] and especially wrong to de-contextualize "the Book," making it available to a spiritually unformed and untrained laity. That is his heresy.[30] Luther sowed the seeds for the advent (and the incoherence) of Liberal modernity—a modernity which lacks the same moral resources that Luther's version of the Church does.[31] To the degree that we live "after virtue," we live "after Christendom" too—and for much the same reasons. The contemporary church lacks the same moral resources which Liberalism lacks. Christendom's "adherence to foundationalist epistemologies"[32] leaves it with modernity's Enlightenment dilemma. It lacks articulacy; it lacks narrative coherence. The Church would need to recover "the gospel" in order to rediscover its own moral resources—

unavailable, as they are, to the secularized, liberalized, posttraditional, "modern" world.

Now—here is the odd thing, and I think that it is very easy to miss—Hauerwas is not at all worried by this superficially sad constellation of facts. In fact, he seems to take a peculiar delight in it all. He has recently "discovered" Foucault, he tells us,[33] but I suspect that he *uses* him, much as he uses most thinkers in a variety of philosophical traditions—as more grist for his own antimodern milling. Foucault is but one more weapon in Hauerwas' antimodern and antifoundationalist crusade. It was Foucault's early delight to have "discovered," so he thought, that the world as we now envision it was about to disappear. His is a very engaging and benign sort of (post)modern apocalypse:

> As an archaeology of our thought easily shows, man is an invention of recent date. And one perhaps nearing its end.
>
> If those arrangements were to disappear as they appeared, if some event of which we at the moment do no more than sense the possibility—without knowing either what its form will be or what it promises—were to cause them to crumble, as the ground of Classical thought did, at the end of the eighteenth century, then one can certainly wager that man would be erased, like a face drawn in sand at the edge of the sea.[34]

In the space opened up by the collapse of that older "order of things," that older way of thinking, we have the freedom to find new ways to think about our "selves" and our lives. Foucault anticipated a dawning "aesthetics of existence,"[35] which—here's the irony of it all—was neither so novel nor so *postmodern* as he wanted it to be. It had, and continues to have, profound roots in the classical Greek tradition, especially in the kind of Hellenism which Nietzsche proclaimed. The question, then, if we really *are* living in the great moment of modernity's demise, is: Which way to turn? *Backward,* to a "premodern" way of looking at things? Or *forward,* toward an uncertain future, more open seas, and a gayer moral science? Foucault, by ignoring certain key contours of Nietzsche's thought, as well as Nietzsche's profound rootedness in the Classical canon (although this began to change in his unfinished *History of Sexuality*), meant to go forward, toward the gayer science of free-spiritedness, and the playful polemics of postmodernism. Hauerwas, again *precisely* like MacIntyre, turns backward—back to where he thinks we took a wrong turn in the Christian way. "These awkward times," he smiles, perfectly delighted by it all, "give us the opportunity to recover the locality of Christian salvation called the Church."[36]

MacIntyre went back, as I have said, to the Greeks, specifically to his own idiosyncratic understanding of heroic society and the way that communitarian sensibility is recapitulated in Aristotle's moral philosophy. Hauerwas is a Christian theologian. He can *make use* of Aristotle, but he can't go back there. After all, the messiah had not yet come.[37] Instead, Hauerwas wishes to go back to the pre-Constantinian period of "Early Christianity," a period he sees as blissfully prior to the wrong path the Church took when it married the political powers-that-be. The Church should have been more chaste, quicker to understand that singleness is also a Christian vocation, that there ought to be no such thing as an erotic relationship apart from the marriage bond, . . . and that you can only marry one person, one time.[38] Sexuality was *political* activity, significant to the Christian *polis,* and ought to be revisioned as such.[39] Any other perspective is "romantic" and "bourgeois."[40] So he says.

What, then, does this portrait of the Christian past look like? Sketchy, at best. Hauerwas "shoots from the hip," as Martha Nussbaum notes.[41] But I think Hauerwas has finally begun to see how integrally related his assumptions about Christian origins are to his new-found conviction that "Christendom" is ending, here and now. As I did with MacIntyre's distorted narrative in the last chapter, so I would like to go back now with Hauerwas—ironically enough, back to the Greeks. I would like to turn to his brief narrative of Christian origins, in order to highlight some of its inadequacies. It is my belief that an illustration of what is missing here—*what is missing is, in a nutshell, the eastern Greek-speaking world*[42]—well illustrates the inadequacy of Hauerwas' and MacIntyre's specious brand of antimodernism. Narrative beginnings and endings are of a piece, and if one goes, the other probably has to go with it. That was true of MacIntyre's narrative of our decline and fall into modernity, and it is equally true of Hauerwas' narrative of the decline and fall of Christendom.

III

As I have noted, Hauerwas' story begins with a telling moment, an idyll he calls "the Early Church." Another image which he takes from Alasdair MacIntyre is that of the character-type, the notion that, in a well-ordered tradition, there are certain characters who *embody* the essential virtues of their society. They "were not just social roles; they provided the moral focus for a whole cluster of attitudes and activities." They furnish the society with "a cultural and moral ideal." Characters, in point of fact, are nothing more than "the masks worn by moral philosophies."[43] So in Victorian England these ideals were best symbolized by the public school headmaster, the explorer and the engineer. In Wilhelmine Germany, the essential *characters* were the Prussian officer, the professor, and the social democrat. In our own age, this *modern* age—especially in North America, I suspect, although MacIntyre never locates these latter types geographically, believing as he does that "modernity is everywhere"—the best we have to offer are inarticulate, often solipsistic, characters like the therapist, the rich aesthete, and the bureaucratic manager. The sketchiness of these portraits (is the explorer any less individualistic than, say, the rich aesthete? weren't they often the same men?) is a problem to which I have already referred. I want to look now at how they function in Hauerwas' theological narrative.

Hauerwas tends to think oppositionally—in twos, rather than threes[44]— and his portrait of the moral world of the early Christians is best symbolized by two characters I have mentioned before: the evangelist and the martyr. To these two I think we might well add a third, *the classically trained scholar/rhetorician*,[45] but therein lies the tale, a tale to which I will return in a moment.[46] I would like briefly to examine Hauerwas' character-sketches, or better, his caricatures, of these Christian social roles. In doing so, I would like to narrate a rather different story of Christian origins.

If we are to believe the account which Luke tells us in his *Acts of the Apostles,* then the first Jews who spread this new message of God's astonishing graciousness told *stories.* That is a roundabout way of confirming Hauerwas' and MacIntyre's insistence upon the theological and philosophical importance of narrative. Stories help us to communicate, and perhaps even to construct, human meaning. What they both fail to say—this is largely what *this* book is all about—is that narrative has something compellingly artificial about it. That level of artifice is well-illustrated by the fact that the stories these early evangelists tell is not at all the same. When we see Peter preach briefly,[47] and then Stephen at much greater length,[48] we are told a story which begins with Abraham and ends with Jesus. That is to say, these men, all deeply committed to the chosen status of the Abrahamic nation of Israel, tell a story in which the promises made to that community have been realized. The way these evangelists chose to begin their stories *destines* them to a certain sort of ending, a certain way of envisioning the "salvation" which Jesus Christ has made possible.

It is Paul who changes all that. Luther read the Pauline revolution rather well, it seems to me. The story Paul tells, from the beginning, is an entirely different thing. He begins, not with Abraham, but with Adam. It is instructive that only two of the gospel writers give us a genealogy of Jesus himself. Matthew, who is consistently concerned to demonstrate the *continuity* between the Abrahamic covenant and the new covenant initiated by Jesus, traces Jesus' lineage back through David to Abraham (Matthew 1:1–17). By contrast, Luke, who is obviously wedded to the Pauline theology of original sin, traces the genealogy of Jesus all the way back to Adam (Luke 3:23–38). It is telling that Luke describes Adam as "the son of God." In this sense he agrees with Paul, that Jesus closes the circle of world history, a second divine son to heal the wound we owe to the first. Thus, the way he sees Jesus Christ "ending" this narrative of decline and Fall is radically different as well.[49] Paul's "salvation" is a very different kind of ending, a very different solution to a very different problem. Whereas Peter and the other evangelists in the Jerusalem Church are desperately concerned to articulate how and why the most favored nation status which Israel has enjoyed up until now is being subtly altered, Paul is concerned first and last with sin, with the unbridgeable gulf which has separated people from God, *after* Eden. His doctrine of salvation becomes much more individualistic, and he has arguably given up so much of his Jewish identity that he becomes a Jew no longer. That is what the first "ecumenical" council in Jerusalem is all about, after all:[50] How much of our Jewishness can we give up, and still be true to the covenant? Is there any *continuity* to this new covenant if non-Jews (that is, *Greeks*) are to be included in it now? Some argue that circumcision is a requirement.[51] That is to say, one must first participate in the Abrahamic covenant, must become a Jew in effect, in order for Christ's salvation to be available. The Pharisees go much further and insist that the whole Law must be kept as well,[52] that the Mosaic covenant is nonnegotiable and actually sets the boundaries which define this community's self-identity (this would be an essential insight which, once developed, contributed to what we now know as Rabbinic Judaism). Paul and Barnabas, while present at this debate, are notably silent. They are content to describe the successes—"signs and wonders," Luke calls them—they have enjoyed "among the nations" (not *against* them, as Hauerwas would prefer), but they studiously avoid debating theology.[53] They have little authority, and even less credibility, in Jerusalem, certainly not as much authority as Jesus' brother, Jacob, has.[54] Yet their version of the "gospel" wins in certain critical ways—up to a point. Circumcision is no longer taken to be the mark of this community, nor is the whole Mosaic Law. Yet Paul's polemical extremism, his outlandish notion that God gave us the Law as a sort of test He knew we would fail,[55] is simply too much. The Lawlessness of Paul's "gospel" is simply too much for the Jerusalem Church. And so a certain list of "bare minimum" *legal* standards are maintained for the Church in the Dispersion: prohibitions against idolatry (more specifically, against food which has been sacrificed to idols); against cultic sexual activity [*porneia*][56] (Hauerwas makes too much of this one, I think, since it probably applied to cultic prostitution and *not* to the household);[57] and a single dietary requirement regarding the consumption of strangled food [*pniktos*] and blood [*haima*] which come from the first covenant God ever made— an explicitly *universal* covenant—with Noah, and every living creature, *after* the Flood.[58]

Those commentators who end the story of the First Ecumenical Council there fail to notice what happened next. A letter outlining all of this, including the short list of Christian "rules," was drafted and sent north to Antioch. Paul and Barnabas took the letter there, but they are essentially being monitored by representatives of the Jerusalem Church. Presumably, there is concern with how the letter will be offered *and interpreted* outside of Jerusalem, where Paul has been free, too free perhaps, to teach as he pleases. In short, *they are not fully trusted*.[59] And when the watchdogs finally leave to return to Jerusalem, Paul and Barnabas stay away. They do not return to Jerusalem until the end of Luke's narrative, and when they do, their mere presence in the city incites a riot.[60] From their inception, these evangelists are telling rather different stories, and Paul has changed the story so much that it threatens to become a new and very different thing.[61] This Pauline theology—the narrative extending from Adam to Jesus—is a profoundly *nostalgic* theology, a theology of lost innocence, *and* of lost paradise. Other early Jewish-Christian preachers did not make the same argument. Paul's is a theology which seems to me rather far in fact from the forward-looking message of Jesus and John—namely, that "the kingdom of God is at hand" (Mark 1:15). And in any case, Paul's new beginning—with Adam, not Abraham—takes him to a very different narrative end. It was in Antioch, after all, that the word was preached to non-Jews for the first time.[62] So it is, Luke tells us, that here, in Antioch and also for the first time, these followers of Paul (*not* Peter)[63] began calling themselves by a new name: 'Christian.'[64]

Immediately after the watchdogs leave Antioch, a new conflict emerges—this time between Paul and the very man who had originally sponsored him before the Jerusalem Church, Barnabas, and John Mark with him.[65] They part company in Antioch. Another conflict, another schism. To ask it again: "Whose gospel? Which story?" The character-type of the evangelist proves to be an uncannily complex one, which never meant one thing only, and seems at countless junctures to have meant incompatible things to different evangelists. Hence Paul's great distress in Antioch, in Corinth, and elsewhere. The superficial simplicity of narrative theologians who want simply "to tell the story" papers all this over.

One of the things which is markedly different about Paul is his *Greekness*. His gospel is not particular.[66] He is a Jew whose theology renders problematic nearly every tenet of first-century Palestinian Judaism (it may have caused less problems in the synagogues of Greece and Asia Minor, where the Promised Land was no longer functionally a lost Eden, and the Temple was no longer a prominent site for exclusive cultic practices):[67] the doctrine of chosenness, the virtues of Hellenism and cultural assimilation, the status of the Mosaic Law (sin and repentance, primarily). Paul's imagery, his rhetoric, his language, and finally his remarkably individualistic doctrine of salvation are all thoroughly Hellenized—as was Judaism itself, at least in the Dispersion. It is largely through his enduring influence that Christianity (emerging now as wholly distinct from Judaism) became a deliberately global and consciously inclusive faith. That has had a brutal cost in far too many evangelized places, but it has had its brighter moments as well.[68]

IV

The cost was paid first by Paul himself, and by a host of other martyrs. They are the Early Church's second character-type, in Hauerwas' judgment. Now Stanley Hauerwas rarely romanticizes, given his deep suspicion of nostalgia as a political trope in the democratic politics of modernity, but he decidedly romanticizes the martyrs.[69] There is a courage, he argues, which comes only with a lifetime of preparation for death. We are all schooled on the stories we are called to imitate.[70] Hauerwas bemoans the loss of a world, and a worldview, in which martyrdom was a decidedly Christian vocation. The point is, like the vast majority of Hauerwas' work, overdrawn and sadly ahistorical.[71] It is another area in which Nietzsche is extraordinarily insightful, if unmodern. His psychological insights are among his most astute, and his psychology of the martyr bears careful reflection: "Blood is the worst of all testimonies to the truth," Zarathustra reminds us. "Blood poisons the purest teaching; blood puts madness and hatred in the heart."[72]

Hauerwas' martyr-myth seems to depend upon the Mennonite community, in North America—not the early Christians of Asia Minor—whose members are all raised reading *The Martyrs Mirror* . . . [73] all of this in a pluralistic society which may "erosively" threaten their lifestyle, yet which is certainly *not* threatening to take their lives. Hauerwas has long insisted on the essential moral difference between physical and other forms of violence. Those who argue that he cannot be a pacifist and write the way he does really *have* missed this point. I do not mind the manner in which Hauerwas writes, but I remain deeply concerned that he has not kept his own counsel here. Whatever restrictions the Liberal state may or may not place upon religious communities, it is *not* physical violence. Martyrdom is no longer a "political" Christian vocation. And that is a decidedly *good* thing.

In North America, freedom of religion is "a subtle temptation,"[74] Hauerwas argues, because it has made the Church fat and lazy.[75] I suspect he also dislikes our "modernity" because it makes martyrdom an impossibility. In reflecting upon the mass suicide at Jonestown, a sort of pseudo-martyrdom which he uses to uncover certain crucial facts about modern society, Hauerwas opines, "we assume that being modern involves at least the agreement that no one ought to take religion too seriously, especially if it is going to ask any real sacrifice from us."[76] This is not to be taken as a theological counsel to Christian suicide, I know.[77] Rather, it is intended as a nostalgic reassessment of the Christian past. The "tragedy" of Jonestown, as Hauerwas calls it, is that we live in a society which does not care enough about the truth of religious convictions to resist the demonic forces of such cults by offering an explicitly *religious* alternative. The Church should be the first to resist the Jim Jones' and David

Koresh's of our world, he argues. Where religion is privatized, made a simple matter of personal choice, then all religion exists on a specious continuum of degrees of danger. We lose the essential distinction, Hauerwas argues, between suicide and religious witness. There is an insight here, overdrawn though it be. I hope to show in the next chapter that religious extremism, such as that posed by the scriptural fundamentalisms, can indeed be resisted for *religious* reasons. I take the Christian tradition seriously enough to be deeply critical of its excesses. The resources for doing so are still available to us, and the modern age is not nearly so dire as our antimodernists allege. What I want to show in this chapter is that there is a fine line to be drawn, but *emphatically* drawn, between martyrdom and suicide . . . and that many of the early Christians we call 'martyrs', about whom Hauerwas waxes so eloquent, were a good deal closer to suicides than he seems willing to allow.

It was, of course, a compelling concern of the early Church to outline some description of what it called a "martyrdom conformable to the gospel."[78] This language comes directly from the early-second-century *Martyrdom of Polycarp*. In the early decades of the second century, the Christian communities had two competing models of martyrdom before them—that of Ignatius (the Bishop from Antioch) and that of Polycarp (the Bishop from Smyrna). In Polycarp's, the case which was ultimately thought more "conformable," the principle of *imitatio Christi* was applied to Jesus' life as well as to his death. Ignatius' extremism, on this view, derived precisely from the fact that he thought the Christian way to involve solely the imitation of a martyr's death, rather than the life of service and healing which was the Lord's. What I want to suggest is that Hauerwas' storied account of martyrdom owes far more to Ignatius' polemics than it does to the sounder doctrinal model of Polycarp.

In one of his most jarring positions, Hauerwas bemoans the absence of the threat of martyrdom in the modern world. "It was through martyrdom," he insists

> that the church triumphed over Rome. Rome could kill Christians but they could not victimize them. . . . The most determinative witness the Church had against Rome was martyrdom.[79]

Again, Nietzsche serves as a corrective for this kind of bad nostalgia—as a philologist, as an historian, as a *psychologist*. "The martyrs," he insists, "have *damaged* the truth."

> The conclusion of every idiot, woman, and *Volk,* namely, that any cause for which someone would go to their death (or which, as in the earliest Christianity, sparks a veritable death-seeking epidemic) must really have something to it—this conclusion has become an unspeakable hindrance to investigation, to the very spirit of investigation and careful inquiry.[80]

This concern for what Nietzsche calls the "crudity" of the martyr-myth is a tremendous psychological insight, which the Church forgets at its peril. Precisely because I do not see Christendom, whatever that might have been, "ending"—it may well be changing, but then, it has never really done anything else *besides* change—I feel a far greater responsibility to be critical of it. The Church has lost none of its spiritual power, it seems to me—to help or to harm. Part of my disagreement is thus over Hauerwas' narrative teleology, his apocalyptic sense of a modern ending.

Hauerwas seems to prefer the rigors, and the discipline of Sparta—as only a man (like Plato or Aristotle) who never lived there really could. Here, as everywhere, history tells a markedly different tale. Hauerwas tells us that "we can never forget that Christians took their children with them to martyrdom— better to die than to be raised a pagan."[81] What is most shocking about this claim is that it is *not* footnoted.[82] If "Christians" did this, I for one am not aware of the practice. Hauerwas is passing off his own romanticized version of the early Church as "the gospel truth," when actually it is nothing more than a fantasy born of his own rabid antimodernism. With no real sense of the past, Hauerwas cannot appreciate the real horror, as well as the bizarre *ritual* dimension, to the Greco-Roman, and Christian, experience we call 'martyrdom.' When it is all a story, an "enacted narrative,"[83] then the certainty of the ending glosses over the passion of lived (and lost) experience.

Ignatius, the early-second-century bishop of Antioch (and martyred foil to Polycarp), is an excellent case in point. He complains bitterly of the rough treatment he is receiving "from Syria to Rome, on land and by sea, day and night." He says that he is waging a war with wild animals (*thēriomachō*) "bound as I am to ten leopards (that is to say a detachment of soldiers) who only get worse the better you treat them."[84] And yet this complaint is offered by a man who is taken westward, quite leisurely really, from Antioch to Smyrna (where he has time to draft letters to Ephesus, to Magnesia, to Tralles, and on ahead to Rome, where he hopes to be killed), and then north to Troas (where he stops again and roughs out one letter to Philadelphia and two letters back to Smyrna) before crossing the sea to Neapolis in northern Macedonia, . . . where he drops out of sight entirely.[85] If he was actually martyred, we do not know of it. What we *do* know is that he was curiously free to do much as he pleased, to meet with whomever he wished, as he made his way—slowly, slowly, now—toward whatever fate awaited him in Rome . . . if, in fact, he ever got there. Martyrdom is not at all what Hollywood, or Hauerwas, have made of it. It is not a "story." There is an important line to be drawn between religious conviction and a pathological death-wish. "Fanatics are picturesque," Nietzsche quips, "and people prefer looking at postures over listening to reasons."[86] Indeed, martyrdom seems not to have been what Ignatius himself wanted it to be. That is why he projects ahead, in his letter to the Romans—to make martyrdom over in his own idiosyncratic "Christian" image:

> Let me be fodder for wild beasts—that is the way I can get to God. I am God's wheat and I am being ground by the teeth of wild beasts in order to be made a pure loaf for Christ. . . .
>
> What a thrill I shall have from the wild beasts that are ready for me! I hope they will make short work of me. I shall coax them on to eat me up at once and not to hold off, as sometimes happens, through fear. And if they are reluctant, I shall force them to it. Forgive me—I know what is good for me. Now is the moment I am beginning to be a disciple. . . . Come fire, come cross, come battling with wild beasts, rending of bones, mangling of limbs, crushing of my whole body, cruel tortures of the devil—only let me get to Jesus Christ![87]

This is nominally Christian conviction which borders on pathology. It is the kind of stuff which, precisely because it lacks the *humanity* of the Synoptic gospels, renders it not merely difficult, but rather morally repugnant, to be a Christian. "I do not want to live in a human way [*kata anthrōpous*]," says Ignatius.[88] Perhaps not, but his is hardly an angelic alternative; it is beastly. There is a curious paradox here: in the name of the very Christian community of which he is a bishop, Ignatius has left the marketplace far behind. He longs for the mountaintop, the solitude of the arena, and a bloody death. As I argued in the second chapter, it may be that Nietzsche's alternative is less beastly than MacIntyre's. Here we see the kind of manic Christianity Nietzsche (and a host of classical rhetoricians as well) lambasted so roundly, and so effectively. It is based finally on a single conviction: "The greatness of Christianity comes not when it convinces the world, but when it is hated by the world."[89] That is as neat a summary of Hauerwas'most recent narrative as any I know.[90]

There is only one thing in this appalling portrait of torture and mauling which redeems Ignatius for me. It is how he concludes this longest, and grisliest, of all his many tirades. He pleads with his Roman hosts:

> If, when I arrive, I plead with you, believe me: it is what I am now writing to you that I really want. Though still alive, it is with a passion [*erōs*] for death that I am writing to you.[91]

Even Ignatius is not so certain, in a cooler and more reflective moment. It is the only *human* moment in Ignatius' otherwise inhuman and antiworldly corpus.

The other factor notably absent from Hauerwas' brief and glowing account of the martyrs is any sense of doubt, despair, even apostasy. His "storied" Christians march boldly and unflinchingly toward their narrative ends. "A people freed from the threat of death," Hauerwas remarks, "must form a polity because they can afford to face the truth of their existence without fear and defensiveness."[92] Even Ignatius, for all his pathology, knew better. He knew, as the Church knew, that only the select few were ready for martyrdom, were in fact even vaguely capable of it. They were *trained* for it, apparently.[93] And even those so trained and habituated apparently were not always up to the task. So grotesque a problem did it become that the gospels were written—among other things, *to guard against* this crassly romanticized portrait of human suffering. Resurrection does not make Crucifixion any less painful. Even being the Christ does not armor you against the desperate cry from the cross: "My God, my God, why have you abandoned me?" Any theologian who wants to read Ignatius' letters as normative, as Hauerwas' authoritarian positions strongly suggest that he does, would be well-advised to take a longer look at Mark's gospel.[94] Hauerwas has rightly pointed to "Mark's powerful development of discipleship, which takes Jesus' life to be a paradigm for our own lives."[95] But here again we meet the dangerous oversimplification of a narrative.[96] What Hauerwas fails to see, or say, is that none of the disciples in Mark (actually the Greek calls them simply *mathētes,* or "students") understand the story, anymore than they understand the parables.[97] If Jesus is a paradigm—and this is Mark's answer to Ignatius' pathology—then he is a paradigm *no one* understands.

V

My point in retelling Hauerwas' tales—and in doing so with an eye to the distorting ahistoricism of his theological narratives—is not to fault him for not having read enough. Just the opposite: he has been reading too much—too much antimodernism—and reading it back into the history of the Early Church. I question his *narrative vision* for being far too narrow. In the name of locality, particularity, and face-to-faceness, Hauerwas has disastrously narrowed and diminished his narrative world. This hamstrings his criticism. One cannot even *begin* to tell the Christian story without paying careful attention, first to its inherent globalism, and then to the cultural crucible of the Greek-speaking eastern Mediterranean out of which it grew and took its first shape. Hauerwas, by contrast, has never seen beyond the iron curtain of western Europe, and the hegemony of Rome.

My broader theological point is that "Christianity" is *not* a strictly biblical phenomenon.[98] Hauerwas knows this better than most. Yet Christianity seems to me to be an emphatically *Greek* tradition which emerges, through an as-yet complex and poorly understood historical and cultural process, as recognizably and theologically distinct in the second or third century of the Common Era. This Hauerwas does not say. 'Christianity,' as we know that term, requires—

not the New Testament, save for certain parts of the gospels, but rather the Incarnational and Trinitarian creeds of Nicaea (325 CE) and Chalcedon (451 CE). Creeds, not just Constantine, make for 'Christendom.' Christianity, to be truly "Christian," also needs a new question—who was this Christ, anyway?—to replace all the older questions which haunted the debates we saw in the Jerusalem Council. Now, Stanley Hauerwas has admirably sensitized the Christian community to its own rootedness in Jewish tradition.[99] Yet, despite what he says, Jesus is not only, nor even primarily perhaps, the long-awaited Jewish messiah. He becomes the son of God, God Incarnate, finally even *Pantocrator* . . . and that is when the line which separates Judaism from Christianity, as two distinct religious traditions, can be meaningfully drawn, perhaps for the first time. Hauerwas has, ironically enough, and against his own best intentions, made Christianity almost too Jewish.[100] That results, again ironically and quite unintentionally, in a certain insensitivity to those Jews who did not convert, often for excellent and deeply "traditional" reasons. "Christianity" emerges only after it moves west—toward Asia Minor and Greece, to be sure, then decisively so in a new form when it reaches North Africa, and then finally again in Rome itself. In Jerusalem, it never seems to have enjoyed great success. Christianity, that is to say, is an eastern Mediterranean, rather than a Roman or Palestinian, phenomenon.

We have been rightly sensitized to the fact that "Judaeo-Christian" is an unfortunate mixing of terms which should probably be kept distinct.[101] Judaism is one coherent and independent religious tradition; Christianity is another. That is a truism, the merest fact of the North American religious landscape in the late twentieth century. Such nomenclatures point to one way in which narrative histories distort. Yet the term remains *historically* and *heuristically* meaningful— as a descriptive term for *first*-century rather than *twentieth*-century religious realities. To speak of "Judaeo-Christian" peoples in the first two or three centuries of the Common Era *is* meaningful[102]—that is, from a time when what we now call "Christianity" was slowly detaching itself from a Judaism already under enormous pressure from the cultural confluence of Hellenistic and diasporic traditions. This, too, should be an essential part of Hauerwas' historical narrative. It, too, is not.

I want now to turn to the next chapter in Hauerwas' distorting narrative. Historically speaking, the kinds of martyrdom which make Ignatius such an odd character and so difficult to relate to seem to have characterized North African spirituality from its inception. Tertullian is but a rhetorically more sophisticated version of Ignatius. And this points to a far deeper and more profound *stylistic* difference in the Latin- and Greek-speaking churches, the west and the east, which had already been reified by the time of the Constantinian revolution and the foundation of Constantinople. We see it well-entrenched, and thoroughly divisive, at the First Ecumenical Council in Nicaea in 325 CE, a council called by Constantine himself. Debates about the humanity and/or divinity of Christ have everything to do with the humanity and/or inhumanity of this new faith. They have everything to do with the idea of martyrdom, the attitude taken toward embodiment, and beliefs about the soul's destiny after death. Arianism is, perhaps heretical, but surely Christianity with a more human, and thoroughly eastern Greek face. That is one reason it would not go away.

The one figure from the Constantinian era whom Hauerwas wants to keep is Augustine.[103] He is, for Hauerwas, what we are all taught in college: *the* theologian for the Early Church, the man who single-handedly defined what "Christians" now believe. He is surely a profound representative of Latin-speaking, fairly rigorous, and often deeply idiosyncratic North African spirituality. His definition of Christianness, like the Levitical self-definition, is curiously and adamantly *anti*pagan.[104] Augustine spoke no Greek, needed Jerome in Bethlehem, in fact, to translate everything for him—*even the Bible itself.*[105] This Jerome did, giving the Church its Latin Vulgate, although he clearly did not care much for Augustine personally.[106] They were, literally and stylistically, while both Christian, members of different worlds entirely.

The east simply does not exist for Stanley Hauerwas. This is an important point for several reasons. I made a preliminary attempt to say why in my last book.[107] More to the point of this book, we may notice one essential polarity which helps to define the birth of the modern age (a polarity, moreover, which runs throughout much *earlier,* premodern Christian thought as well). This is the polarity between "the thesis of Scholastic Aristotelianism and the antithesis of biblical-patristic humanism."[108] If Dupré is right in laying out this dichotomy, then the "modern" era has been characterized by a series of attempts to synthesize theoretically opposed theological forces. Hauerwas' theological narrative cannot help us to do so, because it denies one of the poles of the Christian synthesis, the eastern pole, so consistently. His solution to "modern" theological confusion comes at the expense of denying the geographical and conceptual complexity of the Early Church's views, by focusing exclusively upon its early Latin, and then its Scholastic, traditions (as MacIntyre also does), and by ignoring Christianity's eastern, humanist face.

To claim that the east does not exist in Hauerwas' narrative might seem an unfair claim, yet it is a claim which Hauerwas himself willingly embraces. The attempt to take Christianity's "eastern face" into his theology would be the very temptation to Enlightenment universalism which corrupted the Church in the first place, a false universalism which gave rise to "Christendom." Hauerwas is speaking to *western* Christians only, and leaves the east to its own affairs. My argument is that Christianity cannot be Christianity this way. Its theological narrative has been *fatally* distorted.

Now there is another reason for Hauerwas' reticence. This is because "the west" does not exist for him, either.[109] It is a false construction, he thinks—this polarity of "east and west"— established by the "modern" world. And that is a game which he is no longer willing to play. But precisely by arguing this way, Hauerwas ironically privileges developments in post-Enlightenment Euro-America out of all proportion to their global and historical impact. That is clearest here, in *After Christendom?*, where for the first time he explicitly, if sketchily,[110] traces out the narrative of Christendom's decline and fall—*the* narrative which has everything to do with his antimodern theology. Theology, after all, is a kind of godly story-telling. He conveniently ignores what was, culturally speaking, clearly the highest achievement of the Constantinian era— namely, Byzantium. At roughly the same time that Augustine is launching his tirades against the paganism he was raised on (shades of a very Pauline schizophrenia, here), the Cappadocians in Asia Minor were talking about Christianity's golden opportunity: namely, to marry two very different worlds, the Hebraic and the Hellenistic, the Jew and the Greek.[111] Paul, ever the extremist, had said that in the new world which was dawning, there would be *neither* Jew *nor* Greek.[112] That is a part of his extremism, his emphatic desire to negate. The Cappadocians have it all a little differently: in the new age which they are helping to build, they hope, there will be *both* Jew *and* Greek. That too is the cultural, philosophical, and theological enterprise which we now know as "Christianity."

For a man who complains so eloquently and so bitterly about the parochialism of North American theology ("the subject of Christian ethics in America continues to be America," was a haunting refrain which I heard almost daily in the graduate seminar where we first met), Hauerwas' theological speculations lack the very *globalism* which is a key component of this Greek gospel. He sees the modern trend toward globalism and universalism as erosive, and wrong-headed.[113] These are MacIntyre's categories translated directly into Christian theology. I see this as, among other things, an essential ingredient of the gospel. Hauerwas senses that, although he does not know quite what to make of it. I suggest that an awareness of where it comes from—the Greco-Roman Mediterranean ("eastern," not "western") environment—would advance his thinking on these, as on many other matters. He seems to see Rome—in *this* country, in *this* day and age—as the source of a sectarian stance "against the nations."[114] He seems not to see Constantinople, or the many-splendored histories of eastern Christendom, at all. The subject of his Christian polemics continues to be Euro-America, and a variety of philosophical and theological developments which simply do not possess the erosive global impact he wants to ascribe to them. I grow impatient—much as Jerome did, and for much the same reasons— with theological discourses on Aristotle delivered by a man who will not be attentive to the Greek east, and to the Greek language.[115] I grow tired of being preached an antimodern, sectarian gospel by a theologian who participates so fully in the (post)modern intellectual environment. Modernity itself, not the gospel, has turned antimodern. And in that sense, Stanley Hauerwas is as modern a theologian as any.

VI

The east does not exist in this theological narrative because the focus of this Christian ethic continues to be North America. What we really see when we chart out the intellectual career whose culminating statement comes in *After Christendom?* is the gradual development of an anti-American theological perspective. In Stanley Hauerwas, we have watched an un-American gospel turn increasingly and virulently anti-American. This is what separates him most profoundly from the Protestant fundamentalists of North America, of whom he otherwise often speaks rather appreciatively.[116] He argues that the U.S. flag does not really belong in any church[117] (I tend to agree with that claim), and he refuses to recognize "patriotism" as a churchly virtue or practice (I cannot agree to that claim, nor could the eastern churches). Hauerwas' real enemy is neither Liberalism nor something called "modernity"; it is the United States of America.[118]

"The subject of Christian ethics in North America continues *to be* America," Hauerwas reminds us. This is a sneer, like a great many of his poses, which sticks to Hauerwas' own work. If one examines the matter with some care, then it becomes clear that Stanley Hauerwas' work shares something essential with precisely the turn-of-the-century Protestant Liberalism of which he is otherwise so roundly critical. Precisely like Walter Rauschenbusch, whose "Social Gospel" was so deeply influential at the time, Hauerwas insists upon the *continuity* of Christianity with the Hebraic-prophetic tradition.[119] Precisely like Rauschenbusch, Hauerwas emphasizes the *social* vision embodied in the political ministry of Jesus.[120] And precisely like Rauschenbusch, Hauerwas identifies the Early Church we meet in *Acts of the Apostles* as a sort of Christian Golden Age, one in which real community, real responsibility and answerability to and for one another, were possible.[121] In all of these areas, Hauerwas' is a probing reinterpretation of the reformative conceptual zeal of the Social Gospel. So deeply does modernist schizophrenia run. We become the very thing we claim not to be. Hauerwas' work is an eloquent example of modern antimodernism. It is also, much like MacIntyre's work which I explored in the last chapter, a curious sort of antiliberal Liberalism.

Of course, Hauerwas will not accept this identification, precisely because he decries the unholy marriage of Protestantism and Liberal North American culture. He decries the Unitarianism, and the vague anarchist presuppositions, which underlie such an account. He decries the wedding of the Kingdom of God to this entity "we just so happen" (his words) to call the United States of America. And he decries, as I said, the presence of U.S. flags in too many North American churches.

Hauerwas' broader concern, I suspect, is that Rauschenbusch's account of Jesus' ministry does not culminate in the Cross. As H. Richard Niebuhr put it in a stunning criticism of the Social Gospel: "A God without wrath brought one without sin into a kingdom without judgment through the ministrations of a Christ without a Cross."[122] Rauschenbusch's rather rosy portrait of the Early Church allegedly does not mention martyrdom, either. These are the essential Christian categories—crucifixion and resurrection, that is, a paradigmatic kind of martyrdom—which inform Hauerwas' portrait of the Early Church.

In making these criticisms, Stanley Hauerwas begins to sound ironically very like Reinhold Niebuhr, criticizing that same tradition.[123] Yet Hauerwas would surely object even more vociferously to that equation. For him, Reinhold Niebuhr was the one who most successfully poisoned the well of Christian ethics in the United States, in part by focusing so doggedly on North America.[124] Hauerwas' disagreements with Reinhold Niebuhr are complex, many of them having to do with the well-worn distinction between "Love and Justice."[125] But here again, the larger issue is the "Liberal" conviction that North America was, and continues to be, "a Christian nation." Such claims, Hauerwas feels, serve only to place the flag in front of the cross. And once you allow a U.S. flag into a Church, you will have a devil of a time getting it out again.

Hauerwas' quarrel, I am suggesting, is ultimately with the United States of America—not with modernity, despite the fact that his rhetoric, like MacIntyre's is couched in a a zealous brand of antimodernism. If he believes that the moral course charted out by the North American cultural mainstream is indicative of the way the world is moving, then perhaps he should say this more clearly. I, for my part, would have serious reservations about such a thesis, claiming a centrality for matters North American which the global evidence cannot entirely support. To the degree that he is critical of U.S. political realities, I share a good many of his concerns. Yet increasingly Hauerwas leans toward the rhetoric of antimodernism, and in so doing, makes a caricature of his own better insights. His is a *negative* theology, at its best, a *prophetic* theology, a *critical* Christian ethic. He is an un-American, increasingly anti-American, critic of North America. But he waxes far more eloquently about the social problems in contemporary North America than he does about the key Christian alternatives. These alternatives too often degenerate into syrupy prescriptions for martyrdom and an odd kind of martyrologized nonviolence.

It has been my contention that a fuller account of a more *positive* position— Christian or otherwise—will involve us necessarily in a dialogue with the very

Greek tradition which has been so thoroughly marginalized in Hauerwas' (and most Euro-American) narrative account, the invocation of Aristotle notwithstanding. Understanding why this might be so will require two more chapters, I think.

For now, the matter may be fairly simply stated.[126] My reaction to this distorting theological narrative is twofold. First, I insist that any western theologian as committed as Hauerwas is to telling "the Christian story" simply *must* take a long look at the Orthodox tradition, at Christianity's own *eastern,* not western, face. Therein lies its origin, its beginning. Hauerwas' story could not help but end quite differently, if he had taken the time to begin it more truthfully, with the Greeks.

Here is where, it seems to me, there is some real merit to the charge that Hauerwas' is a tribalistic portrait of the Church, radically sectarian, which some have gone so far as to call "fundamentalist."[127] These criticisms are often made in a rather *ad hominem* and superficial manner. Yet there is a significant point here which I would like to underscore. Fundamentalists, like Hauerwas himself, preach truthfulness rather than truth. They conceive of theology as a telling and retelling of "the story." Fundamentalism is practically communitarian, and thus narratively constituted. Fundamentalism—here is the curious thing—*very much like the modernism which attempts to grapple with it,* is a unique phenomenon of western, not eastern Christendom. In its Christian guise, it is originally a U.S. invention. There are no Orthodox Christian "fundamentalists." It is not some list of alleged "fundamentals" which makes one a fundamentalist—the Catholic and Orthodox Churches, for their part, uphold all five "fundamentals." No, it is not doctrine which makes a fundamentalist. Rather it is a tone, an antimodern state of mind. It is ultimately a posture. There are two things which characterize sectarian and fundamentalist religious commitments in the three major scriptural faiths: first, a heady nostalgia for some allegedly purer scriptural past; and second, an emphatic rage against the alleged evils of the modern age. That is, a narrative of golden ages and a myth of origins which contribute, in their turn, to antimodern despair. I have attempted to address the first of these points, the caricatured fiction of Christian origins, in this chapter. In the next, I would like to explore the second idea, the virulent antimodernism which lies at the heart of so much contemporary theory, and so many theological positions of protest. Most modernists, and nearly all fundamentalists, are *anti*modern. It is my hope that, by exploring the ways in which scriptural fundamentalism has been studied by the academic community, we will gain a better awareness of how this fiction—the fiction of "modernity"—has been narratively constructed, and then construed as a problem in need of solving. To that task, I turn now.

Notes

1. This is directed against Alasdair MacIntyre, who explicitly claims the opposite in *After Virtue,* 2nd ed. (South Bend, IN: University of Notre Dame Press, 1984), 265–72.

2. MacIntyre, *After Virtue,* 212.

3. Friedrich Nietzsche, *Wir Philologen,* 5[115]; *Sämtliche Werke,* VIII. 76.

4. The canonical statement of this position comes in *Beyond Good and Evil,* §4; *Sämtliche Werke,* V. 18, where Nietzsche admits that his new language "rings strangest." I am indebted to James J. Winchester's *Nietzsche's Aesthetic Turn: Reading Nietzsche After Heidegger, Deleuze and Derrida* (Albany: SUNY Press, 1994) for making this and other texts accessible to me.

5. This is perhaps clearest in the essay "From System to Story: An Alternative Pattern for Rationality in Ethics" (with David B. Burrell) in *Truthfulness and Tragedy: Further Investigations in Christian Ethics* (South Bend, IN: University of Notre Dame Press, 1977), 15–39 and reprinted in his *Why Narrative? Readings in Narrative Theology* with L. Gregory Jones (Grand Rapids, MI: William B. Eerdmans Publishing Company, 1989), 158–90.

6. Such a process of acquisition clearly takes *time.* Building upon Aristotle's conviction that "happiness" is a moral impossibility until you are well into your thirties, Hauerwas insists, "what must be said is that most students in our society do not have minds well enough trained to be able to think—period" (*After Christendom? How the Church Is to Behave if Freedom, Justice, and a Christian Nation Are Bad Ideas* [Nashville, TN: Abingdon Press, 1991], 98). His conclusion, that he "cannot think of a more conformist and suicidal message in modernity than that we should encourage students to make up their own minds" is, by his own admission, "morally undemocratic" (*After Christendom?* 102). But then, that is hardly surprising in this polemical era of antimodern antiliberalism. He adds: "Does this mean that I am an 'elitist'? Am I committed to some account of hierarchy? Am I questioning the presupposition that freedom and equality are the fundamental principles of social life? The answer to each question is 'Yes.' " (*Dispatches from the Front: Theological Engagements with the Secular* [Durham, NC: Duke University Press, 1994], 105–6).

For a more moderate viewpoint, which allows for a certain kind of genius even in adolescence, see Martha Nussbaum, *Love's Knowledge: Essays on Philosophy and Literature* (Oxford University Press, 1990), 11ff. For more on this, see Alasdair MacIntyre, *Three Rival Versions of Moral Enquiry: Encyclopedia, Genealogy, Tradition* (South Bend, IN: University of Notre Dame Press, 1990), 82–84, but compare 232.

7. I am deliberately playing on the title of Alasdair MacIntyre's *Whose Justice? Which Rationality?* (South Bend, IN: University of Notre Dame Press, 1988), a seminal influence on Hauerwas' recent books.

8. Stanley Hauerwas, *The Peaceable Kingdom: A Primer in Christian Ethics* (South Bend, IN: Notre Dame University Press, 1983), 145, emphasis mine.

9. While I will be drawing on Hauerwas' major works, I am specifically addressing the claims he makes in one of his latest books, *After Christendom?* What I want to emphasize is that his story hangs or falls according to how well he defines this thing, 'Christendom,' which we are supposed now to be living "after."

10. The term is Clifford Geertz' from *The Interpretation of Cultures* (New York: Basic Books, 1973), 3–32.

11. Hauerwas, *After Christendom?* 16–19, 26.

12. Hauerwas; *The Peaceable Kingdom,* 99–102. See also *A Community of Character: Toward a Constructive Christian Social Ethic* (South Bend, IN: University of Notre Dame Press, 1981), 1, 10, 12.
As will become clear, I think that this phrase nicely captures the tension in his work. It is a glib and penetrating insight at first glance. Yet upon further reflection, one cannot help but wonder what it really means.

13. I am borrowing this phrase from Charles Taylor, whose masterful *Sources of the Self: The Making of the Modern Identity* (Cambridge, MA: Harvard University Press, 1989), 18–19, 53–90, makes the point that this "ethics of inarticulacy" pretty well defines us in the "modern" moment.
For a competing, far more balanced, account of our modern challenges *and* possibilities, see his *The Ethics of Authenticity* (Cambridge, MA: Harvard University Press, 1991). For an appreciative reading of Taylor's work, see Hauerwas, *Dispatches from the Front,* 169–74. I will turn to Taylor's work in the last chapter.

14. See Alec McGowen, *Personal Mark: An Actor's Proclamation of St. Mark's Gospel* (New York: Crossroads, 1984). McGowen performed a one-man recitation of Mark's gospel on Broadway, which is now available in video format from the American Bible Society, 1865 Broadway, New York, NY 10023.

15. I use this word deliberately as I did in the preface, since I will make much of it in the next chapter, where I argue that schizophrenia is widely held to be another key element of our modernness.

16. "The Testament of Friends," in James B. Wall and David Heim, *How My Mind Has Changed* (Grand Rapids, MI: William B. Eerdmans Publishing Company, 1991), 9.

17. Hauerwas, *After Christendom?* 14.

18. Here, as elsewhere, MacIntyre best makes the point in a passage which I used as the epigraph to chapter 2:

Aristotelianism is *philosophically* the most powerful of pre-modern modes of moral thought. If a pre-modern view of morals and politics is to be vindicated against modernity, it will be in *something like* Aristotelian terms or not at all. (*After Virtue,* 118).

19. It is fascinating that Hauerwas titles each chapter of this book as "The Politics of . . . " All activity, even our sexual activity, he now defines as "political." Such sweeping generalizations seem to me to cover over deep and abiding moral distinctions which simply must be made in this, or any, age.

20. An interesting, and particularly troubling, aspect of Hauerwas' ever-growing corpus is the increasing speed with which he writes. One of the most frustrating aspects of this latest book is that he surely has some important points to make, but *he has not taken the time* to make them more carefully and with greater nuance. I will return to this idea.

21. MacIntyre, *After Virtue,* 1–5.

22. Hauerwas, *The Peaceable Kingdom,* 2–12.

23. I should say, too, that Hauerwas is at his most eloquent when he is calling the Church, not the United States and not modernity, to task for its failure in self-understanding. One of the most moving essays he has ever written is a devastating criticism of the way Christians let "their" tradition of Just War Theory be used and abused in the service of wholly secular, national interests.
See "Whose Just War? Which Peace?" in *But Was It Just? Reflections on the Morality of the Gulf War,* ed. David E. Decosse (New York: Bantam Doubleday Dell Publishing Group, 1992), 83–105. Hauerwas preaches in the same vein when his audience is, again, *his* church. See the collection of sermons in *Unleashing the Scripture: Freeing the Bible from Captivity to America* (Nashville, TN: Abingdon Press, 1993).

24. Stanley Hauerwas, *Against the Nations: War and Survival in a Liberal Society* (New York: Winston Press, 1985), 1–2. See also *After Christendom?* 166n8, where Hauerwas says that "[he has] no wish to return to a 'golden age' in which Christians ruled, and [he does not] harbor a desire for a 'Christian culture.' "
Clearly Hauerwas does *not* romanticize the Constantinian moment, which is a profoundly ambiguous one for him (*After Christendom,* 15–19, and 168n18). What he *does* romanticize is what came *before* all that—namely, the martyrs (38).

25. Yet another idea from MacIntyre's *After Virtue,* 28–30.

26. Hauerwas, *Unleashing the Scripture,* 15–18, 25.

27. Philippians 2:12.

28. Is the problem with Luther that his is a deeply anti-Jewish argument against any collective notions of salvation? See Hauerwas, *After Christendom?* 37–38.

29. See Hauerwas, *After Christendom?* 29, for a scathing indictment of "that new creature we have learned to call 'the individual.' "

30. This is the main thesis of *Unleashing the Scripture.* Again, there is an insight here, and again it is overdrawn. What leaves me frankly stunned is Hauerwas' refusal to

see or say that *he himself* would have been considered insufficiently trained for the theology he is doing, since he reads neither Greek nor Latin nor Hebrew. He has effectively admitted that he has no "good response" to the troubling question of his own authority (*Unleashing the Scripture,* 10, 157–58n10).

31. And Reinhold Niebuhr was his greatest exegete. See *After Christendom?* 180n5.

32. Hauerwas, *After Christendom?* 15.

33. Wall and Heim, *How My Mind Has Changed,* 2, 8. See also *After Christendom?* 164n5.

34. Michel Foucault, *The Order of Things: An Archaeology of the Human Sciences* (New York: Random House, 1979), 387. I will return to this idea in the last chapter.

35. Michel Foucault, *Politics, Philosophy, Culture* (New York: Routledge and Kegan Paul, 1988), 49.

36. Hauerwas, *After Christendom?* 35.

37. "For if you believe that Jesus is the messiah of Israel," Hauerwas opines, "then 'everything else follows, doesn't it?' " (*A Community of Character,* 35).
Of course, as the Church discovered almost immediately, "everything" else does not simply "follow." That is the implicit danger of narrative oversimplification.

38. Hauerwas' contrast is, as always, starkly overdrawn: "In a world where we are taught that all human relations are contractual, what could be more offensive than a people who believe in life-long commitments?" (*After Christendom?*, 118 and 26). Actually, in *this* society, the cheapened sexuality of the free-spirit seems to be far more of an offense than "life-long commitments." Here again, with no attention paid to what the AIDS epidemic has done to our sexual consciousness, we are provided with a portrait of our modernness which is, to my mind, virtually unrecognizable.

39. Hauerwas, *After Christendom?*, 20, 113–31, esp. 118–19.

40. I think that Hauerwas' caricature of our modernness suffers from this willful disregard of the Romantic tradition, an aspect of our modernity at least as central to us as "Enlightenment." See Charles Taylor, *Sources of the Self*, 393, and my own essay on Platonic erotics called "A Funny Thing Happens on the Way to Mantineia," in *Soundings* 75.2 (1992): 97–127, especially 118–20. As I have said several times, I think that the Greeks' most enduring legacy comes in their *tragic* and *erotic* literature, not in *moral* philosophy.

41. "A Reply," *Soundings* 72.4 (1989): 765.

42. I am deeply indebted to Vassilis Lambropoulos' *The Rise of Eurocentrism: Anatomy of Interpretation* (Princeton: Princeton University Press, 1993), especially 3–96, for some of the profound implications of this anti-Greek, anti-Eastern "Christian" bias.

Hauerwas argues that only people who are "constituted by the unity found in the Eucharist" have any real access to the Bible. He suggests that "any churches divided from Rome" are actually "divided from themselves" (*Unleashing the Scripture,* 23). He knows this sounds odd to Protestants in North America. But he seems *not* to sense how positively offensive and alienating this same rhetoric is to an Orthodox Christian.

43. MacIntyre, *After Virtue,* 28–30. See also Robert N. Bellah et al.; *Habits of the Heart: Individualism and Commitment in American Life* (Berkeley: University of California Press, 1985), 41–48, 144–47, for a fleshing out of several American character-types, among them the entrepreneur, the manager, the therapist, and of course, the private eye and the cowboy.

44. It is deeply instructive when MacIntyre thinks oppositionally in twos, rather than in threes. These are some of the most pivotal moments in his analysis. The most telling moment is his pivotal chapter in *After Virtue* entitled "Nietzsche or Aristotle?" Clearly, he is demanding a choice of us, a choice I am arguing that is unnecessary for us to make.

45. See George A. Kennedy, *New Testament Interpretation Through Rhetorical Criticism* (Chapel Hill, NC: University of North Carolina Press, 1984), and Burton L. Mack and Vernon K. Robbins, *Patterns of Persuasion in the Gospels* (Sonoma, CA: Polebridge Press, 1989) for more on the centrality of these character-types in the Early Church.

46. For my own work on this character, in which I argue that these men had a foot in each of two cultures—classical and Christian—*and* that most scholars miss this, because we no longer know the Greeks, see "Athenagoras the Christian, Pausanias the Travel-Guide, and a Mysterious Corinthian Girl," *Harvard Theological Review* 85.1 (1992): 35–49.

See Jaroslav Pelikan, *Christianity and Classical Culture: The Metamorphosis of Natural Theology in the Christian Encounter with Hellenism* (New Haven: Yale University Press, 1993).

47. Acts 3:12–26. For the Greek text I am using *The Greek New Testament,* ed. Kurt Aland, Matthew Black, Carlo Martini, Bruce Metzger, and Allen Wikgren (Münster: Institute for New Testament Research, 1966, 1975).

48. Acts 7:2–53. I am deliberately avoiding a discussion of the much more complicated preaching of Philip (Acts 8:26–35) which, on the face of it, *seems* to support Hauerwas' point of view. An Ethiopian Jew is reading the scripture, but admits that he cannot understand what he is reading, "unless someone guides [him]" (8:31).

For my purposes, two points are significant:

First, Philip's actual preaching is not recorded at all (8:35). We are shown the passage from *Isaiah* which the Ethiopian has been reading, and then we are told simply that Philip "opened his mouth" and "preached Jesus to him."

Secondly, this Ethiopian eunuch is meant to symbolize the fact that this gospel is spreading literally to the known ends of the earth, even to those who had been excluded under the Law. That is to say, he is a symbol of the Church's inherent *globalism,* not a paradigm for what to preach.

See the remarkable essay by Clarice J. Martin, "A Chamberlain's Journey and the Challenge of Interpretation for Liberation," *Semeia* 47 (1989): 105–35.

49. Romans 5:12–14, but compare Acts 13:16–41.

50. Acts 15:1–29.

51. Acts 15:1. And circumcision is identified as within the *ethos*—the custom, rather than the law—of Moses.

52. Acts 15:5. And here the word is *nomos* (law), not *ethos*.

53. Acts 15:12.

54. Acts 15:13ff.

It remains a mystery to me why the Latin-speaking western Church knows this man as 'James' when his name was clearly alliterated in Greek, as *Iakobos*. Jesus was named Joshua. And his brother was named Jacob.

Here is another little-known case of narrative distortion. Some interpretive communities, it seems, feel it within their rights actually to change people's names. That the Lord can do so is a Jewish and Christian conviction. That *we* can do so is another matter.

55. For more on this see Martin Buber's classic *Two Types of Faith,* trans. Norman P. Goldhawk (New York: Macmillan, 1951).

56. The history of mistranslation and misinterpretation of this word well illustrates my larger point. In Attic Greek, *porneiai* were houses of male prostitution, in which the *pornos* practiced his trade with little resistance and official government sanction, so long as the relevant tax, the *pornikon telos,* was paid. In the Koine Greek of five centuries later, it is less clear what the term denotes. I tend to think that it still refers to (probably male, probably cultic) prostitution in this passage, since *pornē* retained the meaning of 'prostitute' in Koine, and since cultic concerns clearly define the Council's overarching interests in this discussion. Translations—like the Authorized Version which renders this as 'fornication' (the Latin *fornicatio* also denoted 'prostitution' at least through the High Middle Ages) or the Revised Standard Version's 'unchastity' (whose very vagueness begs the question)—do not help matters much.

What I worry about here, as I worry elsewhere, is the complete lack of cultural and linguistic sensitivity in these debates. Hauerwas takes twentieth-century ideas, and imposes them upon his idyll of the past. We need to think our way back into the extraordinarily complex cultural (and sexual) milieu of the first-century eastern Mediterranean if our readings of such phrases and legal decisions are to have any meaning. The setting here is clearly one of pagan sexual, cultic, and dietary practices which challenge and offend some members of the Jerusalem Church. The setting clearly is *not* a scholastic roundtable debating sexual mores. For more on the historical problem generally, and the linguistic problem of *porneia,* see John Boswell's *Christianity, Social Tolerance and Homosexuality: Gay People in Western Europe From the Beginning of the Christian Era to the Fourteenth Century* (Chicago: University of Chicago Press, 1980) 102–105, 114, 335–337.

57. See Hauerwas, *After Christendom?* 113–31, where marriage and sex are "political" activities. I think this is one of the many points where the *polis* is invoked with such alarming facility that it, too, begins to mean nothing precisely because it means *all* things.

58. Genesis 9:1–7.

59. Acts 9:26.

60. Acts 21:27–33.

61. Galatians 2:11–14.

62. Acts 11:19–20.

63. Acts 13:2.

64. Acts 11:26.

65. Acts 15:37–40.

66. Romans 2:11. The term is *prosōpolēmpsia,* a certain favoritism, or "face-to-face-ness." That is something the Creator of the universe cannot grant, Paul insists, in marked contrast to the way God relates to Moses, say, or Adam.

67. E. P. Sanders makes this same point in *Paul and Palestinian Judaism* (Philadelphia: The Fortress Press, 1977), although his methodology has one peculiarity which I do not pretend to understand. Surveying the extensive literature on Paul, Sanders notes that "what is needed . . . is to compare Paul on his own terms with Judaism on its own terms, a comparison . . . of a whole religion with a whole religion" (12). Sanders' exploration of first-century Palestinian Judaism is exhaustive. *But Pauline theology is not "a whole religion,"* not yet. He is simply one among many evangelists, whose views became determinative some decades later.

68. I think it admirable that Hauerwas, for his part, appreciates the profound *ambiguity* of the Church's globalism, at *After Christendom?* 18–19, 133–52.
Even here however, the whole question is papered over with the claim that "the gospel is a story, the story of Jesus" (152). "Whose gospel? Which story?" "Traditions" are themselves pluralistic. Liberalism did not invent that fact.

69. The topic of early Christian martyrdom has, of course, generated an enormous bibliography. One classic statement is W. H. C. Frend's *Martyrdom and Persecution in the Early Church: A Study of a Conflict from the Maccabees to Donatus* (Garden City, NY: Doubleday, 1967). His conclusion is most relevant to this discussion: "The ultimate legacy of the persecutions was the lasting division of Christendom into its eastern and western parts" (418). The argument here is that martyrdom served as a "mirror" far more

clearly in the Western, Latin-speaking Christian self-understanding than it did in the Greek-speaking East.

For more on the Greek and Roman background to the practice, see Anton J. L. van Hooff, *From Autothanasia to Suicide: Self-Killing in Classical Antiquity* (New York: Routledge, 1990).

For the relation to Paul's views, see David Seeley, *The Noble Death: Greco-Roman Martyrology and Paul's Concept of Salvation* (JSOT: Sheffield Academic Press, 1990). Finally, an excellent and wide-ranging recent work is Arthur J. Droge and James D. Tabor, *A Noble Death: Suicide and Martyrdom Among Christians and Jews in Antiquity* (San Francisco: Harper Collins, 1992). This book accomplishes two essential tasks for our discussion: first, it makes problematic any neat rhetorical distinction between suicide and martyrdom; and second, it points out how the Latin, post-Augustinian prohibition of suicide did not derive from a biblical mandate at all, so much as it did from a curious misreading of the classical tradition.

70. Hauerwas, *After Christendom?*, 104.

71. In arguing this way, I am trying to demonstrate that Hauerwas, MacIntyre, et al., are really the ones (not the "Liberals" at all) who have read a whole range of "modern" assumptions and concerns back into the past. Hauerwas, for his part, is remarkably untroubled by this, because his "authority" derives from his own interpretive (read: antimodern) strategies, *not* from the texts.

72. This passage is quoted by Nietzsche himself in *The Antichrist,* §53, one of the most remarkable psychological investigations of the martyr known to me (*Sämtliche Werke,* VI.234–35).

73. The full title of which is, instructively, *The Bloody Theater of Martyr's Mirror of Defenseless Christians Who Baptized Only Upon Confession of Faith, And Who Suffered and Died For the Testimony of Jesus, Their Saviour, From the Time of Christ to the Year AD 1660.* See Hauerwas, *Dispatches from the Front,* 212–13n3.

74. Hauerwas, *After Christendom?*, 69–92.

75. He would do well to attend to the Catholic "Declaration on Religious Freedom" (*Dignitatis Humanae*) in *The Documents of Vatican II,* edited by Walter M. Abbott and translated by Joseph Gallagher (Piscataway, NJ: New Century Publishers, 1966), 672–700. This document's chief assumption—about "the dignity of the human person" and the "freedom from coercion" by any political body ecclesiastical or otherwise—seems grounded in the very kind of Liberalism which Hauerwas criticizes so roundly. Doubtless he will see that as a *necessary* outgrowth of the document's emergence from the American Catholic hierarchy, under the auspices of Father John Courtney Murray's sponsorship. I prefer to see it as a logical outgrowth of the Church's profound commitment to speak to the entire human family, Christian and otherwise, whereas Hauerwas is explicitly speaking "for Christians and to Christians only" (*After Christendom?,* 13).

76. Hauerwas, *Against the Nations,* 91.

77. See *Suffering Presence: Theological Reflections on Medicine, the Mentally Handicapped, and the Church* (South Bend, IN: University of Notre Dame Press, 1986), 100–13, and *Christian Existence Today: Essays on Church, World, and Living in Between* (Durham, NC: The Labrynth Press, 1988), 199–219.

78. *to kata to euangelion martyrion.* For the Greek text of "The Martyrdom of Polycarp" I am using the Loeb Classical Library edition of *The Apostolic Fathers,* volume II (Cambridge, MA: Harvard University Press, 1992), 312. It is interesting that the author of this letter suggests that the Lord sent this "from above, *in order to show forth a martyrdom conformable to the gospel."*

79. Hauerwas, *After Christendom?,* 38.

80. Nietzsche, *The Antichrist,* §53; *Sämtliche Werke,* VI.235. I hope it is clear enough that when I quote Nietzsche's insight approvingly, I do not mean to support the unfortunate misogyny in which his insights were so often couched. That was already an issue in Nietzsche's lifetime, and I think it telling that so many women spoke in his defense. See Sander L. Gilman, *Conversations with Nietzsche: A Life in the Words of His Contemporaries,* trans. David J. Parent (New York: Oxford University Press, 1987), 52, 88–89, 116–25.

81. Hauerwas, *After Christendom?,* 129.

82. In personal correspondence, Hauerwas mentions Dom Gregory Dix' magisterial *The Shape of the Liturgy* (New York: The Seabury Press, 1983), where I do not find mention of this practice, but rather the predictable anti-eastern bias which so infects western Christian scholarship, writing off "the fascinating *but in the last resort stagnant and suffocating history of Byzantium and its strange frozen civilisation,* where Diocletian's empire dressed in Christian vestments *continued immobile for another thousand years"* (386, emphasis mine).

He also mentions H. E. W. Turner's *The Pattern of Christian Truth: A Study in the Relations Between Orthodoxy and Heresy in the Early Church* (London: A. R. Mowbray & Co., 1954), where the only mention of martyrdom (159–160) comes with the judgment that Gnostic heretics seemed as adverse to martyrdom as the Orthodox were eager for it. Hauerwas has yet to retract this misstatement.

83. Hauerwas, *After Christendom?,* 38. See also MacIntyre, *Three Rival Versions of Moral Enquiry,* 83.

84. Ignatius, *Letter to the Romans,* V.1, translation mine. For the Greek text of Ignatius' letters, I am using the edition of T. E. Page and W. H. D. Rouse in the Loeb Classical Library, *The Apostolic Fathers,* Volume I (New York: Macmillan, 1914), 230–33. In every case, I have checked it against the translated text in Cyril C. Richardson, *Early Christian Fathers* (New York: Macmillan, 1970), 104.

This is, oddly enough, the first reference to 'leopards' in Greek or Latin literature.

85. I am indebted to my former student, Mr. Rick Carter, for research which demonstrates how little we know about Ignatius' journey, save from sources which were written literally half a millennium later.

86. Nietzsche, *The Antichrist*, §54; *Sämtliche Werke*, VI. 237.

87. Ignatius, *Letter to the Romans*, IV.1 and V.2–3. See also Richardson, *Early Christian Fathers*, 104–5.

88. Ignatius, *Letter to the Romans*, VIII.1. See also Richardson, *Early Christian Fathers*, 105. We should compare the martyrdom of his friend Polycarp, bishop of Smyrna, to see how different it all could be, *Early Christian Fathers*, 141–58.
It should be clear, in light of the discussion of her views in the second chapter, that this is precisely the attitude which Martha Nussbaum finds justly worrisome about some—but I am quick to add, not all—of Christian thought.

89. Ignatius, *Letter to the Romans*, III.3. See also Richardson, *Early Christian Fathers*, 104.

90. "[We] are no longer subject to the powers that pretend to rule this world. They are not accepted. Does that not sound like good news indeed?" (Hauerwas, *Unleashing the Scripture*, 83).

91. Ignatius, *Letter to the Romans*, VII.2. See also Richardson; *Early Christian Fathers*, 105. The mention of *erōs*—*a word which does not appear in the entire New Testament*—in this connection should be another reminder of precisely why Nussbaum worries about certain forms of Christian self-abuse as she does, although I do think she goes too far in her criticisms, as Nietzsche did.

92. Hauerwas, *A Community of Character*, 50.

93. See Maureen A. Tilley, "The Ascetic Body and the (Un)Making of the World of the Martyr," *Journal for the American Academy of Religion* 59.3 (1991): 467–80.

94. For an explication of Mark's Passion-narrative as, in part, an antimartyrdom document, see my "Mark's Tragic Vision: Gethsemane," *Religion and Literature* 24.3 (1992): 1–25. See also my *Tragic Posture and Tragic Vision: Against the Modern Failure of Nerve* (New York: Continuum Press, 1994), 181–229.

95. Hauerwas, *The Peaceable Kingdom*, xxiv.

96. See Hauerwas, *A Community of Character*, 46–52, for a telling misreading (he would call it a retelling) of Mark's story of Jesus. In essence, Hauerwas argues that we are shown the disciples, especially Peter, "getting it wrong" in order that we can get it "right." But Mark's whole gospel is meant to show that *no one* gets it right . . . and the minute you lay claim to having it right, you're *wrong*.

97. Mark 4:10ff. For more on this troubling claim, see Frank Kermode, *The Genesis of Secrecy: On the Interpretation of Narrative* (Cambridge, MA: Harvard University Press, 1979), 23–47.

98. With Vassilis Lambropoulos, I am resisting "the assimilation of Christianity back into its biblical roots" (*The Rise of Eurocentrism,* 352n85).

99. See Hauerwas, *Against the Nations,* 61–90.

100. And his Christ too contingent. For a stunning admission of just how Arian his Christology really is, see Hauerwas, *Unleashing the Scripture,* 89–91. For more on Arius and contingency, see Robert C. Gregg and Denis E. Groh, *Early Arianism: A View of Salvation* (Philadelphia: Fortress Press, 1981), 176–83.

101. Alasdair MacIntyre, *Whose Justice? Which Rationality?* (South Bend, IN: University of Notre Dame Press, 1988), 10–11; and Hauerwas, *Against the Nations,* 61–90.

102. Peter Brown, *The Body and Society: Men, Women and Sexual Renunciation in Early Christianity* (New York: Columbia University Press, 1988), 198.

103. And MacIntyre, for his part, has gone so far as to identify himself as an *Augustinian* Christian (*Whose Justice? Which Rationality?*, 10). Nussbaum would clearly object to this, as the imposition of a distorting lens through which to read Aristotle, particularly since she objects to the Augustinian theology of original sin. For my purposes, I merely want to point out that she does so in the name of a very different reading of the Greeks, one much more in accord, in my judgment, with the traditions of the eastern Church.

104. Lambropoulos, *The Rise of Eurocentism,* 78–96.

105. See Valery Larbaud's lovely *An Homage to Jerome: Patron Saint of Translators* trans. Jean-Paul de Chezet (Marlsboro, VT: The Marlboro Press, 1984).

106. See Peter Brown's marvelous description in *Augustine of Hippo* (Berkeley: University of California Press, 1967), 272–75, as well as *The Body and Society,* 366–427. See also J. N. D. Kelly, *Jerome: His Life, Writings, and Controversies* (New York: Harper & Row, 1975), 148, 217–20, 263–72, 317–23.

107. Ruprecht, *Tragic Posture and Tragic Vision,* 168–74.

108. Louis Dupré, *Passage to Modernity: An Essay in the Hermeneutics of Nature and Culture* (New Haven: Yale University Press, 1993), 199, a quote taken from Auer's *Die vollkommene Frömmigkeit.*

109. Hauerwas, *After Christendom?* 164n8.

110. *Ibid.,* 35–39.

111. See Werner Jaeger, *Early Christianity and Greek Paideia* (Cambridge, MA: Harvard University Press, 1961), especially 72–75, for an elegant summary of this remarkable, unAugustinian tradition.

112. Galatians 3:28.

113. Hauerwas, *After Christendom?*, 133–35. See also MacIntyre, *Whose Justice? Which Rationality?*, 326–48.

114. Hauerwas, *After Christendom?*, 88, and the Roman Catholic Church is in danger of losing that stance, again eroded by the ineluctable forces of "Liberal modernity."

115. One of the many cases of too hasty thinking and writing comes at *After Christendom?*, 49, where he refers to Aristotle's conception of justice. Aristotle normally conceives of two extremes, which are vices, for every virtue which normally serves as the mean between them. Hauerwas refers to *dikaeosiene* (*sic*) as one of these extremes. Actually, that word, transliterated correctly (*dikaiosunē*) is actually Aristotle's word *for* 'justice,' an idea which did not really have two "extremes" which assist in defining it.

116. For an appreciative sketch of fundamentalist antimodernism and its authoritarian understanding of the Church, see Hauerwas, *After Christendom?* 110–11, 144.

He has seen his way clear to be critical of some aspects of fundamentalism in *Unleashing the Scripture,* but only because he feels that they participate in Liberal Protestant presuppositions: namely, the individual's right and duty to interpret scripture without ecclesiastical guidance (15), and the notion that there is a single "real meaning" (20) in something called "the text" (19). Liberal so-called "higher education" does claim the first and third things, but not the second. Fundamentalists claim all three. In no case is it easy to say, as he does, that "fundamentalism and biblical criticism are two sides of the same coin when looked at from a political [that word again!] perspective" (19). *Where they are similar is in grounding their antimodern polemics in a nostalgic religious vision of a scriptural Golden Age.* And this remains as true of Stanley Hauerwas' work as of any.

117. Hauerwas, *Dispatches from the Front,* 80–88, esp. 87.

118. *Ibid.*, 1–28, 91–106.

119. Walter Rauschenbusch, *Christianity and the Social Crisis* [1907] (Louisville, KY: Westminster/John Knox Press, 1991), 1–43.

120. *Ibid.*, 44–92.

121. *Ibid.*, 93–142. "[Modern interpreters] seem more anxious to emphasize that it did not occur twice than to show that it did occur once," he says (120)!

122. H. Richard Niebuhr, *The Kingdom of God in America* (New York: Charles Scribner's Sons, 1930), 193.

123. See, most particularly, Niebuhr's, *Moral Man and Immoral Society: A Study in Ethics and Politics* (New York: Charles Scribner's Sons, 1932).

124. Hauerwas, *Unleashing the Scripture,* 156n2; and *Dispatches from the Front,* 26–27.

125. I note especially the lovely collection of shorter topical writings, *Love and Justice: The Shorter Writings of Reinhold Niebuhr,* ed. D. B. Robertson (Gloucester, MA: Peter Smith, 1976).

126. The "death" of Christendom in North America has one enormous implication which Hauerwas has yet to face clearly. That is, precisely, the need for *apologetics* on the one hand, and *dogmatics* on the other. Christians, when they once again become a minority in North America and elsewhere, will begin to sound very much like Symmachus, the great pagan apologist of Imperial Rome, and Athenagoras, the philosopher who attempted to make Christianity palatable to the Roman intellectual elite.

127. Hauerwas, *Dispatches from the Front,* 197–198n29.

5

After Belief?
Fundamentalism, Secularization,
and the Tragic Posture

Miniver Cheevy, child of scorn,
Grew lean while he assailed the seasons;
He wept that he was ever born,
And he had reasons.

Miniver loved the days of old
When swords were bright and steeds were prancing;
The vision of a warrior bold
Would set him dancing.

Miniver sighed for what was not,
And dreamed, and rested from his labors;
He dreamed of Thebes and Camelot,
And Priam's neighbors.

Miniver mourned the ripe renown
That made so many a name so fragrant;
He mourned Romance, now on the town,
And Art, a vagrant.

Miniver loved the Medici
Albeit he had never seen one;
He would have sinned incessantly
Could he have been one.

Miniver cursed the commonplace
And eyed a khaki suit with loathing;
He missed the medieval grace
of iron clothing.

Miniver scorned the gold he sought
But sore annoyed was he without it;

> Miniver thought, and thought, and thought,
> And thought about it.
>
> Miniver Cheevy, born too late,
> Scratched his head and kept on thinking;
> Miniver coughed, and called it fate,
> And kept on drinking.
>
> —Edward Arlington Robinson, 1907

Fundamentalism is a religious phenomenon that has been much in the news in recent years. Many have suggested that it is another important ingredient of our modernness, a key color on the intellectual palate we are using to paint the self-portrait of modernity. Attention was perhaps most dramatically drawn to the phenomenon as a global phenomenon after the Iranian Revolution under the Ayatollah Khomeini, and the subsequent taking of the U.S. embassy in Teheran in 1979. But there followed, immediately on its heels, and in partial response to it, the so-called "Reagan Revolution" in this country in 1980. This bloodless revolution was achieved, it was thought at the time, in large measure through the Republican Party's ability to court the conservative religious electorate whose chief spokesperson at the time was (again, so we thought, so we told ourselves) Jerry Falwell and his newly-founded "Moral Majority." In addition to these factors, and as always since 1948, there is the curiously *religious* challenge presented by the reestablishment of the state of Israel. Here is a political event with overtly religious roots and religious implications (the distinction between religion and politics being, itself, a western creation which does not translate very well in this region). Conservative nationalist and ultra-orthodox religious parties within the Knesset have succeeded in manipulating the parliamentary system to achieve power and influence far beyond what their actual numbers would seem to warrant. In any case, taken together the "fundamentalisms" of the three Abrahamic (and scriptural) faiths seem to constitute essential phenomena in the modern world—or better, they are supposed to represent a coherent *reaction against it.* When our modernity is defined as a spiritual crisis—when it is defined, nostalgically, as coming *after* something else, *at the expense* of something else—then the religious response of the fundamentalist is, much like MacIntyre's and Hauerwas' responses, best understood an attempt to reassert a *pre*modern way of life in the face of the erosive forces of modernity. It is this narrative periodization—premodern, modern, and postmodern—that I wish to question again in this chapter.

When the World Trade Center was bombed in 1991, the news reported immediately that this was the work of "Islamic fundamentalists." It is not at all clear that these men would have identified themselves that way. A terrorist is one thing. A religious fanatic is something else. Fundamentalism has something to do, technically at least, with a belief in the inerrancy of a scriptural revelation. Yet the use of the term persists. Why? There is more to fundamentalism, it would seem, than the bombing of buildings or airplanes, more to it than the stoning of Israeli archaeologists by the ultra-orthodox, more to it than the assassination of doctors in North American abortion-clinics. It is nothing less than a way of life and a worldview which is at stake. So to this short list of overtly *political* resistance—which I suspect is the real issue which troubles us so, and seems worth analyzing—there are other nominally *cultural* phenomena to be examined in this same light: The Salmon Rushdie affair; the protest linked to the release of the film, "The Last Temptation of Christ"; contemporary debates concerning the annexation of the so-called occupied territories which the biblically-minded continue to call by other names. The question of what views and standards link these disparate movements in three separate, however related, religious traditions, has occupied the attention of scholars in religious studies for some time. What links them, it is widely believed, is a revolt against modernity, which is to say, a nostalgic desire to return to a time before this modern "after-time." And that is the larger interpretive viewpoint I mean to question in this book.

I

The debate about fundamentalism and its modernist implications has been greatly advanced by the appearance of a long study devoted explicitly to a "modern" understanding of it. It is a long book, a fascinating book, a challenging book, an *academic* book. That last observation—that this is an academic book, firmly anchored in the less-firm soil of academic rhetoric and "modern" religious assumptions—is perhaps the most important single fact to keep in mind when grappling with the book and with its message. Or so I would like to argue. The book is an academic study of fundamentalism, designed to provide a comparative assessment of the global impact which fundamentalism among the three scriptural faiths[1] has had in this century. It has been an enormously successful book, distinguished with the American Academy of Religion's Award for Excellence in 1990. The book is subtitled, revealingly, I think, *The Fundamentalist Revolt Against the Modern Age,*[2] and was written by a well-loved former teacher.

I trouble to mention that last point because it seems relevant to everything I will go on to say about it here. I respond personally to this book, because I think it an enormously important book. Bruce Lawrence has performed the long-overdue service of putting the issue of fundamentalism into a global and cross-cultural context.[3] That is his great gift, as an historian of world religions. It also represents the most personal element of this book, since I was fortunate enough to have participated in a seminar at Duke University in 1982 when Professor Lawrence was coming to these ideas for the first time, ideas which crystallized into this book some eight years later. It is also a task, a self-consciously *global* task, which had been neither conceptualized nor performed by anyone else. The comparative chapters of the book—Lawrence calls them "Countertexts,"[4] and they constitute the second half of the volume—treat Jewish, Christian, and Muslim fundamentalisms in successive chapters, and are some of the most enlightening in the book. They reiterate, and take much further, insights which I first took from Professor Lawrence over a decade ago. Yet they come on the heels of the first half of the book, a much denser and less satisfying half in which the theoretical framework is laid out, the lens through which Lawrence has chosen to view the global phenomenon of scriptural fundamentalism.

That lens is, it seems to me, actually a distorting mirror—a mirror in which we see nothing quite so clearly as our own assumptions, "academic" and "modern" by turns. The two terms are related, it seems, if for no other reason than that the scholarly community today has made such an issue of "modernity"— that ragbag category which wants to mean everything and ends up signifying nothing, due to the academic sound and fury with which it is too often described. Modernity is, in the final analysis, a catch-all phrase used to register *academic* discontent, and as such, it highlights the degree to which academics and fundamentalists share the same problem—that of "modernity" itself— however widely their solutions to it may diverge. For the purposes of this book, I have been calling that attitude—which most modern theorists and virtually all scriptural fundamentalists share—"the tragic posture."[5] I will also be calling it, in this chapter and only half in jest, the gospel of Miniver Cheevy. Simply put, the idea is that "we" are living somehow *after* the age of belief, whatever that means, and that fundamentalists are trying to turn back the clock. It seems to me that the way academics have confronted the fundamentalist phenomenon is a telling indication of nothing quite so well as an essential modern posture. In a word, I think that this allegedly (anti)modern global phenomenon—of a resurgent scriptural fundamentalism—tells us less about our "modernity" than the theorists think it does. The way these same academic theorists construe *both* the fundamentalist phenomenon *and* our modernness tells us a great deal more about academic Quixotism and the tragic posture, it seems to me.

To its credit, Lawrence's analysis is not reductionist. That is enormously important when the issue is as broad as "modernity." The "modern age" cannot be summarized so neatly as the curious constellation of technology, technical rationality, bureaucracy, the mass media, and the nation-state. These constitute what Lawrence calls 'modernity.'[6] These are, in some important ways, the windmills against which many theoreticians are tilting. And this is academic Quixotism.[7] Rather, throughout this century (and probably long before then, as I will argue) "modernity" has been viewed as a *spiritual* crisis of enormous proportions, as an age somehow "beyond belief" (meaning *after* belief, no doubt). That is, in deeper ways, the modernist windmill against which both the fundamentalists and the sociologists of religion are tilting. Modernity, so defined, is characterized by an odd sort of spiritual schizophrenia.[8] We are, at one and the same time, committed to a sort of *rationality* which is explicitly universal[9] ("scientific" and therefore fundamentally antireligious, when the religion is particularistic[10]), as well as an ideology of *pure tolerance,*[11] which is inherently relativizing. Lawrence's deliberately oxymoronic catch-phrase for this modern schizophrenia is "restrictive universalism."[12] Lawrence seems to see it as uniquely "modern."[13] I have been arguing that it is an essential ingredient of human socialness, a necessary corollary to living forever between the mountaintop and the marketplace. "The political animal" *always* lives with a foot in two worlds, a little schizophrenically, and there is *always* a penultimacy to the *polis.*

The implications of that kind of double-mindedness are legion. In some important ways, Lawrence's study is itself a product of that scholarly schizophrenia, insofar as he feels obligated to take fundamentalism seriously, respecting Hans-Georg Gadamer's "call for excising prejudice against prejudice."[14] But Lawrence's, and our own, commitment to respecting the fundamentalist's prejudicial agenda comes at an intellectual cost. He devotes a book to the phenomenon, even though he finds it an ultimately unconvincing response to the contemporary world. A telling moment thus appears in his discussion of the doctrines of the late Rabbi Meir Kahane.[15] They are written off as "counterfeit fundamentalism." Why they are "counterfeit" remains unclear to me, save that "we" in the academy find them particularly objectionable. The phrase which introduces the very next section of Lawrence's discussion, on the same page, reads "from the modernist viewpoint." It is an impossible perspective to shake off, he is suggesting. That is to say, "we" want to take the fundamentalist phenomenon seriously, but to do so, we must willingly suspend a great deal of academic disbelief. And then we must explain away, or rather define away, what stubbornly refuses to go away.

If the fundamentalist agenda is unconvincing, it is also doomed finally to failure, Lawrence tells us.[16] That failure is defined by the religious movements' being co-opted by the very means of modernity—mass media, democratic rather than theocratic politics,[17] and finally by the forces of globalism themselves—which they mean to combat. Compulsion cuts two ways, and the fundamentalist is attracted to the very hegemonic practices he[18] abhors. Fundamentalists are waging a war, Lawrence suggests, in which they are attempting to use the weapons of *modernity* to undo moder*nism*. It remains to be seen which of the principle actors in this historical farce will be hoist by the petard of their own assumptions. Probably the fundamentalists . . . and quite possibly the academic theorists of religion at the same time. For fundamentalism had a funny way of sneaking up on the theorists, and we are all still trying to be topical, to be better at predicting its next developments. In so doing, it seems to me that academic theorists of religion have made fundamentalism finally more important and theologically credible than it really is.[19] After all, most every theorist agrees that the fundamentalists are engaged in a battle they cannot finally win.

Such a battle is called "tragic" by the modernist.[20] This battle could be construed "tragically" only by a participant in the posture. It is a gross mistranslation of a venerable Greek idea. It is a word which also serves as the focal point for a constellation of crucial cultural ideas. Tragedies are not battles against impossible odds (that is *fatalism,* not tragedy, another key dimension of the tragic posture as I tried to show in the third chapter), nor are they disasters in which doom and disappointment loom larger than humankind.[21] There is a parable indeed in the fact—the *fact*—that *nearly as many Greek tragedies ended well as ended badly.* The manner in which these plays "ended" had little to do, at least in the Greek mind, with how a play was characterized, as "tragedy" or "comedy." Aristotle, that great Hellenic encyclopaedist of the received Classical wisdom, knew this well. Other things being equal, he observes, it would be absurd to *prefer* an unhappy ending to a happy one.[22] Yet that preference was crucial to MacIntyre's definition of "Homeric heroism." We academics—nowhere are we so "modern" as in this—are absurd in just this way. Pining away for a lost era of wholeness and religious belief, we are nostalgically *pre*modern.[23] Or else we are manfully, pridefully forward-looking, staring into the blank slate of the future, the boudoir and the abyss which have so captured the *post*modern imagination.[24] Either way, buying into the gospel of Miniver Cheevy, we want to be anywhere but *here* and *now*. Even this catch-all word 'modern' derives from the Latin *hodiernus,* which meant simply "here and now, contemporary, of today."[25] *It was not, and should not be made, a proper noun.* That fact is, in large measure, what this book is all about.

Fundamentalism, I want to suggest, can and should be resisted. To do so is hardly irreligious (although it can easily be so motivated,[26] there are *other* motivations, explicitly *religious* motivations, for doing so). Fundamentalism is an heretical hyperscripturalizing of religious traditions which are at once more nuanced and more pluralistic than the written word alone will allow.[27] It relies upon an equally specious redefinition of 'modernity', which becomes, on the tautologously fundamentalist view, the source of all our "modern" woes. This is a battle which, unlike the fundamentalists', *can* be won . . . and the possibility of success does not make it untragic. Rather, I think it would take precisely the tragic *vision* to combat the tragic *posture* in the modern age—*a posture which a great many academic theorists of religion and most scriptural fundamentalists ironically share.* That is why Mark's gospel played such a crucial role in my criticisms of Stanley Hauerwas' work in the last chapter. Mark's gospel— along with the prophecies of Hosea, and the story of Job, perhaps—are some of the most eloquent statements of the tragic *vision* in the entire scripture.

As I say, it is not only the fundamentalist who is "antimodern." Many, if not most, modernists are as well—hence the schizophrenia of so much modernist discourse to which I have referred. Fundamentalism and modernism are not "opposite templates of the world in which we live," as Lawrence suggests,[28] but rather flip sides of a common currency, similar attitudes taken to the complexity of the human situation. Hating what we are, we become what we hate. The gospel of Miniver Cheevy, again. One thinks of Max Weber, writing endlessly about religious thought—locked within the "iron cage" of the bureaucratic university, bars which "fate" had forged for him—all the while claiming to be "unmusical in matters religious"[29] (when was there ever a time when religiosity came as easily, or as happily, as "music"?). One is reminded of Alasdair MacIntyre waxing eloquently about the blissful unawareness of the Homeric hero, whose identity *was,* quite simply, his social role[30] (has he not read the poem? what in the world is Achilles so *angry* about?). One is reminded of Stanley Hauerwas proclaiming the end of Christendom, and with it the rebirth of the essential political organization called "church" (has he not seen how riven by contests for authority and power the Early Church was? can he really miss the likelihood of martyrdom?) One is reminded again of Michel Foucault, imagining a day, which may be dawning now, when the very image of "man" as our century has defined him will be washed away like pictures drawn in the sand before an advancing tide[31] (who drew the picture? when was it drawn? and whence cometh the tide?). As I tried to suggest in the last chapter, one is also reminded of a second-century Christian, like Ignatius, wanting "to be ground into bread for Christ,"[32] insisting that faith in Jesus Christ takes all your pain away (here was a Christian who had surely never read the Gospel of Mark). And one is reminded finally of a twentieth-century bumper-sticker proclaiming that "Christ is the answer" (but what was the question?).

What no one—neither the modernist nor the antimodernist—(who are so often the same people) seems prepared to say is that none of this is really new. Such periodizing may make for thrilling narrative philosophy and theology, but it is poor history. Narratives are not histories, and ought not to be presented as such. We seem not to want to see, or say, that this kind of schizophrenia, this experience of having one foot in two disparate worlds, has always been with us. It is as old as the *Iliad,* or the book of Genesis, or the Gospel of Mark. What is new, and really quite novel, is the way we hang a label on it—"modern"— and then pine away for a world either lost to us (*pre*modern) or yet to be (*post*-modern). Contented to be anywhere are we, anywhere but here (and now). It is only "here and now," *hodiernus,* that we claim to be *dis*contented. What is new is the tragic posture, the academic whimsy and the modernist nostalgia. What is new is the gospel of Miniver Cheevy. And the answer, it seems to me, is neither some sort of scriptural fundamentalism, nor some kind of self-congratulatory postmodern playfulness, but rather some hard-nosed history, some hard-nosed willingness to search for the truth (another word at which academics blanch, and fundamentalists cheapen through overuse).[33] What is needed is the tragic *vision*—a hard-nosed willingness to spit on our hands and get on with the serious business of living, here and now—not the tragic posture which has so characterized positions on both sides of the modernist fence.

II

And we are decidedly straddling a fence. On that the academic theorist and the scriptural fundamentalist agree. Lawrence agrees; his analysis of the funda-mentalist phenomenon hinges on that assumption. Religion is at heart, he says, reflective of the "*pre*modern temper."[34] *That is the problem; we are no longer premodern.* "A drastic change has been transforming the entire world during the Technical Age,"[35] we are warned. There is a "seismic divide separating the High Tech from antecedent eras."[36] Both modernists and fundamentalists— nowhere more alike than in this—share a "pervasive concern with the end of 'ordinary' time."[37] They are both *apocalyptic* to the core. That is to say, they take contemporary experiences—that of living with a foot in two worlds, at once—and absolutize them, claiming that it is somehow unique and unparal-leled. No other age has been so schizophrenic as ours. No other age has faced the seismic crisis in worldview and in expectations which ours has. So says the tragic posture.

   Secularization theorists,[38] like their fundamentalist counterparts, are long on rhetoric and long on theory; they are dismally short on details. When every fact is viewed through the distorting mirror of modernism then the novelty of the modern situation is essentially granted before we begin.[39] The whole elab-orate construct remains at the level of assertion, not argument. The only way to *argue* that we today are straddling a great historical divide (or have crossed over it already, with Foucault), would be to do our historical homework, and to demonstrate the manner in which our own age represents an unparalleled chapter in the evolution of human society and the human spirit. That would be no small feat. It has not been done. And I will attempt to show in the next chapter that it simply cannot *be* done.

Instead, because so much of the argument remains at the level of theoretical assertion ("we moderns are different, *fundamentally* so"), we face a situation of uncommon intellectual ambiguity. We have told one another these same things for so long that no one thinks to question them anymore. They are academic orthodoxies as resistant to critical introspection as any list of scriptural "fundamentals." We have told ourselves that they are so, and they are so, *for us*. We have told ourselves these things about our "modernness" for so long that we have begun to believe them. Or rather, we have refused to question them anymore.

Lawrence's definition of 'modernity' is, in this environment, pretty standard. "*Modernity,*" he says,

> is the emergence of a new index of human life shaped, above all, by increasing bureaucratization and rationalization, as well as technical capacities and global exchange unthinkable in the premodern era.[40]

Several things about this definition are worth noting. First and foremost, it is important to realize how much of it is a theoretical veneer painted over a fairly short list of social facts. We are living in the presence of "a new index of human life," an index which would have been "unthinkable in the premodern era." The tautology is pernicious: we are "modern," different. Why? Because we are no longer "*pre*modern."

What are the "indices of modern life" which are cited to make good that extraordinary claim? There are, first of all, the inevitable social markers from Marx, Durkheim, and Weber—the twentieth-century shibboleths of bureaucratization and technology, as well as a new kind of rationality which they allegedly bring in train. Our world has grown smaller, economic markets overlap, and we are confronted on a daily basis by the extraordinary complexity, differentiation, and—here's the trick—simultaneous interrelatedness of our world. Schizophrenic double-mindedness, again: we are "differentiated," yet interrelated at the same time. The existence of global markets has enormously complicated our lives, while it simplifies them materially at the same time.

I gloss this argument because I have always found it a bit self-serving. While it is unquestionably the case that I can drive several miles from my home to the local Farmer's Market and purchase (using hard currency, not barter) almost any kind of produce from all over the world, I am not sure what difference those facts make to my personal life or to my spiritual self-understanding. The bazaar has long been a fascinating area in the city. The marketplace has always been the counterpoint to the mountaintop. While I am bombarded by fleeting images of other parts of the world on the nightly news, I am not so naïve as to assume that I really know anything about those places.[41] To learn a place, like learning a language or culture—as any decent anthropologist or traveller knows—you need to *live* there, for years.

In the philosophical idiom of which we have all grown so fond, the deeper issue is our confrontation with *difference*. That confrontation has made all the difference, in the modern age. So we assert; so we tell ourselves. Yet it remains unclear to me that I am confronted by "difference" in a way that a young boy growing up in the first century of the Common Era in Roman Palestine—let's say in the hill-country around Nazareth—would not have been. In fact, in a world where overland trade-routes were well-established (one passed through the valley outside of Nazareth), designed to link the geographic interior with the major eastern Mediterranean port cities, such a young boy would have been confronted by "difference" on a daily basis far more profoundly than am I in the "modern" world. My French cheeses, my Greek and Bulgarian wines, my South Pacific fruits and vegetables—all arrive by airplane and by truck, vehicles which scream overhead or on late-night interstate highways while I am asleep. I never *see* the "difference"; I see and consume the produce. When a caravan stopped overnight in the neighborhood of an eastern Mediterranean town, *then* they would have been confronted by difference. Ancient peoples would have come to know its face, to learn a bit of its language and its dress. Recent archaeological work on ancient shipping confirms the astonishing fact that the eastern Mediterranean world was linked to regions as distant as southern Spain and the mountains of Afghanistan *already in the fifteenth century* BCE.[42] These trade-routes, and the inescapable confrontations with difference they brought along with their wares, are *at least as old* as the three monotheistic, scriptural traditions which so concern the secularization theorists today.

To that inevitable list of bureaucracy, technology, capitalism, and secularization, Lawrence adds several interesting factors to *his* portrait of our modernity. They are intriguing, and really quite brilliant additions. The first is the existence of the nation-state, and the forces of nationalism[43] which have become so explosive in political affairs in the east bloc since the publication of this book. Nowhere is Lawrence more prescient than here. And yet there is a broader ambiguity which remains largely unaddressed here: nationalism is "the archenemy of fundamentalism,"[44] we are told. And yet all three scriptural fundamentalisms are deeply nationalistic, insistent, in fact, upon the *local* nature of their religio-ethnic reforms. Iran is simply the most extreme case, because it actually has a word for this kind of regionalism. "*Iraniyat*," as Lawrence notes, is "an untranslatable code word for what it is to be distinctly Iranian."[45] That is a paradox worth careful study. It is not undertaken. Instead, we are privileged to a deep insight into contemporary geopolitics, which is then glossed over in a footnote. We do not need to see explained how problematic the modern ideology of the nation-state is to all of us, because it has *already* been masterfully done—by Anthony Giddens.[46] Assertion, not argument; we footnote, then move on.[47]

Lawrence also makes frequent mention of the role the mass media plays in the fundamentalist revolt. It is another fascinating insight. It is also not developed, except to say that fundamentalists cannot use the tools of modernity without having their hands dirtied by printer's ink and their message muted by televangelical double-speak. Fundamentalism becomes inexorably bound to the very world, the *modern* world, it means to subvert. That is part of the hegemonic force of the modern world.

Now, the subtext here is also academic, I suspect. No one group is so enslaved to the tools of technology as the modern academic guild. Given the institutional realities of publishing demands, there is a seemingly limitless sea of books and articles to be read. Nietzsche is, as he so often was, a premonition: "These scholars have read so much . . . " he quips, "when did they ever get the change *to think?*"[48] Assertion, not argument; it remains unclear to me *why* the fundamentalist (or the academic theorist, for that matter) *must* be corrupted by the mass media, although I agree that in most cases we have been. Here again, some hard thinking—and some personal resistance to these same forces—remains to be done.

III

There is one other fascinating suggestion in Lawrence's survey, another key dimension of our modernness. It concerns the way we moderns wage war.[49] Scholars debate when and where we crossed over that great divide, when casualties on an unprecedented scale became first acceptable, then commonplace. All agree that the First World War was a watershed, specifically at Verdun and the Somme.[50] As I suggested in the Preface, those who have benefited from the recent "Civil War" series on PBS may well wonder if the curiously North American brand of civil warfare wasn't in fact the moment which forever changed the waging of modern war—the first war in which casualties on such a scale became acceptable and common. However and wherever one draws that line, we "moderns" clearly do live on the far side of that great divide. The sea-change came with *gunpowder* (and possibly, now, the Bomb—although we have taken several giant steps back from that nuclear abyss in the last four years).

One of the great virtues of Lawrence's study is that one meets so many other theorists worth knowing through him. The Ayatollah Morteza Mutahhari, and his *Fundamentals of Islamic Thought*,[51] was one such person, at least for me. But clearly the most profound thinker, for Lawrence's purpose, is the late North American Islamicist Marshall G. S. Hodgson, to whom Lawrence's book is dedicated. Hodgson's three-volume study, *The Venture of Islam*,[52] is a case study in how religious history can and should be written—from a *global* perspective. Lawrence's globalism, his chief virtue as a scholar, and his clearest difference from Stanley Hauerwas, is deeply indebted to Hodgson's work. Moreover, his definition of the great divide which separates our modernness from the premodern order of things *is* Hodgson's. Hodgson called it "the Great Western Transmutation" (GWT),[53] and viewed it as that constellation of events which form a prelude to nineteenth-century "European World Hegemony" (the title of his next chapter). What happened to "the generation of 1789"[54] has made us, in large measure, who we now are.

It would take us too far afield to give Hodgson's work the attention it deserves. His is, quite simply, the most nuanced, sober, and well-*argued* discussion of our modernness with which I am familiar. I am indebted to Lawrence, first as a student and now as a reader, for calling Hodgson's work to my attention. What is instructive for my present purposes, however, is where Lawrence diverges from or adds to Hodgson's ground-breaking work.

Hodgson is quite prepared to admit that we have in fact crossed over a watershed in the west, somewhere between 1600 and 1800 C.E.[55] So dramatic has been the global impact of industrialization, that the entire complexion of world relations has been changed. Hodgson goes so far as to equate this revolution with the domestication of wheat at Sumer (c. 6000 BCE), that technical innovation which made what we now call 'civilization' (and which he calls the "Agrarian Age") possible. With the GWT, "a new sort of historical process was loosed upon the world."[56] Now, one essential factor to keep in mind about these global developments, Hodgson insists, is their relatively *accidental* character.[57] There had been similar cultural and technical fluorescences in other regions at other times—Hodgson makes most of that in Sung China—but they had always tapered off. There have been many renaissances and enlightenments in world history,[58] but "the Occidental fluorescence," by contrast and for whatever reasons, "did not taper off."[59] The mention of China is pivotal. Hodgson makes much of the peculiar historical irony that so many of the crucial inventions which paved the way to western modernness were Chinese; Europeans simply put these technologies to more intensive and long-standing use. On any short list of such seminal innovations, Hodgson argues that gunpowder (modern warfare), the compass[60] (global trade), the printing press (mass-participatory society), and the civil service exam (the bureaucratic nation-state) all must have a place. All came from China.[61] But they all found a home, and intensive application across key sectors of society, in the west.

Gunpowder is, in some ways, the most influential innovation of the four. Hodgson goes so far as to title this third and last volume "*The Gunpowder Empires* and Modern Times." Between that crucial period from 1600 to 1800, we witness the rise of the hegemonic and colonial western powers. Only one non-western power, in fact, was able to maintain its Agrarian-Age position of "rough parity" with its western rivals. That was the Ottoman Empire. And the First World War signaled its end. So it is that gunpowder, and the compass, and the bureaucratic nation-state ushered in that era of colonialism which has had such devastating effects in the regions we now know as "the Third World." That kind of ranking itself—first world, and third—would not have been meaningful in the Agrarian Age, Hodgson suggests. It is another by-product of the gunpowder empires and of European world hegemony.

One now begins to see why Hodgson, as an Islamicist, is so deeply concerned to portray the *accidental* character of the rise of the Occident. Lawrence is an Islamicist, as well. "Evolutionary" historians of "progress" have tended to attach a moral valence to these changes, to valorize "the rise of the west" as a vindication of western religion, or ethnicity, or culture. All the more important, then, for us to keep in mind that most of the material innovation for this extraordinary "transmutation" came from elsewhere. *It just so happened* to take root in the Occident. *It just so happened* that the European Renaissance did not taper off. *And it just so happens* to be in the nature of this kind of technical advance that, once it has begun in one place, changes occur with such rapidity that the rest of the world no longer has time to catch up. If it took a millennium for the domestication of wheat to spread from Sumer to Britain, then that was not so very long "as ancient time-spans go."[62] "But once one such [industrial] transmutation had been completed in one place, *there was no time* to wait for the like to happen elsewhere."[63]

I am particularly impressed, and troubled, by that image of there being "no time." It is that aspect which speaks most intensively to the modern scholar (and probably to the Christian fundamentalist, too, if he is one who believes that "the end" is imminent).[64] I would have liked to see Hodgson, or Lawrence, reflect upon the fact that the pendulum clock was invented, *not* in China, but in western Europe.[65] Is *that* the difference the Occident makes? If so, then was the Occident *really* just an accident?

I do not mean to be coy about that. This is a matter of the deepest significance. I am thinking of the Euro-American first-worlder who feels so tempted, and tied, to the horological romance of the third world. That is where she goes to recreate. Why? For the simple reason that "time moves more slowly there," somehow. Those Occidentals, like Hegel, who spoke of Greece (and implicitly, of "the east") as "the childhood of Europe" knew whereof they spoke. A child's days are long and full. Ours today are merely full. I trouble to mention that because I am deeply concerned that we have translated our own academic breathlessness into our theories. Even Hodgson, who is on the whole so balanced, seems himself to have been a slave to the clock.[66]

While hesitant overall to do more than reflect upon the material and technical implications of the GWT, he cannot ignore its spiritual implications. Many of them are quite positive, and Hodgson admits that "for an unbiased devotee of Shar'î Islam there was much to admire."[67] But he notes one other crucial implication which had farther-reaching, far more ambivalent consequences. That is "an *expectation of continuous innovation,*" an attitude founded

> on encouraging an attitude of willingness to experiment, taking as little as possible for granted of what had already been thought and done, rejecting established authority of every sort, and running the inherent risks of error that such rejection entails.[68]

That is a depiction of the breathlessness of having *too little time,* and too much to do. "Innovation," a codeword for technical inventiveness and academic publishing deadlines, translates into never standing still. That is an essential aspect of our (western, academic) modernness which Hodgson does not discuss.

Lawrence's book is a product of this same innovative restlessness. While Hodgson cautiously admitted that there had been a "transmutation" which was a prelude to the modern age, and while he even made mention of all the standard Weberian categories in doing so—bureaucratization (civil service), technology (gunpower), globalism (the compass), and mass participation (the printing press)—he was really rather reticent about making global claims for their *spiritual* impact. It is as if Hodgson were saying, "All right, surely something *has* pretty clearly changed in the 'modern' age. But it is as ambivalent— good and bad, by turns—as *every* innovation. There is much for a Muslim to applaud, and much to be leery of. But for God's sake let's tread lightly on the theory."[69] Lawrence treads a little heavier on the theory, a little too heavily for my taste. Much like Michel Foucault, who "multiplied events,"[70] or like George Steiner (the *academic's* academic, to whom we will turn in a moment), Lawrence *multiplies* these transmutations. That, too, is an essential part of "the fissive trend" which helps to define the twentieth century.[71] Hodgson spoke of two transmutations: one in Sumer some eight thousand years ago; another in Western Europe some three hundred years ago. Lawrence suggests—and again it is asserted, nailed down with footnotes, never explained—that the GWT has given way in its turn to "the *third* wave,"[72] what he calls "the High Tech Era."[73] Shortly thereafter, Lawrence wonders if perhaps it is not better to have *four* waves: agrarian, medieval (1450–1890 . . . the nineteenth century as *medieval*?!), modern (1890–1955), and now contemporary (1955–?).[74] Theory on top of theory, transmutation on top of transmutation, with no end in sight. Even the words fail us, since 'modern' *means* "contemporary." It is *not* a proper noun, and should not be made into one. Yet that is precisely what the "modernist" and the "fundamentalist"—much like Miniver Cheevy—*must* do.

IV

So it is that this "expectation of continuous innovation," and the alienation from the natural pulse of *time* which it brings in train, has plagued and distorted modern thinking.

> Had we but World enough, and Time
> This coyness, Lady, were no crime . . . [75]

We do not have time enough for this, and such modernist coyness—the posture itself—is virtually a crime, in its extremity. It has spiritual implications, for all of us. When we tell ourselves these things long enough about ourselves, we begin to believe them. We *become* them. The gospel of Miniver Cheevy, again. Lawrence is as willing to draw out the spiritual implications of the modern age as Hodgson was hesitant to do so. Lawrence *must* do so, else his theoretical framework—that fundamentalism is *anti*modern, that it stands *in revolt against* the modern age[76]—makes no sense. I prefer to see modernists and fundamentalists engaged in a squabble between people who look at our world in much the *same* way—as a spiritual crisis of unparalleled proportions. They are both tilting at the windmills of modernity. That is Miniver Cheevy's world, a product of the very scholarly "Quixotism" which Nietzsche endeavored to unmask.

Another dichotomy which is always bandied about by the secularization theorist is that between *rational* and *traditional* societies, allegedly rival ways of looking at the world. This maps the allegedly enduring conflict between Homer and Plato, as we will see in the next chapter. Hodgson explicitly rejects this viewpoint, as a simplistic and self-serving way to talk about our modernness.[77] Lawrence, despite some important disclaimers,[78] seems closer to accepting the distinction. Once again, he *needs* some form of this assumption in order to make the case that fundamentalism is, at heart, an *antimodern* movement. Fundamentalism attempts to revert to a *pre*modern, highly *traditional* view of the world, and that sets it at odds with the highly technicalistic, rationalist, innovative, and scientific perspective of the modern age.

So says the tragic posture, in both its fundamentalist and modernist guise. Still, I worry here, as I worry elsewhere, that an academic construct, a theory-laden construct, has been imposed upon the phenomena. It is surely not accidental that the groups which Lawrence identifies as "fundamentalist" are all *scripturally* grounded.[79] The Muslim community knows this well, when it identifies all three scriptural traditions—in contrast to most of the other world religions—as "people of the book." The "books" may differ in every case (or rather, they build upon one another in a series), yet this impulse—to put religious truth *in writing,* in a definitive *book*—is a constant in all three faiths. We no longer understand immediately, in this era of too many books and too little time, the quasi-mystical quality which the well-worn phrase "it is written" must have had, in an only marginally literate cultural setting.[80] The scriptural fundamentalist claims that he has this premodern sensitivity and sense of wonder which other moderns have lost. They are in the business, so they say, of "reenchanting" the world. But they may be as wrong about that as the secularization theorists are wrong about them.

It remains unclear to me that *any* fundamentalist, a *scriptural* fundamentalist, if asked, would reply by way of self-identification that he is "antimodern," or that he is in revolt against "the modern age." He would argue, instead, that he is a rightly-guided adherent to *the* textbook for holy living. Other issues are tangential; this *scripturalism* is essential.[81] We misrepresent these people when we lay our theoretical antimodernism upon them, just as they misrepresent the scripture when they make of it a fundamentalist handbook. I prefer a simpler perspective. I am content to define fundamentalism (which I deliberately do not capitalize) as *the attempted politicization of an allegedly inerrant scriptural mandate.*[82] Our intellectual integrity is on the line when we bend over backwards in the attempt to understand that which is intellectually offensive.[83] Scriptural fundamentalism is very nearly idolatrous and *untrue,* and the academic community ought to have the integrity to say that, if that is what it believes, not to patronize fundamentalism by patting its head and endeavoring to "appreciate" the good points it has to make about "modern society." If we want really to represent the phenomenon, then we owe it our respectful and insistent *dis*agreement. One cannot help but wonder if the real sympathy which so many academics seem to have for the fundamentalist phenomenon derives from their shared sense of apocalypticism, and of *crisis.*

While I very much appreciate Lawrence's perspective on the debate about "religious ideology,"[84] it would go too far to say that ideologies are all alike, that every ideology needs to be dealt with in every case. That takes Gadamer's dictum about "prejudice against prejudice" to unnecessary extremes, in the direction of that very pseudo-Liberalism which MacIntyre and Hauerwas write off as a sham tradition. The insight that religious thought is one among a range of competing (and regnant) ideologies has indeed helped to "remove religion from the garbage heap of history to which early ideologues had consigned it."[85] The ironic turnabout, however, is that modernist ideologues will end up casting religion *back* on the garbage heap if they insist upon legitimating theologies which actually belong there. We are not in the business of understanding every religious idea. There are noxious religious doctrines worth opposing. *The fact that truth is a complex category does not mean that there are not lies.* "The not-so-simple critique of ideology"[86] to which Lawrence refers so sensitively is also not-so-difficult as to be impossible. We are not committed to the garbage heap of pure tolerance. There is something noxious in the Gush Emunim's (the "Bloc of the Faithful") use of a scriptural mandate to define latter-day Israeli territorial policies in the Occupied Territories.[87] That is an idolatrous and wrong-headed attempt to read the Book ahistorically, as though its categories translate directly into the twentieth century.[88] "Biblical borders" are precisely what the scriptures do *not* provide.

Such an idolizing of the written word is equally destructive, and often self-destructive, when it speaks in a Christian idiom. It has served, by quoting one verse (Matthew 27:25) out of context and with no historical understanding whatsoever, to brand the Jewish community with the stigma of "Christ-killers." It has served, by quoting another verse (Mark 16:18, which has the added irony of probably not being genuine, but a later addition to this gospel[89]) to justify the cults of snake-handling in which participants die each and every year—and whose deaths are then explained away as due to unfaith. It led as well to Ignatius' pathology, which I examined in the last chapter. It has served, through the expectations it fosters—namely, that a book can provide a "total" guide to "modern" life—to force the issue in the various Muslim communities which attempt to ground their legal codes in Qur'anic precedent. Of the 6,666 verses in the *Qur'an*, Lawrence notes, somewhere between 200 and 500 deal with explicitly legal matters.[90] What the Islamic fundamentalist refuses to see, or say, is that he is of necessity cast outside of the *Qur'an*, cast back upon the subsequent traditions of *hadith* (oral sayings of the prophet) and *ijtihad* (canonical judgments of scriptural scholars) in rendering contemporary judgments. A book, while doubtlessly crucial in every tradition, is merely one part of the past—a very important part, but only a part, of a *living* religious tradition. Despite what Luther, and a host of other scriptural nominalists have insisted, a book is not "all you need." *Sola scriptura, sola conundrum.*

Sensing that, Lawrence devotes his chapter on "American-style Protestant Fundamentalists"[91] not to the abortion-debate,[92] or to the interminable constitutional debate over Church-State relations and the First Amendment, but rather to the historic debate over creationism and evolutionary theory, a debate Lawrence explicitly urges the Christian fundamentalist to give over.[93] Lawrence goes further still. "The response that fundamentalists have made to the problem of evolution entails its own excesses," he tells us. "Often fundamentalists seem to abuse both the Bible and science."[94] Moreover, he insists, "the shortcomings of creation science are easy to score, whether as science or as religion."[95]

In light of these convictions, why make so much of the fundamentalist creationist challenge, going so far finally as to say that "the deemphasis on evolution [in the name of millenarian apocalypticism?[96]] by fundamentalists or those who study and try to understand them, needs to be redressed?"[97] Ironically enough, because, in Lawrence's judgment, this is where the fundamentalists really have something to say. These people know who their enemy is, know where the "modern" threat is really coming from. Our "experts" in the modern era are therapists and research scientists, not priests. MacIntyre and Hauerwas argue in much the same way. Today it is the cosmologist, like Carl Sagan, who tells us that he has solved "the God problem."[98] Science is our civil religion; this, our whole worldview, our whole *faith,* blew up when the *Challenger* did in the skies over Cape Kennedy.[99] In the creationist-evolutionist debate, one religious faith is pitted against another. And we owe it to the fundamentalists for having pointed out to us how much academic scientism is asserted (in footnotes not so very different, in their way, from scriptural proof-texting),[100] rather than posited, argued, and tested. Gratefully, Lawrence notes that fundamentalists have helped win a space back for God-talk in the public domain, such that even a Harvard astrophysicist can now acknowledge "the crisscrossed relation of science to religion in the Technical Age," on National Public Radio.[101] In fact, Lawrence concludes his massive study with precisely this image.

It did not take the fundamentalist challenge—if that is what it is—to accomplish this. In fact, fundamentalism will never fully accomplish this. Fundamentalism will surely *lose* the religious voice any space it continues to enjoy in the public domain, in the long run, by making religious values unpalatable and frankly incredible.[102] Walker Percy, as intelligent a spokesperson for religious values as any we have had in this country—and a convinced antifundamentalist— has levelled equally devastating criticisms at what he terms Sagan's crude brand of sophomoric scientism.[103] And no one spoke more presciently to the implicit *hybris* of "the new science" than Friedrich Nietzsche.[104] His criticism of Darwin, confined to a single aphorism in a late work, is worth more than all the vitriol heaped on him by a host of savvy fundamentalists.

> *Anti-Darwin.* As far as the well-known "struggle for existence" [*Kampf um's Leben*] goes, it seems to me that he has simply asserted, rather than proved, it. It certainly exists, but only as an exception; the full reality of life is not captured in ideas like the drives of instinct [*Nothlage*] and of hunger [*Hungerlage*], but rather in excess, profusion, even and especially in absurd squandering—where there is struggle, people struggle for *power.* . . . One should not mistake 'Malthus' for 'nature'.

Given, though, that this struggle exists—and in actual fact, it certainly does exist—it unfortunately results in the exact opposite of what Darwin's school desires, of what one *might* possibly desire with him: namely, the triumph of the strong and the privileged and the fortunate exceptions. .

Species do *not* grow in perfection. The weak will always assert their mastery over the strong, since they are the majority, and they are *more clever....*

Darwin forgot the spirit [*Geist*] (now that is English!). *The weak have more spirit.* One must need spirit to acquire it; when one needs it no longer, one loses it. Whoever has strength gives up on spirit ("Let it go!" they say in Germany today. "The *Reich* must remain to us.")

By 'spirit' I mean what all can see—caution, patience, cunning, simulation, great self-control, and all that is mere mimicry (to this last category belongs the lion's share of virtue).[105]

This aphorism deserves careful scrutiny, much more than I can give it here. Nietzsche does what he so often does, at his best. He points out to us where, and why, we assert rather than argue. In our desire to assert and move on, we attempt to cover our eyes from the truth (admittedly, a deeply problematic concept in Nietzsche's later thought). Here, we get a brilliant insight into the theoretical heart of evolutionary theory—the so-called doctrine, "survival of the fittest"—as well as Nietzsche's mature philosophy of "will to power," which argues the opposite. The strong do not prosper, he insists; the herd customarily kills them. We do not want to admit to the amorality of nature, the illusory quality of virtue, the tragic truth that nature revels in its own (anti-Malthusian) abundance, and in (Dionysian) destruction. The tragic hero revels in this reunion with nature, even at the cost of his own life. Those who have strength, Nietzsche insists, *tragic* strength, do not need spirit.

We can debate the nuances of Nietzsche's insights. For my part, I have been extremely critical of him in this later period, where I think he has grown *anti*modern, rather than *un*modern, as he was earlier in his career. His later bow to the tragic posture comes in passages like this one, where he insists that it is somehow in the nature of human reality that the weak shall triumph over the strong, that the mediocrity of the herd is always validated against the excellence of the few. It does not take a person of Nietzsche's psychological acumen to hear, here, the discontent of a man who wrote brilliant book after brilliant book, and was completely ignored by the academy of scholars. But Nietzsche's better insights also make clear that it does not take a fundamentalist Christian to take issue with the crude scientism of the popular mind. One of Nietzsche's earliest insights—it is the central thesis already of *The Birth of Tragedy*[106] and continues to be the presupposition behind *Wir Philologen*—was that scientism is "decadent." He also called it "Alexandrian." He wanted to rehabilitate a *tragic* vision whose goal is wisdom, and the practical skill at being human, somewhere *in between* the marketplace and the mountaintop—not scientific or, worse still, philological "truth." It remains one of my surest convictions that the Christian tradition, underscored by the tragic *vision* rather than the *posture,* gives us essential critical leverage against the excesses of the fundamentalist, the scientist, and the later Nietzsche, alike.

V

"Universalists are modernists swimming against the tide,"[107] Lawrence tells us, fairly early in the book. I think he is probably right about that—and the tide is decidedly antimodern.[108] I suspect that Lawrence is right about the intellectual climate within the high walls of the academy, but *outside* of them I am not quite so sure. That fact has had far-reaching (and to my mind disastrous) consequences. It leads to the intermittencing of world history, the imposition of radical breaks and fissures in the never-smooth course of human history. It establishes great cultural divides, fissures, *transmutations*—across which we have lost sight of one another, and of the past. It has led to the contemporary hypostatizing of *difference,* and a psychedelic fascination with the alleged dilemma of our modernness. Living on the verge of yet another transmutation—in Lawrence's view they seem to be coming so fast now that there is no avoiding them—we are doomed to the kinds of schizophrenia which so characterize our modernity, on the academic view. We are all forced to live, and struggle to keep our balance, with one foot planted none-too-firmly in each of two separate worlds—and the ground keeps shifting under our feet. Yeats stood at this same crossroad, or thought he did, in 1921, and his tortured vision of "the end" speaks eloquently to our own academic discontents.

> The best lack all conviction, the worst
> Are full of passionate intensity.[109]

Knowing him personally, and indebted to him for so much of what I know, I consider Professor Lawrence one of "the best." But the academic rhetoric of modernism has shaken his conviction, as it has shaken all of us, encouraging us to forget what we know best. When he is treading lightly on the theory—in the second half, the concrete half, of this study—his work positively shines. The first half of the book, I think, could be greatly reduced, since it does not contribute, really, to his concrete analyses. Our "context" is modern, "here and now," not modernity.

I have mentioned George Steiner several times in passing, as the *academic's* academic. I have used Steiner's work elsewhere, along with that of Alasdair MacIntyre, to trace out the contours of the tragic posture.[110] Steiner makes his first appearance early in Lawrence's argument, and he returns intermittently in the footnotes throughout. Lawrence mentions only a single book, however, *After Babel*,[111] which is an extraordinarily dense, theory-laden, and overlong[112] investigation of the phenomenon of human language. But it is also, as are all of Steiner's books, an investigation of our modernness, our *problematic* modernness—a problem which is asserted throughout.[113] Steiner begins with a sense of wonder, fascination really, that human language should be so varied. There is no reason, he notes, that the phenomenon of human language shouldn't be confined to four or five major examples. But this wonderment quickly turns to (modernist) despair.

> *There is a centrifugal impulse in language.* Languages that extend over a large physical terrain will engender regional modes and dialects. Before *the erosive standards of radio and television* became effective, it was a phonetician's parlor-trick to locate, often to within a few dozen miles, the place of origin of an American from the border states or a north-country Englishman.[114]

There is a doctrine of *entropy* which lies at the heart of this troubled perspective. Human language itself is something which tends toward disorder. When we cut against that natural grain, we get ourselves into trouble. Language's *natural* state is particularity, locality, regionalism, narrowness. Bigger and broader is decidedly *not* better; in fact, it is a good deal worse. It is, in Steiner's idiom, "erosive." Cosmopolis, while clearly "the hidden agenda of modernity,"[115] is a dream endlessly deferred. Hence, universalism is *always* swimming against the tide. That tide is modernist and fundamentalist alike.[116] It is, in a word, *anti*modern.

This well represents the tragic posture *in nuce*. Local forms of community—the ancients had them; we do not—are the ideal, those bounded face-to-face communities which are hard to understand from the outside (much like the idiolects they speak). Alasdair MacIntyre, too, refers to "the internationalized languages of modernity,"[117] those being German, French, and English. He does not mean this as a compliment. Internationalism and cosmpolitanism, like Liberalism itself, is "erosive" by definition. The National Socialists argued much the same way, as we saw in chapter 1.[18]

All of this is asserted; *our modernness begins in some important ways with that assertion.* Why assert the "erosiveness" of the modern moment? Turn this assumption around, stand it on its head in fact, and the whole portrait of our modernity seems to me to look very different indeed. "Bigger" and "broader" can be *constitutive* rather than erosive, a thrilling beginning rather than a cataclysmic end. Here too, a genuine dose of real cultural history seems to me to undo most of those assumptions which, taken together, I am calling "the tragic posture."

After the Alexandrian conquests of the fourth century BCE, it became pretty clear pretty quickly that the Macedonian empire needed a common language. It was also clear that Greek, as it was then spoken on the mainland, was far too complex to serve that purpose. And so the Greek language itself—under pressure of global necessities—was changed. Change, as I suggested in the last chapter, wants always to be evaluated negatively by the anti-modernist. The language was not eroded or corroded, but simply *changed*. It became *koinē*, a Greek word which means, quite simply, "common." This was a language—be it noted, a *second* language—which *everyone* could learn, a language everyone *did* learn. Now, an "internationalized" language is never simply imposed upon a passive world.[119] It is necessarily changed in the process of encountering differences, both cultural and linguistic. It is often changed *for the good*. In fact, this internationalized language of *koinē* Greek has given us some of the most exciting literature of the antique world—Plutarch, and Pausanias, and the New Testament, among countless other things.[120] If we are not prepared to write off the phenomenon of *koinē* Greek as somehow "erosive"—as Nietzsche did,[121] and as I hope that we are not—then why are we so quick to write off "modern English"[122] this way? The answer, it seems to me, is the tragic posture. This judgment is what we assume and assert at the outset. We seem to have no other way to think about ourselves.

The tragic posture concludes, as Lawrence's provisional[123] study does, that modern people "believe beyond belief,"[124] and that is what is novel about us. Most academic responses to scriptural fundamentalism take much the same form as Alasdair MacIntrye's antimodern polemics: "then they had it, and now we don't." Stanley Hauerwas seems to be arguing that "they [the Early Church?] had it, and we [Liberals? moderns?] have lost it, *but* we can get it back again." The fundamentalist is arguing in much the same way. Lawrence, for his part, seems to agree that fundamentalism is a local, sectarian attempt to "get it back," an attempt which is ultimately doomed to failure. Once it is gone, there is no bringing it back again. Max Weber made that conviction the cornerstone of his sociology. No clock, no matter how sophisticated, runs in reverse.

In every case, we seem to be remarkably inarticulate about what "it" is. It is only when 'religion' is defined as a seamless sacred canopy[125] which provides all the answers and holds our lives together (another definition which modernists and fundamentalists implicitly share), that the modern age (defined essentially as an age of schizophrenia and disenchantment) can be termed unreligious or even *anti*religious. If we speak of "belief, beyond belief' *as the modern condition,* then we are poor judges of human attitudes, and even poorer historians. Unless by 'modern' we mean, as we ought to mean, simply "contemporary"—in which case, it is an attitude which was "modern" for Mark, too. His followers implore Jesus, "I believe . . . but help my unbelief" (Mark 9:24). More, it seems, has *always* been enormously difficult to say.

The same poet who spoke of "belief beyond belief" speaks of a far more bracing human fact. Wallace Stevens was a lovely spokesperson for the tragic vision; he was no posturer. Only by quoting him out of context can we make him so. Let the last word, so to speak, be his:

> . . . How cold the vacancy
> When the phantoms are gone and the shaken realist
> First sees reality. The mortal no
> Has its emptiness and tragic expirations.
> The tragedy, however, may have begun,
> Again, in the imagination's new beginning,
> In the yes of the realist spoken because he must
> Say yes, spoken because under every no
> Lay a passion for yes that had never been broken.[126]

Notes

1. For an interesting worry about the appropriateness of the term 'fundamentalist' for cross-cultural comparisons, see William Shepard, "Comments on Bruce Lawrence's *Defenders of God*" as well as Lawrence's convincing reply in *Religion* 22 (1992): 279–85.

2. Bruce B. Lawrence, *Defenders of God: The Fundamentalist Revolt Against the Modern Age* (San Francisco: Harper & Row, 1989).

3. Lawrence, *Defenders of God,* 90ff.

4. As "countertexts," Lawrence means to set them up as reactions to the "context," which is precisely *the modern world.* See Hans G. Kippenberg; "Revolt Against Modernism: A Note on Some Recent Comparative Studies in Fundamentalism," *Numen* 38 (1991): 131.

5. See my *Tragic Posture and Tragic Vision: Against the Modern Failure of Nerve* (New York: Continuum Press 1994), 11–25.

6. Lawrence, *Defenders of God,* 27. Lawrence contrasts this with 'modern*ism,*' which he identifies as "the search for individual autonomy driven by a set of socially encoded values emphasizing change over continuity . . . ". I am uneasy still about distinguishing these forces this way, although it is crucial for Lawrence's thesis. He wants to demonstrate that fundamentalists oppose *modernism,* not modernity (with its technical accoutrements), most all of which they happily use.

7. I worry that Lawrence has himself taken a step in that direction when he defines 'modernism' as a worldview which finds its "utopian extreme" in "consumer-oriented capitalism" (*Defenders of God,* 27). That definition of the problem plays right into the hands of MacIntyre and Hauerwas, it seems to me.

8. See Louis A. Sass' *Madness and Modernism: Insanity in the Light of Modern Art, Literature, and Thought* (New York: Basic Books, 1992), 1–16, 355–73.

9. Kant is a key figure here, despite his insistence over and over again that this universal rationality is rather hard to get hold of. The key Kantian texts are *Critique of Pure Reason,* trans. Norman Kemp Smith (New York: St. Martin's Press, 1929, 1965), "The Transcendental Dialectic." III.4–7; and *Religion Within the Limits of Reason Alone,* trans. Theodore M. Greene and Hoyt H. Hudson (New York: Harper & Row, 1934, 1960). See also Lawrence, *Defenders of God,* 161, 170.

10. Lawrence, *Defenders of God,* 111.

11. See Herbert Marcuse, Barrington Moore, Jr., and Robert Paul Wolff, *A Critique of Pure Tolerance* (Boston: Beacon Press, 1969) for an eloquent criticism of this sort of bland, ill-informed, and catch-all "tolerance." It is a brand of thinking which is, incidentally, neither preached nor practiced by anyone in the modern world that I can see, save perhaps certain unsophisticated elements of the ACLU.

Yet this remains the very notion which Alasdair MacIntyre cites as the proof of Liberalism's fundamental incoherence. He calls such tolerance a "reckless generosity" in *Three Rival Versions of Moral Enquiry: Encyclopedia, Genealogy, Tradition* (South Bend, IN: University of Notre Dame Press, 1990), 30–31. And yet his own confessedly utopian vision of the university is equally as committed as the Liberal to devising "new ways to allow these [untolerated, un-encyclopaedic] voices to be heard" (236). I have pointed to this as one of the chief ironies of the tragic posture, that few, if any, of these people can manage to be as antimodern or as desperate as their rhetoric compels them to be.

12. Lawrence, *Defenders of God,* 155.

13. *Ibid.,* 186, 229.

14. *Ibid.,* 172. See also 64–69.

15. *Ibid.,* 132.

16. A failure which will be defined on the fundamentalists' own terms. See *Defenders of God,* 152, 226–27, 232.

17. See Arthur E. Farnsley II's remarkable *Southern Baptist Politics: Authority and Power in the Restructuring of an American Denomination* (University Park, PA: Pennsylvania State University Press, 1994), ix–xvi, 35–54, 139–43.

18. When discussing the fundamentalist, I am intentional in my refusal of inclusive language, which I will use elsewhere. The lingering sexism of most "premodern"

worldviews is one of the many aspects of that world which are painted over by nostalgic and antimodern polemics. Of course I am aware that a great many fundamentalists are women.

19. I take George M. Marsden's really fine and careful work to be symbolic of this paradox. See his *Understanding Fundamentalism and Evangelicalism* (Grand Rapids, MI: William B. Eerdmans Publishing Company, 1991).

20. Lawrence himself uses the word to connote "universal patterns of expectation" which end in "disappointment." And he contrasts it to "utopian" thought, which is waiting on an apocalyptic or Hollywood ending. See *Defenders of God,* 97. The relationship between this idea and MacIntyre's tragic posture is, I hope, clear enough.

21. George Steiner, another key modernist in the portrait Lawrence is painting, defines tragedy this way in *The Death of Tragedy* (NY: Hill and Wang, 1961), 8–9, despite what he himself knows about the Greeks (7). I will be returning to Steiner's work at the conclusion of this chapter.

For a elegant criticism of this position, see Walter Kerr, *Tragedy and Comedy* (New York: Simon & Shuster, 1967), 13–56; and Walter Kaufmann, *Tragedy and Philosophy* (Princeton: Princeton University Press, 1968, 1979), §§11, 16, 29, 41–42, 57–61.

22. Aristotle, *Poetics* 1453bl–1454a8.

23. Lawrence, *Defenders of God,* 24.

24. *Ibid.,* 233.

25. *The Oxford English Dictionary,* 2nd ed. (Oxford: Clarendon Press, 1989), IX.947–49.

26. Lawrence, *Defenders of God,* 233–35.

27. I well understand that the so-called "higher criticism" of the Bible was one of the chief forces which prompted the fundamentalist response in *this* country, at the turn of *this* century. But I have also been a teacher of the Bible, and know well that without some such historical sensitivity, we are lost in a sea of scriptural conundrums. So, a modern approach to the biblical texts is inescapable, however problematic it may also be.

28. Lawrence, *Defenders of God,* 24.

29. See Max Weber, *The Protestant Ethic and the Spirit of Capitalism* (New York: Charles Scribner's Sons, 1958), 181–82; and H. H. Gerth and C. Wright Mills, *From Max Weber: Essays in Sociology* (New York: Oxford University Press, 1946), 25.

30. Alasdair MacIntyre, *After Virtue,* 2nd ed. (South Bend, IN: University of Notre Dame Press, 1984), 121–30; and *Whose Justice? Which Rationality?* (South Bend, IN: University of Notre Dame Press, 1988), 12–29.

31. Michel Foucault, *The Order of Things: An Archaeology of the Human Sciences* (New York: Random House, 1979), 387.

32. Ignatius, *Letter to the Romans,* IV.1. See *Early Christian Fathers,* ed. (Philadelphia: The Westminster Press, 1953), 104.

33. See Martha Nussbaum, *Love's Knowledge: Essays on Philosophy and Literature* (New York: Oxford University Press 1990), 228–29.

34. Lawrence, *Defenders of God,* 24.

35. *Ibid.*

36. *Ibid.,* 230.

37. *Ibid.,* 244.

38. "Secularization," says Lawrence, "more than any other term, captures the pervasive ambiguity that characterizes institutions, as well as individuals who have become heirs to the Enlightenment" (*Defenders of God,* 94, also 98). That "pervasive ambiguity" is neither institutional, nor new, on my view. See Mary Douglas, "The Effects of Modernization on Religious Change," in *Religion in America,* ed. Mary Douglas and Stephen M. Tipton (Boston: Beacon Press, 1983), 25–43, as well as Peter Berger's "From the Crisis of Religion to the Crisis of Secularity," in the same volume, 14–24.

For an interesting, and much-qualified, defense of secularization theory, see Frank J. Lechner, "The Case Against Secularization: A Rebuttal," *Social Forces* 69:4 (1991): 1103–19.

39. Jeffrey K. Hadden, "Toward Desacralizing Secularization Theory," *Social Forces* 65 (1987): 587–611.

40. Lawrence, *Defenders of God,* 27.

41. I also do not mean to be sanguine about the hierarchies and poverties which First World capitalism and colonialism have imposed upon the Third World. So I take Lawrence's important point at *Defenders of God,* 52–53. I am simply hesitant to draw out too many *cultural* and *spiritual* implications from these appalling *economic* facts.

42. The most stunning work has been done by the American George Bass, off the southern coast of Turkey, near Kaş, at a site called Ulu Burun. This shipwreck, the oldest ever excavated (there may be one, I am told, slightly older which was recently found off the eastern coast of mainland Greece), tells a remarkable story about the extraordinary level of linkage and integration of the entire Mediterranean basin at this early date. See Bass' "Oldest Known Shipwreck Reveals Bronze Age Splendors," *National Geographic* 172.6 (December 1987): 693–734.

For some related work, see his earlier reports from a smaller wreck in the same vicinity: "The Cape Gelidonya Wreck: Preliminary Report." *American Journal of Archaeology* 65 (1961): 267–76 and "Cape Gelidonya: A Bronze Age Shipwreck," *Transactions of the American Philosophical Society* 57:8 (1967).

I should also mention that, while I am trying to be inclusive of the Jewish community in my dating (using the categories of "the Common Era" rather than dating global events from the advent of Christ), I have not succeeded in "including" the Islamic calendar this way. I have chosen not to do so only because I think it would not be particularly meaningful to a primarily non-Muslim audience, and would only add another level of complexity to what is already a rather complex and heady argument.

43. Lawrence, *Defenders of God,* 83.

44. *Ibid.*

45. *Ibid.,* 202.

46. *Ibid.,* 227 and note. I should add that this same book, Giddens' *The Nation-State and Violence* (Berkeley: University of California Press, 1987) figures heavily in Hauerwas' antimodern polemics.

I have placed myself in a curious sort of intellectual bind here. If anything I have said up until now is even roughly correct, I cannot simply footnote Giddens' work myself. Hence the singularly academic (and aesthetic) evil of a long note.

Giddens' work is difficult to summarize. For my purposes, two things are worth noting. Giddens is heavily indebted to three thinkers who, taken together, support his self-confessed "*discontinuous interpretation of modern history*" (31–32). He defines this discontinuity as "the coming of a type of society radically distinct from all prior forms of social order." That is to say, the novelty of the "modern" world is simply asserted at the outset, not concluded, tentatively, at the end. As I will hope to show in the next chapter, such "proofs" will always fail, even on their own terms.

From Karl Marx, Giddens has taken the worst, *the hyperhistoricizing of Hegel's far more nuanced historicism* (MacIntyre also does this, as I tried to show in chapter 3, but see Giddens' disclaimers at 335–36). Giddens wants to be "disjunctive," where he feels that Marx was too "evolutionary," but this begs the deeper question. He and Marx agree that "modernity" is something new under the sun, a force to be reckoned with, a way of life in desperate need of explanation. Whether we have evolved to the "here and now" or made a quantum leap into it, "modernity" is always the issue, and its novelty is always assumed. That is precisely the assumption I mean to question in this book.

From Max Weber, Giddens has taken all the modernist buzzwords: capitalism, bureaucratization, secularization and, most important I suspect, *disenchantment.* That is why he quotes Camus appreciatively, concluding that "nobody, surely, can expect [this generation] to be optimists" (294).

Finally, from Michel Foucault (310) Giddens has inherited the peculiarly "modern" interest in *dis*continuities, as well as the suspicion of surveillance and institutional violence—what Foucault alternately blasted as "the panoptic perspective," and "our carceral society."

These are all important points, to be sure. But they lead Giddens to a definition of "modernity" as a period of:

1. Magnified capitalistic enterprise
2. Industrial production
3. Heightened surveillance
4. Consolidation of the centralized control of the means of violence (5).

They also lead him to the eminently modernist conclusion that "the twentieth century world is a bloody and frightening one" (3). Of the four aspects of our modernity which Giddens considers so determinative, the last two have not been dealt with at all, he feels. His discussion of industrial capitalism is too brief by far (122–47), but then, it can afford to be since, as he himself notes, Marx and Weber have already said what needed saying (122–23).

The latter two points—concerning surveillance and the centralized means of violence—force Giddens to the really chilling conclusion that "totalitarianism" is, not merely an anomalie or an excess, but actually "a tendential property of the modern state" (295).

Now that is really an extraordinarily disturbing claim, and I cannot resolve it in a footnote. Suffice it to observe here that the very word, 'totalitarian' (itself a twentieth-century coinage from Giovanni Gentile, the Italian fascist, who referred appreciatively to *uno stato totalitario* in 1920, 295), threatens to become just one more among a seemingly endless series of buzzwords which have been cheapened through overuse by academic theorists and politicians alike. If we want to make the case for the real novelty of "modern" statism and "modern" violence, then we simply must deal with the horrifying historical spectacle of, say, Assyrian military practices, or Egyptian and Roman statist imperialisms. Giddens senses how slippery the terminology is (296), and admits that only Stalinism, Nazism, and Italian fascism (299) really fit the bill (maybe Kampuchea, too, briefly, under Pol Pot, 302). It remains unclear that "totalitarianism" is a response to some sort of modernist spiritual crisis; it seems much more the case that what we worry about is the *technology* (222–54) . . . and the body-counts.

That is Giddens' richest point in the book. His chief concern was and is "the industrialization of war in a radically new world order. Nowhere," he continues, "are the discontinuities of modern history more acute" (339). Now *that* is a prescient insight, particularly when we recall that it was penned in 1985, *well* before the pyrotechnics of Desert Storm and the nauseating rhetoric of self-congratulation in which the Bush administration indulged itself for the next two years. Our allegedly "new world order" looks suspiciously like the Third World colonialism of the gunpowder empires. And the only wars we seem willing to wage are those fought in defense of that *older* order.

The main point, and it remains my chief concern, is that Giddens gets his conclusions—that "we" are all different in the "modern" age, paradigmatically so—too easily. It is asserted at the outset, and assumed throughout the book. Not surprising for a writer who argues that "it is *the* task of 'sociology' as I would formulate the role of that discipline at any rate, to seek to analyze the nature of *the novel world which, in the late twentieth century, we now find ourselves*" (33).

47. One might pursue a fascinating sociological investigation on the manner in which academic writing has itself been distorted by its location within the academy, and the process of tenure review. When Lawrence turns his attention to Charles Darwin, he notes (*Defenders of God,* 173) that there are a variety of ways in which Darwin's contribution might best be measured. What follows is a five-tiered approach which looks for all the world like a tenure review!

48. Nietzsche, *Wir Philologen* 7 [1]; Sämtliche Werke, VIII. 122–123.

49. Lawrence, *Defenders of God,* 49–50, 153. See also Giddens, *The Nation-State and Violence,* 222-254. In a fascinating analysis of the ways in which *technology* has altered the world of modern warfare—with railroads and telegraphs, chiefly—Giddens nevertheless concludes that the modern nation-state, not the technology, is the key factor which makes all the difference. Naturally, I would reverse that: *technology,* not the nation-state, is the chief problem with modern warfare.

50. Lawrence, *Defenders of God,* 53–54.

51. *Ibid.,* 221–24.

52. Marshall G. S. Hodgson, *The Venture of Islam: Conscience and History in a World Civilization* (Chicago: University of Chicago Press, 1961, 1974).

53. Hodgson, *The Venture of Islam,* III.176–222. See also *Defenders of God,* 43–58.

54. Hodgson, *The Venture of Islam, III.205–8.*

55. *Ibid.,* III.176.

56. *Ibid.,* III.179.

57. *Ibid.,* III.183, 196–200; and Lawrence, *Defenders of God,* 42, 47, 190.

58. It is a key factor in my analysis that only the west has had the presumption to capitalize and globalize its own versions. So it is that MacIntyre and Hauerwas can make "*the* Enlightenment" a unique and unparalleled sort of problem in the modernist story of decline and fall they want to narrate. For more in this vein, see Kippenberg, "Revolt Against Modernism," 128–33.

59. Hodgson, *The Venture of Islam,* III.183.

60. In the words of Joseph Glanville, in his *Plus Ultra, or, The Progress and Advancement of Knowledge Since the Days of Aristotle* (1668), the inventor of the compass "is worth a thousand Alexanders and Caesars or ten times the number of Aristotles." As quoted by Louis Dupré in *Passage to Modernity: An Essay in the Hermeneutics of Nature and Culture* (New Haven: Yale University Press, 1993), 155, 275n28.

61. Hodgson, *The Venture of Islam,* III.197.

62. *Ibid.,* III.179.

63. *Ibid.,* III.199, emphasis mine.

64. It is the most fascinating dimension to David Harvey's *The Condition of Postmodernity: An Enquiry into the Origins of Cultural Change* (Oxford: Basil Blackwell,

1989), 201–323, that postmodernism is essentially a constellation of *"new dominant ways in which we experience space and time."* I am naturally worried about books which privilege and problematize our own perceptions this way, but the insight is a fascinating one.

65. The science of timekeeping is a fascinating one in the history of technology and human culture. It is beautifully laid out in Maurice Mayr's *The Clockwork Universe* (New York: Neale Watson Academic Publications, 1980), which is a Smithsonian catalog of an exhibition by the same name which showed in Munich from 15 April to 30 September 1980, and then in Washington, DC from 7 November 1980 to 15 February 1981.

Clearly, people had "kept time" long before the period of European world hegemony. But there was indeed something of an "horological revolution" which coincides with the GWT (the term is from Samuel L. Macey's *Clocks and the Cosmos: Time in Western Life and Thought* [Hamden, CT: Archon Books, 1980], 17–33).

For the purposes of my argument, the crucial moment came in Holland in the winter of 1656–57, when Christiaan Huygens invented the pendulum clock, a device which *regularized* and *revolutionized* timekeeping in a single generation. Huygens' masterwork, *Horologium Oscillatorium* (1673), has recently been translated into English by Richard J. Blackwell as *The Pendulum Clock, or, Geometrical Demonstrations Concerning the Motion of Pendula as Applied to Clocks* (Ames, IA: The Iowa State University Press, 1986).

66. I am indebted to Harry Partin, one of Hodgson's graduate students at the University of Chicago before his untimely death in 1974 (as well as a former professor of mine), for the personal anecdotes which make a real virtue of the man.

For a far less friendly, and really rather unfortunate, characterization, see Saul Bellow's *To Jerusalem and Back* (New York: The Viking Press, 1976), 108–9.

67. Hodgson, *The Venture of Islam*, III.196. See also 190–91, 195.

68. *Ibid.,* III.193. See also Lawrence, *Defenders of God*, 57. Note that this is precisely what Lawrence defines as 'modernism' (*Defenders of God*, 27).

69. For more in this vein, directly related to Lawrence's analysis, I am indebted to Thomas P. Kasulis' "Modernism, Scripturalism, Fundamentalism: Necessary Connections?," an unpublished manuscript which Professor Lawrence passed along to me.

70. Michel Foucault, *The Archaeology of Knowledge,* trans. A.M. Sheridan Smith (New York: Harper & Row, 1972), 199–211.

71. Lawrence, *Defenders of God*, 67.

72. The term, which Newt Gingrich has so popularized, is actually Alvin Toffler's, in *The Third Wave* (New York: Morrow Press, 1980), where he is referring to the inception of the *computer* age. Is that why Lawrence makes so much of the "High Tech Era?" Is it finally *electricity,* and not gunpowder at all, which contributes to "the rise of the west?"

73. Lawrence, *Defenders of God,* 48, 67.

74. *Ibid.,* 54. This kind of periodization is another characteristic, not necessarily of our modernness, but of academic thinking itself. So it is that "Modernism" was born c. 1910–15, and "Postmodernism" sometime between 1968 and 1972. See Harvey, *The Condition of Postmodernity,* 28, 38.

75. Andrew Marvell, "To His Coy Mistress" (Hunton Bridge: The Kit-Cat Press, 1978). It is worth noting which words Marvell saw fit to capitalize—World, and Time, and of course, the Lady.

76. Many scholars now argue this way, among them Nancy Tatom Ammermann, *Bible Believers: Fundamentalists in the Modern World* (New Brunswick, NJ: Rutgers University Press, 1987), 3, 8, 14; Harvey Cox, *Religion and the Secular City* (New York: Simon & Shuster, 1984); and Frank J. Lechner, "Fundamentalism and Sociocultural Revitalization in America: A Sociological Perspective," *Sociological Analysis* 46 (1985): 243–60.

77. Hodgson, *The Venture of Islam,* III.181, 188.

78. Lawrence, *Defenders of God,* 175–81, 188.

79. Jerry Falwell makes the point eloquently: "The Bible is absolutely infallible, without error, in all matters pertaining to faith and practice, as well as in areas such as geography, science, history, etc. The disintegration of our social order can be easily explained. Men and women are disobeying the clear instructions God gave in His Word." *Listen, America!* (Garden City, NY: Doubleday, 1980), 63.

Note the two assumptions which, taken together, constitute the tragic posture: (1) that we are somehow "disintegrating" now; and (2) that the (premodern) Bible can reintegrate us.

80. For this insight I am indebted to the ground-breaking work of Walter J. Ong, *Orality and Literacy: The Technologizing of the Word* (New York: Methuen & Company, 1982).

81. For the importance of biblical inerrancy, see Farnsley, *Southern Baptist Politics,* 55–74.

Farnsley makes use of a distinction (58n3) from the work of Nancy Ammermann, whose *Bible Believers* (pages 1–5, and 215n) distinguishes between those fundamentalists who are scriptural inerrantists, and those Fundamentalists (capital F) who may be more accurately described as "antimodern."

82. This definition is, ironically enough, very close to Lawrence's own: "*Fundamentalism* is the affirmation of religious authority as holistic and absolute, admitting of neither criticism nor reduction; it is expressed through the collective demand that specific creedal and ethical dictates derived from scripture be publicly recognized and legally enforced" (*Defenders of God,* 27). All I have wanted to point out is that there is nothing essentially "antimodern" about such a perspective; it applies as well to Tertul-

lian in Roman North Africa in the second century CE as it does to Jerry Falwell in North America today.

83. Although I take Ammerman's point (*Bible Believers*, 4) that "self-identification is not always reliable," and overall I think the balance she strikes between listening and interpreting is just right. See her "Dilemmas in Establishing a Research Identity," *The New England Sociologist* 4 (1982): 21–27, and *Bible Believers*, 9–14. That balance has resulted finally in her massive survey, "North American Protestant Fundamentalism," in *Fundamentalisms Observed*, ed. Martin E. Marty and R. Scott Appleby (Chicago: University of Chicago Press, 1991), 1–65.

84. Lawrence, *Defenders of God*, 81.

85. *Ibid.*, 82.

86. *Ibid.*, 68.

87. See Thomas L. Friedman's remarkable *From Beirut to Jerusalem* (New York: Doubleday, Anchor Books, 1989, 1990), 262–66, 286–87, 301–2, 316–21, 466–67. Both Friedman's and Lawrence's analyses are characterized by a profound sensitivity to the fact that this picture of Jewish fundamentalisms is complicated considerably by the existence of very eloquent, and markedly apolitical, persons, the so-called Haredim, or "those filled with the awe of God" as well as the Neturei Karta party. For more on this, see Gideon Aran, "Jewish Fundamentalism: The Bloc of the Faithful in Israel (Gush Emunim)," in *Fundamentalisms Observed*, 265–344.

88. Edward Said has eloquently addressed this problem, both in his ground-breaking *Orientalism* (New York: Pantheon Books, 1978), and more recently in "Michael Walzer's *Exodus and Revolution:* A Canaanite-Reading," reprinted in his *Blaming the Victims: Spurious Scholarship and the Palestinian Question*, with Christopher Hitchens, (London: Verso, 1988), 161–78. This debate between Said and Walzer was summarized by M.D. Walhout in his "The *Intifada* of the Intellectuals: An Ecumenical Perspective on the Walzer-Said Exchange," *Soundings* 74.3–4 (1991): 327–50.

89. See my *Tragic Posture and Tragic Vision*, 248–55.

90. "Such a thin base does not foster or sustain a comprehensive judicial system," Lawrence concludes, in notably *non*fundamentalist terms (*Defenders of God*, 214).

91. Lawrence, *Defenders of God*, 153–88.

92. As it appears the fundamentalist Christian Right in America have increasingly decided to do. Falwell's later work is devoted, not to a defense of scriptural inerrancy, but to an argument against abortion, *If I Should Die Before I Wake* (Nashville, TN: T. Nelson Publishers, 1986). The religious Right is driving this point home, as the wedge which will probably disrupt, if it has not already done so, their fragile coalition with the far more centrist Republican party.

93. Lawrence, *Defenders of God,* 187–88.

94. *Ibid.,* 172.

95. *Ibid.,* 183. He does not "score" any himself, preferring merely to footnote "frontier researchers" in geology and biology. Assertion, not argument, again. These are the kinds of arguments we *all* need desperately to *see*. As we all need to see, and discuss, the shortcomings and the anomalies in evolutionary theory itself.

96. Farnsley, *Southern Baptist Politics,* 57–60.

97. Lawrence, *Defenders of God,* 186.

98. *Ibid.,* 183. See also 60–61.
See my review of Carl Sagan, *Pale Blue Dot: A Vision of the Human Future in Space* (NY: Random House, 1994) forthcoming in *JAAR.*

99. *Ibid.,* 154–55.

100. See William Placher, *Unapologetic Theology: A Christian Voice in a Pluralistic Conversation* (Louisville, KY: Westminster/John Knox Press, 1989), 39–54.

101. Lawrence, *Defenders of God,* 243–45. The location of that observation is instructive. The whole debate about public funding for such programs as NPR is a telling confirmation of my central thesis. The argument, simply put, is that public broadcasting is too left-leaning, that it needs to be more representative if we want to fund it "publicly."
All to the good, we want to say (in fact, public television is not nearly so left-leaning as alleged), but such an insight is hardly a counsel to "pure tolerance," as Hauerwas and MacIntyre have argued that it must be. Such a perspective on the role of "public" media is still incompatible with the tolerance of Rabbi Kahane, or the Reverend Farakhan, both of whom assuredly did *not* belong on NPR. Our refusal to grant them a public forum for their curious brands of religious racism does not make Liberalism inconsistent or incoherent.
The truth of the matter is a little messier, and a great deal less apocalyptic than that. It is an excellent example of what Aristotle might have called the exercise of *practical* reason and *practical* wisdom—the realization that truth's complexity does not mean there are not noxious untruths.

102. It is my suspicion that this has already happened to the Christian Right in America. Jerry Falwell was consciously addressing the nation as a whole in books like *Listen, America!* and *The Fundamentalist Phenomenon: The Resurgence of Conservative Christianity* (Garden City, NY: Doubleday, 1981). Having cast the fate of his community upon the lot of politics, he just as quickly gave this over, contenting himself to the subsequent agenda of *Finding Inner Peace and Strength* (Garden City, NY: Doubleday, 1982). That was his last book with Doubleday, and his subsequent attempts to recover a political voice and influence have fallen on comparatively deaf ears.

103. See his *Lost in the Cosmos: The Last Self-Help Book* (New York: Farrar, Straus, Giroux, 1983), 172–74, 201–2.

104. Who simply cannot be labelled an "idealist philosopher" (*Defenders of God,* 29).

105. Nietzsche, *Twilight of the Idols,* "Skirmishes of an Untimely Man," §14; *Sämtliche Werke,* VI. 120–21, translation mine.

106. Nietzsche, *The Birth of Tragedy,* §18.

107. Lawrence, *Defenders of God,* 35.

108. That is the point which MacIntyre and Hauerwas cannot grant. Their whole antimodern argument presupposes that *they* are the minority, swimming *against* the tide. Hauerwas goes so far as to call Christians "resident aliens" (much as Aristotle was in Athens). See MacIntyre, *Three Rival Versions of Moral Enquiry,* 217.

Ironically, *they* are the academically fashionable ones. If not actually an academic version of "the moral majority," they are an outrageously vocal minority. It is their posing which defines our dominant *academic* worldview. They have largely incapacitated any academic ability to use language like "human nature," or the "human situation."

As Martha Nussbaum is quick to remind these latter-day Aristotelians, there are some Aristotelian virtues which are pretty clearly *non*relative. See her "Non-Relative Virtues: An Aristotelian Approach," *Midwest Studies in Philosophy* 13 (1988): 32–53.

My book is largely an attempt to rehabilitate that language, and a refusal to grant Hauerwas and MacIntyre *their* language—the words "tragic" and "liberal" and "modern"—without a fight.

109. William Butler Yeats, *The Collected Poems of W. B. Yeats* (New York: Macmillan, 1952), 185.

110. Ruprecht, *Tragic Posture and Tragic Vision,* 11–25.

111. George Steiner, *After Babel: Aspects of Language and Translation* (New York: Oxford University Press, 1975).

112. As Steiner himself later admitted, *George Steiner: A Reader* (New York: Penguin Books, 1984), 16, although he cannot resist adding the rhetorical question: "Ought one not, at least once in the course of work, write a book which *is* too long?"

113. See especially his *In Bluebeard's Castle: Some Notes Toward the Redefinition of Culture* (New Haven: Yale University Press, 1971), 1–9, 68–71, 134, for the postured nostalgia of academe.

114. Steiner, *After Babel,* 31, emphasis mine.

115. The phrase is Stephen Toulmin's, from *Cosmopolis: The Hidden Agenda of Modernity* (Chicago: University of Chicago Press, 1990).

116. Lawrence, *Defenders of God,* 111.

117. Alasdair MacIntyre, *Whose Justice? Which Rationality?* (South Bend, IN: University of Notre Dame Press, 1988), 379. See also 327ff. and Stanley Hauerwas, *After Christendom? How the Church Is to Behave if Freedom, Justice, and a Christian Nation Are Bad Ideas* (Nashville, TN: Abingdon Press, 1991), 133–135.

118. For more on this see Luc Ferry and Alain Renaut, *Heidegger and Modernity,* trans. Franklin Philip (Chicago UP, 1990) 4–6, 17, 53–55.

119. I am fascinated by the fact that each of the three *scriptural* languages—Hebrew, Greek, and Arabic—has gone through this internationalizing process to one degree or another. I have chosen to focus on the Alexandrian example because it is the only case in which this process of "internationalization" took place *before* the language becomes "scriptural."

In other words, the Christian movement opted for the most global, international language available to it, when it came time to spread "the word."

120. We are indebted to Vernon K. Robbins, *Ancient Quotes and Anecdotes* (Sonoma, CA: Polebridge Press, 1989) for providing us with a collection which amply illustrates the tremendous vitality and literary sophistication of this cultural achievement. For more on this enormously rich, and poorly understood, tradition (with suggestions on how to teach it), see David Ricks, "Greek *tout court?,*" in *Arion, Third Series,* 1.3 (1991): 29–44.

121. "It was subtle [*Feinheit*]," he chuckles, "that when God wished to become a story-teller, he learned Greek—*and* that he did not learn it better." *Beyond Good and Evil,* IV.§121; *Sämtliche Werke,* V.94.

122. See Bill Bryson, *The Mother Tongue: English and How It Got To Be That Way* (New York: William Morrow and Company, 1990).

123. Few have noted that Lawrence explicitly sees his study as provisional, as a sort of working hypothesis (*Defenders of God,* ix–x). It is alarming to see how many academics claim that he has "proven" any number of things which he meant merely to suggest. This chapter is intended, in part, to raise questions and thus to further that ongoing debate.

124. This is from Wallace Stevens' poem "Flyer's Fall" (1945), as found in the posthumous collection, *The Palm at the End of the Mind* (New York: Random House, 1972), 270.

125. See Peter Berger, *The Sacred Canopy: Elements of a Sociological Theory of Religion* (Garden City, NY: Doubleday, 1967). See also Lawrence's comments in *Defenders of God,* 144, 172.

126. Wallace Stevens, "Esthétique du Mal," in *The Palm at the End of the Mind,* 257–58.

Premonition Fulfilled

6

Aftermath?
On Modernist Prejudices and the Past

> No! Don't come to me with science when I ask for the
> natural antagonist of the ascetic ideal, when I demand:
> "where is the *opposing ideal?*" . . .
>
> This pair, science and the ascetic ideal, both rest on the
> same foundation—I have already indicated it: on the same
> overestimation of truth. . . .
>
> *Art*—to say it in advance, for I shall return to this sub-
> ject at greater length—art, in which precisely *the lie* is
> sanctified and the *will to deception* has a good conscience,
> is much more fundamentally sensed by Plato, the greatest
> enemy of art Europe has yet produced.
>
> *Plato versus Homer: that is the complete, the genuine
> antagonism!*
>
> —Nietzsche, *On the Genealogy of Morals*

The last chapter concluded with Wallace Stevens' plea for a recovery of *passion*, "the passion for Yes." In poeticizing this idea, Stevens is striking a profoundly Nietzschean chord, making the kind of unmodern music which I
suggested Nietzsche was making in the 1870s. It was unmodern music, to be
sure, but not at all *anti*modern, as it later became. Nietzsche's mature philosophy expressed itself as a powerful process of Yes-saying, even to life's most enduring and hardest problems. Chief among those problems was the *fact* of
human society—a fact which is as inescapable as it is ennervating, at times.
Nietzsche, in his early period, said yes to this fact and embraced it. His philosophy traces out the complex and circuitous paths which lead from the marketplace to the mountaintop, and back again.

I spoke of Nietzsche's development—from unmodern to antimodern—as
a "premonition." It is a premonition of ideas yet to come. It is a premonition of
how things stand now in contemporary philosophical and theological circles, I

think. There was nothing nostalgic in Nietzsche's earlier period; thus the idea of *decadence* had not yet achieved the prominence it was to achieve in his later writings. I would like now to examine the work of a contemporary modernist whose career traces out this same complex trajectory, from unmodern to antimodern, and who does so, moreover, by grounding a number of key arguments in his philological portrait of the Greeks. The thinker is Charles Taylor. And what we find in his work, I think, is a Nietzschean premonition fulfilled, a sophisticated kind of unmodern thinking which gives way, at the last, to the enormous pressure exercised by antimodern posturing—Nietzsche's and MacIntyre's chiefly.

I

The appearance of Charles Taylor's *Sources of the Self*[1] has been hailed as a decisive event in the debate about what ails us in the "modern" world. The debate itself hinges upon an ironically Nietzschean equation of values with symptoms—that is, a cultural diagnosis of sorts.[2] That is something which everyone I have been reading in this book has been attempting, however much they may disagree on the extent of our illness. Where does our moral incoherence come from?, Taylor want to ask. What are the sources of our frustration and our curious inability to answer when once we ask quietly who we are, what we are doing, what we may fairly hope for. The modern dilemma—the *crisis*, if you will—is tied to this moral incoherence, what Taylor calls our "ethics of inarticulacy."[3] When asked about our "selves," when asked about our "vision," when asked about the "good," we fall strangely and paralytically silent. *We no longer know what to say.* Now that our notions of "identity" and of the "self" have been problematized—another key component of our modernness[4]—we as a culture are essentially experiencing an identity-crisis, writ large. Like the middle-aged executive who suddenly leaves home, career, and family behind in desperate search of the self he or she presumably has lost, modern culture has taken to the road, looking for we know not what.[5]

It was not always so, Taylor insists, and as such, his book represents a self-confessed exercise in *recovery*[6]—that is, an attempt to trace out several of the trajectories which constitute the "modern" way of thinking about our selves, as well as the genealogy which will help us to understand that it was not always so. In that exercise, what stands out most graphically is our novel language of *inwardness*.[7] This idea, too, derives from MacIntyre's polemics. In heroic societies, he insists, the distinction between inside and outside does not really exist yet. One's "self" is precisely defined by one's social role. What one *is* is what one *does*. And if there is no "inside," then there is no "outside" either. In our emotive modernity, where we have all been driven outside—away from the marketplace and off to the mountaintop—there is nowhere left to turn, save within.

My use of the term 'identity-crisis' in reference to the modern age is deliberate.[8] That self we are seeking, that elusive essence which makes us who and what we are, is found *within*. Introspection—to say nothing of therapy and self-help—represent the road to (self)recovery. On this view, Augustine becomes an essential character in the unfolding drama of our modernness. His *Confessions* represent a whole new way of writing, a new way of centering and locating the self, all couched in terms of a psychology of "the will" which was not available to his predecessors.[9] In that section of Taylor's book entitled simply "Inwardness"—a section which constitutes fully one-fourth of the entire work—Taylor traces out the *inner* topography of the modern self from its alleged and incomplete beginnings in Augustine, through Descartes, as well as some of its expressivist and solipsistic extremes in Montaigne and, quite differently again, in the Reformation. We have seen many of these same narrative turning-points before, in MacIntyre's and Hauerwas' work.

Yet this section on "Inwardness" begins with a chapter on Plato and the poets—where this "modern" self is allegedly *not* to be found. This chapter is, to my mind, the most instructive in Taylor's entire book—it is, after all, *his* narrative beginning—and I will perhaps make more of it than he does. It is my own belief that, through it, we may better understand what is right, and important, *and* importantly wrong, with his impressive phenomenology of the modern soul. I want to highlight several implicit assumptions—*assumptions about the past vis-à-vis our modernness*—which Taylor shares with a whole host of "modern" critics: Friedrich Nietzsche, Alasdair MacIntyre, Stanley Hauerwas, and Michel Foucault, among others. These thinkers, different as they all are, share certain assumptions which make their similarities far more illuminating than their differences. Their "modernity" is constituted, in large measure and in Taylor's own language, by the assumption that "the moral world of moderns is significantly different from that of previous civilizations."[10] That is precisely the claim—the *modernist* claim—I want to question.

What is right and what is wrong with Taylor's account is perhaps best understood by recognizing what is right and wrong in Alasdair MacIntyre's epoch-making *After Virtue*, a book to which Taylor is finally too deeply indebted.[11] MacIntyre's is a far more despairing, and far less kind, account of our modernness. In it, as I have argued in chapter 3, MacIntyre's rather apocalyptic portrait of our modern perplexity depends upon a whole range of loosely grounded assumptions about the past. MacIntyre's description of our "Fall" *into* modernity needs some account of the Garden, a primordial beginning—a place and a time which provides the measure of our fall from grace and innocence, the object of our cultural longing, the paradise which we have lost. His

Ithaca is Greece: Homeric and heroic societies, or more to the point, the manner in which such a seamless social world is recapitulated in Aristotle's moral and political philosophy. In the modern world—where the battle-lines are drawn decisively between Aristotle and Nietzsche[12]—the Greeks represent the only sane road back to cultural and moral recovery. Theirs is, in fact, the only moral vision worth "recovering." Like the prodigals he claims we all are today, MacIntyre is calling us back from the mountaintop, back to the fonder fold of the marketplace. As we shall see again in a moment, life there was none-too-fond in the first place—for the heroes, or for anyone else.

Yet MacIntyre's is a recovery of a different sort, recovery from a sickness which is far more threatening and has spread throughout the system. As Sophocles' Ajax remarks, shortly before his own suicidal "recovery":

> No good physician quavers incantations
> When the malady he's treating needs the knife.[13]

The cure MacIntyre prescribes matches the illness in its severity. If Nietzsche philosophizes with a hammer, then MacIntyre does so with a knife.

Charles Taylor does not, happily enough. Indeed, the greatest difference between his own work and Alasdair MacIntyre's is one of style and of tone.[14] *Sources of the Self*, in tandem with Jeffrey Stout's *Ethics After Babel*,[15] represent what are to my mind two of the most sophisticated attempts to take MacIntyre's full measure *and* to offer a stylistic corrective. Neither of them feel the need to minister to our modernity with a knife. They both argue that MacIntyre's symptomatology of modern culture—ironically enough, so very close to Nietzsche's own—is too severe. There are rich moral (re)sources evident in the topography of the modern self. Life in the post-Enlightenment world, with its own attendant problems to be sure, is also free of many of the errors and extremities of antiquity. We are freer (if not yet free enough) from religious wars, inquisitions, and intolerance, Stout is careful to remind us.[16] We are committed to the elimination of human suffering, committed to the ideals of universal human rights—all of which provide tremendous critical leverage against oppression unavailable to the ancients, says Taylor.[17] International travel today is comparatively safer than it was when Odysseus took to the road, and journeyed among the Cyclopes. The rich language of inwardness provides us with exciting new personal possibilities. And Taylor concludes his survey with an appreciative sketch of some trendy, "modern" ideas—from human potential movements, through ecology-consciousness, to New Age phenomena—all of which MacIntyre treats with an ill-disguised philosophic scorn.[18] There is a crucial element of despair lacking in Taylor, hence little need for the knife.[19]

Both of these correctives, rich and suggestive as they are, miss what I take to be the fundamental point. That has been my point in writing this book. Both take on MacIntyre's rather postured portrait of our modernity, and correct it in important ways. What they do not say—what *no one* has said, to my knowledge—is that an Apocalypse is always linked to a Genesis, the beginning to the end. That is the subtle artifice of any good narrative. Hence the importance of the notion of a *genealogy*, particularly in moral matters, *pace* Nietzsche. "The beginning and the ending are shared in the circumference of a circle," Heraclitus remarks. [20] Nietzsche was to reify this same image in his doctrine of the eternal recurrence.

For a philosopher who argues for the centrality of *narrative* in the construction of philosophical arguments and of moral lives, MacIntyre's own narrative must be examined in detail. His starting point has never been seriously questioned[21]—not only does Taylor not question this, his argument actually *hinges* upon it, as we shall see—and without that, MacIntyre essentially wins by default. By granting his initial premises about Homeric seamlessness and exteriority, we are doomed to some version of his conclusions about the decadence of modern inwardness and incoherence. If MacIntyre's narrative beginning is overdrawn, as I will show that it is, then his apocalyptic conclusions cannot be right, either.

What I have been arguing is that MacIntyre cannot be right about the uniquely "inarticulate" nature of our modern perplexity, and our modern identity, if he is wrong about the past. If the Greeks have an uncanny way of sounding both "modern" and perplexed, then it becomes impossible to make the apocalyptic, *anti*modern case which MacIntyre so badly wants to make. Both Stout and Taylor highlight important omissions in MacIntyre's picture of *the present*. But both fail so much as to address his portrait of *the past*. And until they do so, it seems to me that MacIntyre wins by default, because he has set the terms in which the debate takes place. Until thinkers apply their critical powers to analyzing our prejudices about *the past*—as Nietzsche's philology did so prophetically, and as I tried to demonstrate in chapter 1—then all our talk about the present will continue to suggest the illusory need for a knife. Modernism is Quixotism cloaked in academic dress.

II

We live in an academic environment which has become obsessed with the idea of *difference*.[22] Cosmopolitans are, in Lawrence's terms, modernists swimming against the tide. The important first step in any cross-cultural conversation is the articulation of what is *different* about "the other," what sets others at such a distance from our ways of thinking about our selves and our world. There is a long tradition of sociological theory which operates on this presumption of difference and its role in constituting different kinds of "selves." In a world where culture creates consciousness, different cultures and different times cannot help but construe consciousness differently.

An absolutely fascinating restatement of this idea came from Michel Foucault, in his own ground-breaking book, *The Order of Things*.[23] And Foucault is a thinker who is *at least as* important to Taylor's agenda as Alasdair MacIntyre. In this, Foucault's first book, he sought to trace out a changing set of cultural constellations which articulate radically different visions of the relationship between "words and things" (the French title of the book), between language and reality. Such a constellation, or *episteme*, represents not just a way of thinking, *but rather the only way to think*, at a given time. With astonishing rapidity, and for no real reasons which we can ever understand,[24] this "order of things" breaks down. An *episteme* collapses, and a whole new way of construing our cultural and subjective reality emerges in the space created by this collapse.[25] If this really is an "archaeology" of the human sciences, as Foucault insisted that it was, then it is archaeology of a rather bizarre sort. It is an archaeology of *radical breaks*, what the archaeologists call 'destruction-layers.' Foucault's whole project is "an archaeology of cataclysm." One such cataclysm took place in Europe in the seventeenth century, and we are living—so says Foucault—in the space created by another such collapse right now. Bruce Lawrence made a similar suggestion in the last chapter. That collapse, an epistemic crisis of enormous proportions, is a crucial criterion of our modernness. Our words and things no longer correspond. We are living amid fragments. *We no longer know what to say*. We saw this same image at the outset of MacIntyre's antimodern narrative as well.

Foucault spent much of his subsequent life analyzing various constellations of cultural ideas—madness and criminality, punishment and correction—and their implicit notions of the individual across this "great divide" which separates the seventeenth century from ourselves. They are his great, his most *critical*, and his most psychedelic, books.[26] Yet at the end of his life, in a massive four-volume *History of Sexuality*, Foucault returned to the Greeks, and discovered a world there in many ways surprisingly like our own—certainly closer to us in many ways than the European seventeenth century which he had sketched out so well before. Hence the ambivalent reception of these last books. For those who had appreciated the radical critique implicit in his archaeological investigations, this project could not fail to look like a violation. I prefer to view it as symbolic of Foucault's dawning recognition of my central thesis: that any cataclysmic reading of the modern situation needs to clarify its own assumptions about the past.[27] And precisely in going back—back to *Greece*, which is our own, "western" past—we are no longer able to be quite so apocalyptic about our epistemic "difference" in the modern age.[28] If Greece was not a Garden, then modernity is no Apocalypse. The archaeologist of cataclysm is forever digging in the wrong places, forever digging his own grave.

Taylor shares this characteristically modern interest in epistemic breaks. All of his metaphors invoke them: breaks, fissures, destruction layers, *discontinuities*.[29] He also shares a fascination with Foucault's favored time-period: the France which spans the great divide separating Descartes and Pascal from Montaigne.[30] His own notion of an intellectual "break" is as radical as Foucault's. It is an oft-told tale, which we have seen many times now. A primitive, premodern way of looking at the world broke down in the eighteenth century. In an increasingly denaturalized, mechanized, "outer" world, the important human truths were sought "within"—the old issue of "inwardness" again. Kant's philosophy of radical autonomy and the Romantic fixation upon (human) nature as a moral source represent the far side of this great intellectual divide. Taken together, the Enlightenment and Romanticism "have made us what we are."[31] This is a statement of extraordinary significance, tracing out as it does Taylor's one great disagreement with Foucault: we are *not* living in the midst of another epistemic break today. "Perhaps we are going over another watershed," he admits, "although I have my doubts. . . . We still instinctively reach for the old vocabularies, the ones we owe to Enlightenment and Romanticism."[32] Modernity is not an unparalleled crisis—*contra* MacIntyre and Foucault, and the later Nietzsche—rather, it is more of the same. "We live still in the aftermath of modernism," he notes, "indeed, *we are still in the aftermath of almost everything I have been talking about.*"[33]

Now, Taylor's position *could* be radicalized much further, if he cared to do so. He could conceivably have given up the philosophy of epistemic breaks altogether, and the episodic, cataclysmic philosophy of history which is its corollary.[34] In so doing, he would have been turning an eminently "modern" idea on its head: the notion of historical *dis*continuity, and *différance*. In so doing, he would be moving very far indeed from MacIntyre and Foucault and the later Nietzsche, the direction in which I suspect his inclinations truly lie.[35]

Alasdair MacIntyre has suggested that "the introduction of the word 'intuition' by a moral philosopher is always a signal that something has gone badly wrong with an argument."[36] His reasons for saying so accord well with the early Foucault: there is no such thing as "human nature," since there is no "universally human" way of intuiting or doing or being anything at all. Taylor stands rather far from such an extreme. Or rather, he wishes to do so. His book is *grounded in* intuitive moral evaluations, as he himself has the candor, and the deep philosophical conscience, to admit.[37] His willingness to discuss moral intuition, like Martha Nussbaum's, flags a deeper commitment to principles of cultural *continuity*, not a modernist ideology of discontinuities and difference. It is the most *un*modern, and "untimely," aspect of Taylor's work.[38] But he fails to apply this—his own intellectual intuition—to this inherited portrait of the past. And that failure results in the very "inarticulacy" he identifies as our greatest "modern" dilemma.

III

In fact, so far is he from doing so that Taylor actually *posits* differences in the past. Yet these posit-ions—are always kept at the level of assertion, not argument.

> Our modern notions of inner and outer are indeed strange and without precedent in other cultures and times. In order to see how strange and different it is, it will be useful to trace its genesis from a previously dominant localization.
> *I find a paradigm statement of this in Plato*.[39]

Plato is a paradigm and a test-case in two ways. As Taylor notes, Plato (allegedly) embodies a very different way of thinking about our selves—outer, not inner—where the language of inwardness is not yet available to the speaking subject.

But it is more than that, it seems to me. One thing which runs like a *leitmotif* throughout Taylor's work, eternally recurring, is the contrast between a heroic, aristocratic, and warrior ethos over against more egalitarian, "Platonic" ideals: polemic versus dialectic.[40] *Plato himself straddles "a great divide*," and that is what makes him so oddly and ironically contemporary. Not that his answers resemble ours, but the nature of his *problem* does. He is becoming as schizophrenic as most moderns, we are told. He consciously inhabits two very different ways of looking at the world—one poetic, heroic and "outer," the other philosophically introspective—living and writing as he does at an epistemic and moral rupture, what Taylor will call, in a different context, "a crisis arising in the transition between identities."[41] Plato has a foot in each of these two worlds, a fact which lends ironic force to Nietzsche's epigram: "Plato versus Homer!" In fact, the schizophrenia is even more complex than that: "Plato versus himself!"

Taylor's whole intellectual program assumes this. And Nietzsche's is a small, stilled voice always lurking beneath the surface of these modernist arguments. But if it is excessive and wrong, as I am arguing that Nietzsche's later views are, then the whole philosophy of modern "decadence" which characterizes so much of the argument must go with it. Apocalypses and Geneses hang or fall together. Beginnings and endings are of a piece. Plato was not the first to live with a foot in two worlds, nor the first to find that fact problematic in construing his own "identity." The poets had already done so, Homer perhaps best of all.

Taylor lays this all out quite clearly at the outset:

> In a sense, Plato can be seen as the key figure in the establishment of *this dominant moral philosophy*. In the process, other moralities, other maps of our moral sources, had to be either discredited or annexed and subordinated. There is, for instance, *a warrior (and later warrior-citizen) morality*, where what is valued is strength, courage, and the ability to conceive and execute great deeds, and where life is aimed at fame and glory, and the immortality one enjoys when one's name lives on forever on men's lips. . . . Indeed, in some more primitive cultures, this access is seen as a kind of possession or mania.
>
> This is an utterly different view from Plato's about the site of our moral sources, about where one has to go to accede to a higher condition. It has something in common with *another rival view, one which exalts a state of manic inspiration in which poets create*.
>
> The author of the *Republic* has to deal with both these views in order to establish his own. His line is to discredit the second one almost entirely, or at least to make us very wary of it, and to subordinate the first.[42]

Three things are important about this discussion. First is the fact that Plato is made simply "the author of the *Republic*." Taylor needs to do this, because it is central to his argument that Plato bans the poets. "Plato versus Homer," again. He ignores essential texts like the *Symposium* and the *Phaedrus*,[43] where the passions—with their potential for "manic inspiration"—are not only rehabilitated, but made virtually indispensable to the moral life.[44]

Now this would all be a rather simple matter of factual disagreement, but for the fact that Plato still has a foot in the other worlds which Taylor sees him banning. He has, already, a wide range of moral sources upon which to draw. So too, for that matter, did Homer. *That fact cuts to the heart of this entire epitaph written over modernism's aftermath.* These rival maps of our moral sources which Plato allegedly discounts—the heroic, warrior-ethic and the aestheticism of poetic inspiration—are not merely historical footnotes which help us to understand how Plato argued and whom he was fighting. Rather, they continue to represent the great alternatives in "modern" moral philosophy. This is what makes the argument in the *Republic*—to say nothing of the *Iliad*—seem so refreshingly close to us. The warrior-ethic, of course, has been upheld by Nietzsche in his anti-Platonic and anti-Christian polemics. Hence his formula, "Plato versus Homer," and his revelling in such a "complete, genuine antagonism." Nietzsche's later thought is the agonistic, conflictual philosophy *par excellence* (so is MacIntyre's, for that matter). And it has gained an astonishingly wide currency today—particularly in its fixation upon contests of *power*, as analyzed so probingly by Foucault.

But so, too, has a new-found *aestheticism* won a place in modern moral discourse, and here again Nietzsche is prophetic. What both MacIntyre and Taylor call 'Emotivism'—although MacIntyre is uniformly critical of it in a way that Taylor is not[45]—is another chief feature of our modernness. Our emphasis on individuality, on "becoming what we are" and on creating a purely subjective, deeply personal sort of beauty—all of those things which, taken together, Foucault labelled "an aesthetics of existence"[46]—are intended to fill the enormous and unsettling gaps left in our lives by the hyper-rationality of a thoroughly technicalized world. In the midst of our modern "disenchantment"— another one of Taylor's preferred descriptive terms, borrowed this time from Max Weber—the poets, singers, and aesthetes of existence provide the means to put the magic back into our lives. They present us with "epiphanies."[47]

So it is that "Plato's work should probably be seen as an important contribution to a long-developing process," according to Taylor. It is a process "whereby an ethic of reason and reflection gains dominance over one of action and glory."[48] Yet it is as deceptive to call Plato "the first," as it is to call him "transitional." That is a very modern way of thinking and story-telling, which seems to me to lack the very historical sensitivity which it demands elsewhere. Homer *already* initiates "a long-developing process." Or, to put it more appropriately, in Taylor's own idiom, Homer already draws upon a number of moral sources, and dramatizes the process whereby we attempt to sort them out. Not "Plato *versus* Homer" but rather "Plato *and* Homer"—engaged in a fascinating quest for "articulacy."

The modernist denies all of this, insists in fact upon the opposite. We assume that Homer is nothing at all like us, and Plato at best only vaguely so. The modernist *presupposes* what it is he or she wants to find in the past—difference— then claims that we, decadent "moderns" all, have "lost" it. We presuppose a ludicrous transparency and instinctive one-dimensionality—what Nietzsche alternately called "greatness of spirit" and "immoralism"—in Homeric society, and in the warrior-ethos one allegedly sees vindicated by the *Iliad*. It is almost as though *power* were all that mattered, an idea which is as old as Thrasymachus or Thucydides, and as "modern" as Nietzsche or Foucault.[49] Yet the entire force of the *Iliad* hinges upon the way in which the poet puts this *ēthos* to the question. That is what we moderns miss.

"I find it hard, like everyone, to give a convincing picture of the outlook of Homeric man," Taylor confesses.[50] It is hard, I am suggesting, only if one is *predisposed* to see this world as absolutely seamless,[51] *and absolutely foreign* to our own—the modern myth of cultural difference, again. It is telling that the *only* Homeric scholar whom Taylor mentions is Bruno Snell,[52] a convinced

Hegelian who attempted to apply Hegel's historicism—the conviction that the human spirit evolves, and that the ancient world is therefore different from our own in decisive ways, as prior steps on the ladder of self-consciousness—to the Homeric poems. In doing so, Snell outhistoricizes even Hegel himself,[53] and ventures claims about the Homeric Greeks which directly contradict what Hegel himself said.[54] "There is in Homer no genuine reflection," Snell argues, "no dialogue of the soul with itself."[55] Again, one *assumes* the difference, the great cultural divide, and then—not so very surprising—one finds it in the text.

Taylor admits that "some have been tempted to make light of Snell's thesis, and to deny that Homeric man was all that different from us in his way of understanding decision and responsibility."[56] He goes so far as to dismiss the whole Homeric question as irrelevant, as "*prehistory* to the story I want to tell."[57] It is almost as though Taylor senses how shaky is the assumption upon which he has built his argument. Homer cannot be written off as "prehistory"— certainly not to an argument which hinges upon a reading of Plato's *Republic*. I have been arguing throughout this essay that the assumptions these anti-modernists (post- and premodernists, alike) make are always tied to (largely unstated) premises about the past. Thus the Homeric question can be no mere sidelight, particularly not to an argument which identifies "Plato versus Homer" as such a pivotal and decisive moral moment. Homer is our narrative beginning. It is in Plato, given his alleged hostility to the (warrior's and poet's) passions and his apotheosis of human reason, that the first halting step is taken down the long road toward the modern construal of the self as "inner space." The language of the will, or intentionality, of inwardness may not be explicit, but it is implicit for the first time in the moves Plato makes. And it is anti-Homeric to the core.

I would like to argue the opposite. This language of interiority, of inwardness—this whole distinction between the inner and outer, really—is precisely what is at issue in the Homeric poems. The moral sources upon which Achilles draws are already as rich and as variegated as Plato's. And it is to the *Iliad*—toward a demonstration of this in a way which Taylor, MacIntyre, and even Nietzsche for his part, all fail to do—that I should like to return. I promised to do so in chapter 2, and it is now time to do so. I think that this is the essay in *retrieval* which Taylor ought to have undertaken.[58] It would have made his account of modern problems a very different thing, indeed.

IV

It is arguable that Achilles, at the outset, is simply one among a host of warriors who live, and who are even willing to die, by the heroic code. In fact, I think, Homer has gone to enormous lengths to characterize him this way. He is as petty as Agamemnon. And the whole dispute which consumes them both arises over an eminently heroic, and rather petty, controversy. His woman—who means no more (and no less) to him than does his gold, or his chattel, or any of the other trinkets by which he thinks his worth is measured—has been taken from him. He has lost face, and has suffered this ignominity in the most public manner imaginable, in assembly. His refusal to fight any longer for Agamemnon, and his removal from the field for fully seventeen of the twenty-four books of the *Iliad*, is animated at the outset by this simplistic and emotive—what we loosely call 'heroic'—view of things. Those with physical strength enjoy superior honor. Their excellence (*aretē*) is measured by how much they own. When his woman, and hence his honor, is stripped from him, Achilles has little choice but to leave.

We do not meet Achilles again until book ix, and he has presumably had much to think about in the interim. It is the awakening of his inner life—the dawning language of interiority which allegedly cannot exist in the Homeric idiom—which the poet portrays so masterfully now. The Achilles of book ix is nothing like the spoiled child who complained and cried and finally quit in the first scene. Achilles refuses to play the game any more. In leaving his child-likeness behind, *his* identity-crisis has begun. Through an unmistakable series of deft poetic touches, Homer means us to see just how complete Achilles' rejection of the heroic code has become, just how far he has moved from the warrior-*ēthos* of the other Greeks.

Agamemnon has, himself, lost face in turn, has been forced to admit that he cannot do without Achilles—after seven books of disastrous engagement with the enemy. In Achilles' absence, the Trojans have mounted a crushing counter-offensive which presumably would have been impossible were Achilles still fighting. They have driven the Greeks back upon the ships, back behind their defensive fortifications. It is the first time the Greeks have had need of them. In this precarious situation, desperate to save himself and his men, Agamemnon must give away a bit of his honor, and a great many *things*—thereby validating, so he thinks, Achilles' whole *raison d'être*. Agamemnon supposes that he is giving Achilles exactly what he has always wanted, what *everyone* wants: more treasure than any hero has ever dreamed of; his own daughter for a bride; seven Trojan mistresses; seven citadeled kingdoms; and the return of Briseis, the "object" which started it all, with the solemn promise that he has never touched the girl, "as is natural [*themis*] between men and women."[59]

The invocation of *themis*—that Greek word to which I alluded in the second chapter, which connotes intuitive moral norms "naturally" accessible to all[60]—is very important for understanding what takes place next. The Greek troops are very close to panic. "This is the night which makes or breaks our

army," says Nestor.[61] Agamemnon calls a hurried assembly in which he counsels an immediate (and under the circumstances, rather shameful) retreat. Now,
in no more than sixty verses, *themis* is invoked three times.

First, by Diomedes, who responds immediately to Agamemnon's sudden
show of cowardice.

> Son of Atreus, I first of all will fight your heartlessness as it is right [*themis*]
> to do in assembly [*agorēi*]. So, my lord, do not be angered.[62]

Next by Nestor, who affirms Diomedes' steadfast courage and elaborates upon
it, calling Achilles directly to mind.

> Friendless, lawless [*athemistos*], and homeless is he
> who longs for cold conflict among his own people.[63]

Then again by Nestor in the subsequent war council among the leading Greek
chieftains, as he is about to broach the very touchy subject of Agamemnon's
apology to Achilles.

> You are lord and Zeus has given you both the
> scepter and the law [*themistos*] to rule over them.[64]

What is absolutely crucial to understand, it seems to me, is how precisely
Achilles would have objected to each of these three claims, and more specifically that he—as the paradigmatic man caught inescapably between two
worlds—would have objected precisely to the invocation of *themis*. *His* moral
intuitions have turned away from objects entirely, have turned within. To
Diomedes, he would have replied that *themis* counsels us not to fight Agamemnon's sudden loss of heart, but rather to fight Agamemnon himself. There
comes a time when we no longer feel obliged to prop up tottering and unjust
regimes. To Nestor, he would have replied that the conflict he has stirred up
among the Greeks—cold though it is—is all done in the name of *themis*. His
disobedience is hardly uncivil, hardly "lawless." For Agamemnon—and this is
his third answer—rules by the scepter alone, not by "law" at all.

When Agamemnon ticks off the list of things he means to give Achilles,[65]
as I say, he is going out of his way to include every thing any hero could
possibly want. Achilles no longer wants it. Any of it. And it is only now, in
book ix, that the full scope of his rejection becomes apparent to the other Greeks
and to us. At the outset, Homer had promised to sing of the wrath (*mēnin*) of
Achilles. We now discover that he is not angry about what we thought. He is
no longer arguing about women, or wealth, or public recognition. His whole *in-*

ner world has come to life. And he is angry, precisely, about the dramatic inconsistency between what he himself wants and what every other Greek—using the sham logic of the heroic code—tells him he should want. That is how far he has moved from the "heroic" terms of the debate as Agamemnon—and Nietzsche, and MacIntyre, and Taylor—conceive them.

There is probably only one man among the Greeks who is capable of understanding Achilles, because he has entertained these same ideas himself. That man is Odysseus. At the conclusion of Agamemnon's dramatic concession, an embassy is sent off to make the offer official. It is composed of Ajax and Phoenix and Odysseus.[66] Before they depart, Nestor, the aged counsellor who is himself never at a loss for words, counsels these three privately, "but Odysseus most of all"[67]—presumably because he, too, knows what Odysseus knows, or at least knows *that* Odysseus knows. There is a tremendous psychological depth here, a troubled world beneath the surface calm of a hero's words, however, resolute. All sense it, to a degree, and Homer clearly, if subtly, marks out its presence for us.

It is Odysseus then, as it had to be, who bides his time, feasts with his friends, patiently waits for the proper moment to strike—with words. He gets said what needs to be said. He repeats Agamemnon's peace-offer, detail by lustrous detail. And he lends Agamemnon's offer a gentility and graciousness it had not possessed before—he is much more "politic" than the king. He appeals to Achilles' sense of honor: even if you despise the king and his gifts, he says, surely you can take pity on the rest of us who are still your friends. He appeals to the lingering heroic sensibility lodged in Achilles' breast, as it is still lodged within his own: the Greeks will honor you like a god if you agree to come back, and you will win a great honor (*mega kūdos*) if you can kill Hector.[68] Finally, he initiates and concludes Agamemnon's extensive laundry list with a single phrase, which is also the real heart of his argument: *metallēxanti choloio*, "to give over your anger"[69]—since compassion (*philophrosunē*) is better than rage.[70]

This phrase comes straight from Agamemnon. The king had concluded *his* great concession speech as follows:

> All these things I will bring to pass *when he gives over his anger.*
> Let him soften—Hades is hard and never softens;
> that is why he is the most hateful of all the gods, to mortals—
> and let him yield to me, in so far as I am a greater king
> and in so far as I lay claim to an older generation.[71]

Homer means us to remember this, and in fact Achilles' answer—what is probably the finest single speech in all the *Iliad*[72]—is an answer both to Odysseus' speech, which he has heard, and to Agamemnon's, which he has not. He invokes Hades explicitly in both.

To Odysseus, he is abrupt, and brutally frank:

> As hateful to me as the doorways of death is
> the man who keeps one thing hidden in his heart, and says another.[73]

The great depth in heroic societies to which I referred above is precisely what angers Achilles so, the sheer hypocrisy of it all. No one can live as exteriorly as the hero is supposed to live. We are all inward-leaning creatures with secret, inner spaces. "Inwardness" is hardly a "modern" creation. Odysseus is sensitive enough to understand the full depth of Achilles' questions, to sense the profundity of his anger. But even he only understands it, he does not and cannot *live* it. Odysseus has presumably made his peace with the heroic world a long time ago. But knowing what he knows, and feeling what he feels, forces him to speak out of two sides of his mouth. That kind of double-life Achilles is no longer willing to live. Once you have turned decisively inside, every perception of the outside is changed.

Building on this image of Hades, which prompted his outburst, Achilles turns specifically to Agamemnon's peace-offering.

> The same Fate [*moira*] awaits us, whether we wage war or not.
> We are all held in equal honor [*iēi timēi*], the noble with the base.
> We all die the same way—the man who has done nothing and the man who has
>   done much.[74]

And again:

> Not equal in value to my life [*psychēs*] are all the things
> they say that Troy holds within her, that strong citadel—
> in the days before, when there was peace,
> before we Achaeans came . . . [75]

You cannot miss Achilles' irony, tinged with a musing, sad regret.

> There are still cattle and fat sheep,
> tripods to be won, blond-headed horses . . .
> But a man's life [*psychē*] does not come back again . . .
> when once it has flown beyond the barrier of the teeth.[76]

The speech is a rhetorical masterpiece. Achilles takes up each item which Agamemnon has offered, surveys its value objectively, and rejects every one in turn with biting sarcasm. A startling new vocabulary—the language of *equality* and *mutuality*, tied to the *inwardness* of Achilles' quest—has entered into his thinking, and his world will never be so small again. We are meant to see that he is rejecting the "heroic" ethos entirely, this whole way of carving the world up into enemies and friends.

> For my mother tells me—divine, silver-footed Thetis—that
> I have a doubled fate regarding my end [*telosde*] in death.
> If I stay here and fight for the city of Troy
> then my return home is lost, but my glory [*kleos*] is ever-lasting.
> If I return to the beloved land of my fathers
> then my glory [*kleos*] is lost, but a long life will be
> left me, nor will the end [*telos*] of death soon find me out.[77]

This choice Achilles claims already to have made. He is not interested in glory any more than he is interested in treasure. And he is leaving in the morning, for good.[78] He has chosen the destiny he wants—so he says—and in choosing it, he rejects the sham "duties" of heroism. Odysseus does not, cannot, answer— he knows what has happened here and knows that further words would be futile. "So Achilles spoke, and they were all stricken to silence, amazed by his words. He had spoken very roughly."[79] Achilles has broken with the whole show.

But Achilles' destiny is even more "doubled" than he knows. He really does have a foot in each of two worlds—and one of them is still the heroic world he longs to escape. What we witness now through an uncanny series of deft character sketches, is Achilles' gradual concession to his former self, and to the heroic code—a concession which will ultimately cost him his life.

The next speaker is Phoenix, who is just as old, and just as wordy, as Nestor. His speech, by far the longest in book ix,[80] is an extended, hopelessly simplistic appeal to the ethic of helping friends and harming enemies[81]— illustrated with personal anecdotes and superficial myths. You owe me, says Phoenix in effect, since I raised you myself and suffered all kinds of trouble at your hands—when you would spit up your wine on my clean shirts.[82] You owe all of us, since we are your friends. The pettiness of this tired old man is made quite clear in conclusion. Make sure to accept *the gifts*, he counsels his young friend, since if you agree to come back and save us, but don't get anything concrete in the bargain, then your honor [*timēis*] will be less.[83]

Achilles summarily dispenses with Phoenix; he has played this game before. Using the heroic code for his own rhetorical purposes, Achilles asks, in effect, Whose side are you on? *Your* duty, as *my* friend, is to hate those whom I hate—namely, Agamemnon. Stay with me in my shelter tonight, and we will decide what to do with ourselves in the morning. Suddenly, and without our being able to say exactly when or why, Achilles' departure is not a certainty.

Only Ajax is left, and in the *Iliad* he is far from a mental giant.[84] The subtleties, and the hypocrisies—which Odysseus plays with such virtuosity and which have taken Achilles to the limit of his endurance—are all lost on him. He is a simple man, as I have said several times—heroically resolute, but a little one-dimensional. A man of few words, a man of deeds. There *is* a virtue in that, particularly in battle, where too much thinking can get you killed (as Hector will be) or leave you hopelessly torn (as Achilles is now). Ajax tells Odysseus that he doesn't understand any of this, and indeed he does not. His world is defined—as Achilles' no longer can be—by the strict parameters of the heroic code: you help your friends; you hurt your enemies. His argument is extremely simple. First, he mentions the concept of "blood-money" (*poinēn*). Even when a friend has been murdered, the hero accepts the blood-price, and the guilty party is absolved. You do not wallow in your grief. As with Phoenix before him, *things* are what matter to Ajax. Even *personal grief* is erased by gifts. Secondly, Ajax observes that this disastrous conflict, which now threatens the entire Trojan expedition, has taken place *for the sake of a single woman* (of course, so has the whole Trojan War, as Achilles astutely observes)[85]—and that is simply unthinkable.

Now, against all expectation, Achilles makes a desperate concession—to Ajax, of all people.

> Ajax, noble son of Telamon, lord of the people,
> all that you have said seems to come from my own heart [*thymon*].[86]

His *former* heart, we want to say. Achilles seems actually to be making a concession to his own former self—the infinitely younger man he was, mere days ago, and who stands before him now in the towering figure of Ajax. Achilles stands, as we have said, with a foot in two very different worlds, straddling an abyss which will soon consume him. Moreover, the concession is made on behalf of a man to whom he is curiously bonded—by *fate*.[87] It is Ajax, and he alone, who will brave impossible odds in order to carry Achilles' body out of the battle after the latter has fallen. And it is Ajax who will finally suicide himself over the alleged slight of seeing Achilles' armor awarded to Odysseus rather than himself. That is when he speaks of treating certain maladies with a knife. These men are linked in a destiny as awful as the one which binds Achilles to Priam, linked to the heroic code of which Achilles at least is trying to be free. And when they both are dead, a whole worldview will symbolically die with them, as Pindar said, and as we saw in chapter 1.

Now the concession, such as it is, Achilles couches in strictly *negative* terms, at least at the outset:

> I will not think again [*prin*] of bloody battle
> until such time [*prin*] as the son of noble-minded Priam, divine Hector,
> arrives at the ships and shelters of my Myrmidons
> slaughtering Argives as he goes, kindling fire by our ships.[88]

Negative or not, it *is* a concession, and a decisive one. He told Odysseus that he was leaving in the morning. He told Phoenix that he would wait until the morning to decide what to do. Now he is suddenly staying—committed to watching, interminable waiting, and the inevitability of being sucked back into the very game he no longer wants to play. His destiny is now sealed. In every meaningful sense, it is the beginning of the end.

V

There are doubtless those who will not let me leave the discussion this way, which is to say, who will not let this *end*. They will dismiss my reading of the poem as "humanistic" or "romantic," perhaps even "naïve." They will deny that the cultural schizophrenia implicit in any "heroic" society, the schizophrenia of intuitive (inward) appeals and heroic (outward) expectations, have anything at all to do with the *Iliad*. They will refer appreciatively to Alasdair MacIntyre's account of heroic society, where *doing* has a priority over *being*—where you are, in fact, precisely what you do.[89] In such a world, cultural expectations and social roles—of warrior, speaker, chieftain, even wife and mistress—are all that matter, all there is. These same people will cite Bruno Snell, to support their claim that Homer looked at his world and his self very differently than we do.[90] They may even go so far as to argue, with Foucault, that there was no such thing as a self back then, that the 'self'—like the companion-concept of 'man'—is a rather recent construction of the past several European centuries. And some of them, ironically the most eloquent by far, will claim that this period is coming to an end, in *this* day and age.[91] In the void created by this collapse, a space is created in which we may go back to a *pre*modern way of looking at things, or else go forward, toward a vague and ill-defined *post*modernity—toward the boudoir, or the abyss.

Such people will they quote, but not Homer himself, never Homer. They will not do so for the simple reason that the essential role which *inwardness* and intuition play in the evaluation of any society's values, is the very "epiphany" Homer provides. *The inner life*, to say it again, is what the *Iliad* is all about.

When Homer invokes his Muse, in the first line of the poem, he makes us a promise, sets himself a task:

> Sing in me, Muse, the wrath of Achilles . . .

He promises to sing, and in singing to explain, what has made Achilles so angry. It is not very long before we realize that he is not angry about lost women, lost treasure, nor even about lost battles and lost friends. He is angry, frustrated, driven to despair, *by lost innocence*, by the realization that his inner world will never be quite so simple again. He is angry at the hypocrisy of heroism, at the inescapable distance between what his society tells him to be, and what in fact he is. His society tells him that a hero is not afraid, yet everyone fears death. Not to fear in this way is to be a brute, like Ajax, not a hero. Surely it is no accident that the one scene of which Homer never tires is the *inner* debate, a monologue which he privileges us to hear, dramatized for our ears alone, in which the vast majority of Homer's heroes—Trojan and Greek alike—try to steel their hearts to the heroic tasks at hand.[92] If we are honest, as Homer is, then the matter is really quite simple: *they are trying to talk themselves out of running away*. And this for the simple reason that they want desperately to do so—as would any sane woman or man. No less a hero than Hector *will* run away, as I showed in chapter 2, and he is no less a hero in our eyes for doing so. That is Homer's magic, and he is constantly working it on us. Odysseus, Diomedes, Hector, Paris, Sarpedon, Glaucon, Aeneas . . . they all meet in the depths of paralyzing, damning inner conflict. Apart from this—the insoluble conflict between heroic expectations and human intuitions, between duty and destiny—the *Iliad* would make no sense at all.

Yet this is precisely the senseless muddle most modern commentators have made of the poem. These heroes are always debating the same thing within themselves: the relative virtues of the heroic standard of dying by your shield, of refusing to give ground. It is hypocritical to say this about ourselves, when we—we, who have had any experience of real battle, not the pyrotechnical shadow-play of the sham battle we called "Desert Storm"—know that warfare, as Homer understands it, is essentially an eternal see-saw, an ebb and flow of cowardice and high courage. To say anything else is to clothe oneself in what Simone Weil calls "the armor of a lie."[93]

Let me illustrate with one example more—as if more were needed—in a scene which, happily enough, coincides with the last. We begin in the fourth book of the *Iliad*—which describes the first serious stretch of fighting since Achilles' abandonment of the Greeks—and we will end in the ninth. Agamemnon strides into the front ranks in order to stir up the hearts of the leaders of his wildly teetering forces, to convince them, if possible, that the loss of Achilles makes no great difference to the Greek expedition or to its eventual, *inevitable* outcome. Agamemnon is a king, first among all the Greek chieftains at Troy, used to being heeded, used to being heard. He is, as kings so often are, a little rough around the edges, a little too sure of his own mind, a little abrasive—all characteristics which got him into trouble with Achilles in the first place. He is well-intentioned, most of the time, but he has an uncanny talent for saying the wrong thing at precisely the wrong time and in the wrong way, for stepping on other people's toes, particularly the toes of his friends.

The first prince he really dresses down is Diomedes. Now Diomedes is a pure warrior, as will be made abundantly clear in the sixth book, which later bore his name: not the bravest of the Greeks, yet very brave; not the strongest, yet exceptionally strong; not the most heroic or steadfast, but a pure hero. He is the kind of man no army can be long without. Diomedes endures; Diomedes prevails.

In a misconceived (yet really typical) attempt to spur him on to even greater acts of valor, Agamemnon says, in effect, "You're not half the man your father was."[94] He goes on to say—what no man in a society based on shame can bear to hear—that, should Diomedes' father suddenly appear on the scene, the contrast would be dramatic. The son is "much worse in fighting [*machēi*], better only with words [*agorēi*]." Diomedes would do well to be ashamed. He has all the talents, all the tools; yet the deeds are somehow lacking.

Diomedes stifles a fury not so very different from the one which moves both Achilles and Odysseus to speak, a fury which finally inspires Achilles to quit the field—but he does not answer Agamemnon directly. Instead, he speaks to a friend standing nearby,[95] and says, in effect, that the king must be obeyed in everything—that a king has the right, among other things, to be wrong. The capture of Troy will be *his* glory, the loss of the Greek fleet *his* eternal shame. Since he has taken the greater risk, he is free to say what he wishes. In a world of bold sinners, none sins so boldly as a king.

And that, according to the shallow rationale of the heroic code, is the end of the matter. That is the myth every Greek hero tells, and believes, up to a point. *That*, not Liberalism, is the sham tradition. Hot blood makes for hot words, yet only the king may give way to his great heat. And does so, freely, all too often.

Five books later, the Greek tide has turned, as it eventually had to, in the absence of Achilles. The Greek forces, as we have seen, are in full retreat, dug in now behind defensive fortifications it would not have occurred to them to build as recently as one week earlier. Agamemnon, who has been a little too quick to every opinion he has ever had, calls an emergency war council and urges retreat from Troy "this very night." The opportunity may not exist tomorrow. Nestor had said that this was the night which makes or breaks the army. It has already broken Agamemnon. Hector and the Trojans seem suddenly, shockingly invincible.

First to his feet in opposition, if we recall, stood Diomedes. We would expect no less. He tells the assembled princes that, even if they should all consent to leave, he would stay and himself take Troy, alone. But before he goes on to explain this stunning statement of heroic resolve, he breaks stride entirely, giving vent first to what is really on his mind. It has been on his mind for days now, for five full books of the *Iliad*. Through the course of God only knows how many duels and how much destruction, he can speak of nothing else until he has spoken first of this. His heavy heart needs lightening, his wounded honor a salve. Diomedes takes the opportunity to remind Agamemnon of his unjust rebuke from five books earlier.

> Son of Atreus, I first of all will fight your heartlessness as it is right to do . . .
> I was the first of the Greeks whose spirit [aikēn] you slighted
> saying I was unwarlike and lacked it [analkida].[96]

Then, conscience cleared, he can turn to the more pressing matters at hand. But not until then. Zeus has given the king two great gifts, he says—the sceptre and the law—but not a third, the very thing in fact which Agamemnon earlier said that *he* had lacked:

> With the sceptre, he has given you honor beyond all others,
> but he did not give you spirit [aikēn], which is the greatest power of all.[97]

Agamemnon—so great is his own distress just now—does not dispute the point. Here are heroes who use the sham ideals of the heroic code merely to score points in meaningless verbal duels. They are *all* more adept at this crasser war of words.

This same scene, or else one very much like it, constantly plays itself out in the Greek world, past as present. It makes sense of "politics" which would otherwise be senseless. The tension between inner and outer—the lip-service we pay to dutiful obedience versus the realities of festering human resentment—drives the drama throughout the Homeric poems. The *Iliad* itself, this much-touted "tragedy" of Achilles, is also the story of an interminable feud between two megalomaniacal Greek chieftains. Countless smaller feuds dot the emotional landscape of the poem. Diomedes, Odysseus, Agamemnon, Paris, Achilles himself—none of them *ever* forget a wrong word, the merest word, spoken in anger. These Greeks have the longest memories, and the tenderest sense of wounded honor, one can imagine. They feel deeply, and that is the end of the matter. Not only do they indeed *possess* an inner life; the inner life seems at times the only thing worth talking about.

VI

Why are these stories, and this moment in the *Iliad*, book ix particularly, so important? In the first place, they give the lie to this mythology of harmonious origins which constitutes the first step toward what I have been calling "the tragic posture," the nostalgic modern narrative of decline and fall. They provide a much richer, "thicker," portrait of the past. This society, however "heroic" and allegedly "exterior" it may appear, is already seething with *internal* conflicts, and psychological depths, not all of which are to be neatly or happily resolved. Of course, they may be resolved, for a *Greek* tragedy is just as far from a pessimistic story as it is from a naïvely optimistic one.[98] "Tragedy," it seems to me, connotes precisely that tone which Taylor finds missing from most of the modernist debate.[99] It is we—fatalistic, modern, fixated upon apocalypse—who want to read "tragedy" this way. Hence our postured insistence that we are somehow "coming to an end."

Achilles *will* eventually learn what he needs to learn—and Homer stops singing when that happens. But at what a cost does this knowledge come to him! It costs countless lives—Greek and Trojan, and the very best on both sides. It even costs Achilles his. Finally, this story—and all of the *Iliad*, really—illustrates a phenomenon which I have been circling around for a long time now, and have tried to get at in a variety of ways. There *is* already an "individualism"—a profound "inwardness" and an astonishingly "modern" problematizing of the self—in Archaic and Classical societies, the modernist protests notwithstanding. "Plato versus Homer" is, in the final analysis, not so genuine or complete an antagonism. The story which Homer tells in the ninth book of the *Iliad* is a marvel of poetic construction precisely because it sketches out a whole array of individual characters so distinctly. The identity-crises which we are told is so modern a predicament—*our* "inarticulacy"—is precisely the result of this inner/outer dichotomy, and the necessity which we, much like they, experience for living in two worlds at once, speaking out of two sides of the mouth. We all pay lip-service to ideals and ideologies which none of us completely accept. There is no one "narrative" which tells *the* story of our lives.[100] We inhabit many worlds, tell many different stories, wear many different hats—and these all do not, can not, overlap. There are gaps, interstices, identity-crises great or small. We *begin* inside of a "tradition" and we move *necessarily* outside of it. Any "tradition" worthy of the name in some sense *forces* us "outside." Where we go is precisely "inside" *ourselves*, attuning ourselves to certain moral intuitions which Achilles, Antigone, and others describe so poetically and so well.

Yet we must reenter the world again. Zarathustra comes down from his mountaintop; Achilles returns to the battlefield upon which he will eventually lose it all. There is a *penultimacy* to the *polis*, a timelessness to this oscillation, the ebb and flow of identity-crisis.[101]

The intriguing, and troubling, relationship between the individual and the moral sources available in the larger society is not "modern." When Charles Taylor speaks of "the modern language of identity, which would be anachronistic in talking about the ancients,"[102] the burden of proof lies with him to read the *Iliad* differently than I have done, not merely to nod in assent in the direction of Snell and MacIntyre, Nietzsche and Foucault. He must show us, specifically, why this individual whom he calls "distinctively and uniquely modern" does not figure in this, the oldest poem that we in a place called "the west" are heir to. That poem, which has been the narrative beginning of nearly every modernist story-teller I have mentioned in this essay is astonishingly old, yet extraordinarily familiar at the same time. Appeals to epistemic breaks, to secularization and disenchantment, to cultural difference alone will not do. This is a tension as old as human identity, as old as human thought, and I like to think that I have traced out its *pre*-modern contours, albeit sketchily, from Homer to Plato.

"Plato *versus* Homer?" Not at all.[103] To those who worry that we are living at the end, that we are forced to live straddling a great cultural and moral divide, that the threads of our moral fabric have come undone, there is really only one thing to be said. Achilles *already* unravelled it all. He already stood perched over this same great divide. The sacred web of moral meaning was never very tightly woven to begin with. Which means *both* that we need not be overly romantic about the past, *and* that we need not be so pessimistic or desperate about the present. "Tradition" is what it always has been—flawed, imperfect, pluralistic, and deeply divided against itself, but still in place, ready for us to draw upon as *one among a series* of moral sources, if we have the ears to listen and the eyes to look. Our own moral intuitions and sentiments are another. Taylor himself argues this way, at his best. But the constant invocation of MacIntyre and Foucault, and the postures of the anti-modernist, cut away from his case. Soon, we find ourselves "in the aftermath," oddly inarticulate about what it is that we allegedly come "after."[104]

Tradition is an important part of our destiny. It lives when *we* make it live. We are *not* fated to lose it. Yet it will never answer all of our questions. We all inhabit many languages, many worlds, straddling a variety of personal and cultural and psychic divides. There is a *penultimacy* about the *polis*.

If we fail to meet these challenges, if we retreat instead into the heady nostalgia for a bygone era, if we passively resign ourselves to a "modernity" we do not want—then the fault lies, as it has always lain, in our selves and *not* our stars.

Notes

1. *Sources of the Self: The Making of the Modern Identity* (Cambridge, MA: Harvard University Press, 1989).

2. The relationship between therapeutic language and philosophical/critical language is a fascinating one which derives in large part from the major Hellenistic philosophical schools. See Martha Nussbaum, *The Therapy of Desire: Theory and Practice in Hellenistic Ethics* (Princeton: Princeton University Press, 1994), 3–47.

3. Charles Taylor, *Sources of the Self*, 53–90.

4. This development is often taken to be distinctively and excessively "American." See, for example, Robert Bellah et al., *Habits of the Heart: Individualism and Commitment in American Life* (Berkeley: University of California Press, 1985), 55–84.

5. It is interesting to note that such a self-reflective task can itself (much like Hegel's attempt in *The Phenomenology of Spirit*, about which Taylor has written at some length) only be accomplished *at the end of an era*. That is to say, we seem to need the virtues of hindsight to see what we have lost and where we have gone wrong. So at least, says the tragic posture—and I for my part do *not* see this naïve claim in Hegel. See Charles Taylor, *Hegel* (New York: Cambridge University Press, 1975), 3–51.

6. Charles Taylor, *Sources of the Self*, 3, 10.

7. Martha Nussbaum has gone so far as to argue that this novel language is tied to the inward-looking art-form of the novel. But she is quick to add that the *Odyssey* is already the west's first novel. These genres are not so "modern" as we allege. See *Love's Knowledge: Essays on Philosophy and Literature* (New York: Oxford University Press, 1990), 7–10, 390.

8. And it builds upon Taylor's own discussion in *Sources of the Self*, 27ff.

9. Charles Taylor, *Sources of the Self*, 21–22, 121, 137–139. This insight as well is drawn from Alasdair MacIntyre, whose work we will be facing again presently. See *After Virtue*, 2nd ed. (South Bend, IN: University of Notre Dame Press, 1984), 175; *Whose Justice? Which Rationality?* (South Bend, IN: University of Notre Dame Press, 1988), 154–57; and *Three Rival Versions of Moral Enquiry: Encyclopedia, Genealogy, and Tradition* (South Bend, IN: University of Notre Dame Press, 1990), 154.

It is fascinating how, given our need for clear narrative beginnings, scholars love to identify one thinker as "the first" to speak in some given way, and then to trace our own development from this point. *Some nine hundred or one thousand years previously*, Heraclitus remarked: "I went in search of myself." And on that bizarre journey of exploration, he too turned decisively *within*.

For my text of Heraclitus' fragments, I am indebted to Charles H. Kahn's *The Art and Thought of Heraclitus* (New York: Cambridge University Press, 1979). This particular fragment is Kahn's no. 28 (Diels no. 101).

10. Charles Taylor, *Sources of the Self*, 11.

11. See Taylor's "Justice After Virtue," in John Horton and Susan Mendus, *After MacIntyre: Critical Perspectives on the Work of Alasdair MacIntyre* (South Bend, IN: University of Notre Dame Press, 1994) 16–43.

12. Alasdair MacIntyre, *After Virtue*, 109–120.

13. Sophocles, *Ajax* 582–83.

14. "But whether I am right here," Taylor opines, "or whether one of the more gloomy views above is correct, is irrelevant to my main purpose" ("Justice After Virtue," in Horton and Mendus, eds., *After MacIntyre*, 42). Clearly, I think that this is not only relevant, but actually the heart of the matter.

15. Jeffrey Stout, *Ethics After Babel: The Languages of Morals and Their Discontents* (Boston: Beacon Press, 1988).

16. *Ibid.*, 191–93, 224–26.

17. Charles Taylor, *Sources of the Self*, 11–14.

18. *Ibid.*, 495–521.

19. For MacIntyre's complaint that Taylor is, in effect, not antimodern enough, see his "Partial Response to My Critics," in Horton and Mendus, eds., *After MacIntyre*, 286–90. Clearly, in MacIntyre's judgment, one may *not* be both modern and Aristotelian.

20. Charles H. Kahn, *The Art and Thought of Heraclitus*, no. 99 (Diels no. 103).

21. Indeed, in the collection of critical essays entitled *After MacIntyre*, we get a fairly predictable list of complaints: that he is wrong about Aristotle, that he is wrong about Aquinas, that he is wrong about the Enlightenment, that he is wrong about Utilitarianism, that he is wrong about Kant. No one has questioned his account of Homer, or of Nietzsche (the two points are related), and yet that is precisely where his argument is *fatally* flawed in my judgment.

22. An excellent case in point occurs in Taylor's *Sources of the Self*, 111–14, 176.

23. Michel Foucault, *The Order of Things: An Archaeology of the Human Sciences* (New York: Random House, 1979).

24. His thesis stubbornly refuses the question of causality. Contingency—the randomness of "this-then-that"—is all there is.
See Foucault's essay "Nietzsche, Genealogy, History," in *The Foucault Reader*, Paul Rabinow ed. (New York: Pantheon Books, 1984), 76–100. So, too, Charles Taylor, *Sources of the Self*, 199–207.

25. For more on Foucault's cyclical historicism, see Vassilis Lambropoulos, *The Rise of Eurocentrism: Anatomy of Interpretation* (Princeton: Princeton University Press, 1993), 348–49n64.

26. See particularly *Madness and Civilization: A History of Insanity in the Age of Reason* (New York: Pantheon Books, 1965); *The Birth of the Clinic: An Archaeology of Medical Perception* (New York: Pantheon Books, 1973); and *Discipline and Punish*:

The Birth of the Prison, trans. Alan Sheridan (New York: Random House, Vintage Books, 1977).

27. See MacIntyre, *Three Rival Versions of Moral Enquiry*, 44, 49–53, 221, for a similar genealogy of Foucault's thought. The only disagreement I have with MacIntyre is that he is far more critical of "the final Foucault" than I would want to be.

28. As Foucault himself put it, in an astonishing footnote to a discussion about why his encounter with the ancient world had been so determinative to the new direction he finds his thought taking, he identifies an assumption which is "doubtless fundamental to Western philosophy—to examine both the difference which keeps us at a remove from a way of thinking in which we recognize the origin of our own, *and the proximity that remains in spite of that distance* which we never cease to explore" (*The History of Sexuality*, Vol. II: *The Use of Pleasure*, trans. Robert Hurley [New York: Random House, 1985], 7, emphasis mine.) Foucault goes on to insist—so strongly has he come to see it—that those who cannot accept this fact, and the fateful difference it makes for what he is doing now, are "not from the same planet" as he!

29. And this even to the point of the ridiculous, such as *Sources of the Self*, 200, where Taylor refers to "the great prestige of the visual and plastic arts in the Italian Renaissance" as "something which had no precedent among the ancients." One hardly knows what to make of such comments, save that they assume the very thing they mean to prove—namely, the radical *discontinuities* between cultures, across the great divide of time.

30. See Taylor, "Justice After Virtue," in Horton and Mendus, eds., *After MacIntyre*, 19–20.

31. Charles Taylor, *Sources of the Self*, 393.

32. *Ibid.*

33. *Ibid.*, 482, emphasis mine. See also MacIntyre, *Three Rival Versions of Moral Enquiry*, 149–69, 199, for this same specious imagery of life in an "aftermath."

34. As he is, for reasons which remain unclear to me, unwilling to do. See the global claims at "Justice After Virtue," in Horton and Mendus, eds., *After MacIntyre*, 22.

35. See, for instance, *Sources of the Self*, 70–71, 99–100, 488, 518–19.

36. Alasdair MacIntyre, *After Virtue*, 69.

37. Charles Taylor, *Sources of the Self*, 4–8, 75, 496. See also "Justice After Virtue," 37.

38. See Taylor's explicit criticism of Foucault's excesses in *Sources of the Self*, 462–63, 465, 488.

39. Charles Taylor, *Sources of the Self*, 114, emphasis mine.

40. Thus, in *ibid.*, 16, the contrast between a warrior-ethic and Plato is presented as a paradigm. The movement from an honor-ethic to Plato's is thoroughly contemporary (20–21), and the notion of justice-as-power, very much in line with Thrasymachus, is also in evidence at a variety of periods over the past three millennia (22). See similar comments ventured at 37, 65, 85–86, 92–93, 152–54, 196–97, 240, 285–86, 377, 500. In all of this, Taylor is again building upon the work of Alasdair MacIntyre, *Whose Justice? Which Rationality?*, 30–39.

41. Charles Taylor, *Sources of the Self*, 192.

42. *Ibid.*, 117, emphasis and emendation mine.

43. I am currently trying to develop a very different Platonism which is grounded in these two texts. That forthcoming manuscript is tentatively entitled *Symposia: Plato, the Erotic, and Moral Value*.

44. Taylor himself calls this "a semi-suppressed side of Plato's thought" (22), but it remains unclear to me *by whom* this thought has been "suppressed." By we moderns? Or rather by Taylor himself? On art as more than *mimēsis*, see *Sources of the Self*, 419.

45. See Charles Taylor, *Sources of the Self*, 198, 374–90. It is unfair, he admits, when "modernity is often read through its least impressive, most trivializing offshoots" (511). That is precisely what MacIntyre does, on my view. See *After Virtue*, 6–35, especially 11–12.

46. Michel Foucault, *Politics, Philosophy, Culture: Interviews and Other Writings, 1977–1984* (New York: Routledge & Kegan Paul, 1988), 49. See also Charles Taylor, *Sources of the Self*, 117.

47. Charles Taylor, *Sources of the Self*, 422–25, 481.

48. *Ibid.*, 117.

49. For Nietzsche's telling commentary on "Plato Against Thucydides," see *Twilight of the Idols*, "What I Owe to the Ancients," §3.
For a good commentary on Foucault's doctrine of power, see the interview "Truth and Power," in *The Foucault Reader*, 56–57.

50. Charles Taylor, *Sources of the Self*, 120. See also Alasdair MacIntyre, *After Virtue*, 121–30, and *Whose Justice? Which Rationality?*, 12–29.

51. Taylor, "Justice After Virtue," 40.

52. The text is Snell's celebrated *The Discovery of the Mind: The Greek Origins of European Thought*, trans. T. G. Rosenmeyer (New York: Oxford University Press, 1953). Snell's *Entdeckung des Geistes* was originally published in Germany in 1948.

53. Hegel remarked, in his lectures on aesthetics, that sometimes "we get the beginning and perfection all at once." Henry Paolucci, *Hegel: On the Arts* (New York: Frederick Ungar Publishing Co., 1979), 122. That is the Hegelian line on Homer!

54. For an elegant analysis and corrective, see W. Thomas MacCary, *Childlike Achilles* (New York: Columbia University Press, 1982), 3–15, "On Re-Reading Snell's Homer," and 16–34, on "Hegel's Homer."

55. Bruno Snell, *The Discovery of the Mind*, 19. It would take us too far afield to explore this further, but Snell's methodology, confined to this first chapter on Homer, is to pick out words from the Homeric lexicon, see how they were used, and then argue on this philological basis that Homer locates the physiological seat of deliberation in various organs which never mingle. But Homer writes *poetry*, not philosophy, and thus metrical considerations play far more of a role in his word-choice than does physiology. Snell himself admits this (21), but passes it by. See W. Thomas MacCary, *Childlike Achilles*, 4, 14–15. For a concise criticism of Snell's thesis, see Bernard M. W. Knox, *The Oldest Dead White European Males: And Other Reflections on the Classics* (New York: W. W. Norton & Company, 1993) 37–47.

56. Charles Taylor, *Sources of the Self*, 118. It is interesting that Taylor speaks of being "tempted" to this view. Is it impossible *to argue* for it?

57. Charles Taylor, *Sources of the Self*, 120, emphasis mine.

58. Lambropoulos, *The Rise of Eurocentrism*, 17ff.

59. *Iliad* IX.134. My Greek text of the *Iliad* has been edited by Malcom M. Willock (London: St. Martin's Press, 1978). All translations are my own.

60. It is much like what Taylor calls "moral intuition" at the outset of his argument, in *Sources of the Self*, 4–8, as opposed to Alasdair MacIntyre's comments in *After Virtue*, 124 and *Whose Justice? Which Rationality?*, 13–14.

61. *Iliad* IX.78.

62. *Iliad* IX.31–32. Note the use of the term *agora*, or "assembly." As the debate well illustrates, the Greeks did not romanticize the *polis* the way most modern commentators do.

63. *Iliad* IX.63–64. This is the passage which Aristotle quoted in his definition of the "political animal," as I pointed out in chapter 2. What he (and most commentators like MacIntyre) fails to say is that Achilles' conscious decision to quit the field, and therefore to become "a-political," is meant to be a good and necessary thing. According to the demands of *themis*, he has nowhere else to go—save "outside" and "within."

64. *Iliad* IX.98–99. This exact phrase is repeated at IX.156.

65. *Iliad* IX.122–57, repeated at 264–98. It bears mentioning, given the importance of Greek names in this poem, that Agamemnon names his three daughters among the potential brides for Achilles. They are: *Chryso-themis*, or 'golden-justice'; *Lao-dikē*, or 'justice-of-the-people'; and *Iphi-anassa*, or 'rule-by-force'. Only the last of these names really captures the essence of their father.

66. Actually, there is an ambiguity in the manuscripts as to whether there were two or three members of the embassy. All three are named, but when they head off to Achilles' tents, Homer uses the dual voice (*Iliad* IX.182–84) as though they were only two. If there were originally two in this story, then I would suspect that they were Ajax and Odysseus, since Phoenix' presence adds little to the overall dramatic movement of the book, but provides a wonderful opportunity for Homer to flex his story-telling muscle again.

67. *Iliad* IX.180.

68. *Iliad* IX.303.

69. *Iliad* IX.261, 299.

70. *Iliad* IX.255–56.

71. *Iliad* IX.157–61.

72. *Iliad* IX.307–431. It is very much akin to Antigone's great debate with Creon, in Sophocles' *Antigone* 441–526.

73. *Iliad* IX.312–13.

74. *Iliad* IX.318–20.

75. *Iliad* IX.401–03.

76. *Iliad* IX.406–9. It is imagery of this sort which Bruno Snell invokes as "evidence" for how differently Homer understands human psychology and physiology than do we "moderns." When he says *psychē*, he means "life," and he envisions it as a physical thing which "flies" beyond the teeth. But the image is a poetic one, and poetry cannot be used as "scientific" evidence. Words too, after all, according to Homer, are said to have "wings" when they "fly past the teeth."

77. *Iliad* IX.410–16.

78. *Iliad* IX.356–63.

79. *Iliad* IX.430–31, repeated at 693–94.

80. *Iliad* IX.432–605.

81. See Mary Whitlock Blundell, *Helping Friends and Harming Enemies: A Study of Sophocles and Greek Ethics* (New York: Cambridge University Press, 1989) for the argument that what we see in the tragedies is a continuation of this Homeric, heroic moral vision. Impressed as I am by the work, I want to emphasize more than has been done, how *ironic* Homer is being every time he displays this crude warrior-*ēthos*.

82. *Iliad* IX.490–94. This is meant to be ridiculous. Phoenix is using an heroic vocabulary, *polla pathon kai polla mogēsa* (IX.492) to describe the most trivial of troubles.

83. *Iliad* IX.604–5.

84. This poetic image lives on in Shakespeare. See *Troilus and Cressida*, II.i. In this, the poet is fairly building upon Homer's own imagery, at *Iliad* XI.543–64—which is Ajax' moment of terror and moment of truth, when we should expect the inner debate in which most every hero engages at some point.

We do not get it; instead, we are treated to some bizarre similes without parallel in the poem where the sweating hero is compared to an ox and then a donkey—which is to say, *a brute*.

85. *Iliad* IX.337–45.

86. *Iliad* IX.644–45.

87. Recall MacIntyre's comments upon heroic fatalism, to which I alluded in chapter 3 (*After Virtue*, 124–25).

88. *Iliad* IX.650–53.

89. Alasdair MacIntyre, *After Virtue*, 122.

90. Bruno Snell, *The Discovery of the Mind*, 6–7, 19, passim.

91. The canonical text is from Michel Foucault, *The Order of Things*, which I quoted in chapter 4:

> As an archaeology of our thought easily shows, man is an invention of recent date. And one perhaps nearing its end.
>
> If those arrangements were to disappear as they appeared, if some event of which we can at the moment do no more than sense the possibility—without knowing either what its form will be or what it promises—were to cause them to crumble, as the ground of Classical thought did, at the end of the eighteenth century, then one can certainly wager that man would be erased, like a face drawn in sand at the edge of the sea. (387)

92. See, for example, *Iliad* I.188–95; V.166–78, 217–28, 251–73, 596–606, 669–76; VI.440–65; VII.92–102, 123–60, 206–18; VIII.137–71; XI.310–19, 401–10, 461–73; XII.307–28; XVI.485–501; XXII.95–161.

93. Simone Weil, "l'Iliade, ou, le Poème de la Force," in *La Source Greque* (Paris: Editions Gallimard, 1953).

94. *Iliad* IV.365–400.

95. *Iliad* IV.411–18.

96. *Iliad* IX.32–33, 34–35.

97. *Iliad* IX.32–49.

98. This insight is, to my mind, Nietzsche's greatest and most enduring one. The canonical texts for this idea are four: *Twilight of the Idols*, "What I Owe to the Ancients,"

§5; *The Gay Science* §370; *The Birth of Tragedy*, 1886 preface §1; and *Ecce Homo* III.i.§1. See also Walter Kerr's remarkable *Tragedy and Comedy* (New York: Simon & Shuster, 1967), 13–36.

99. Charles Taylor, *Sources of the Self*, ix–x.

100. This last comment is directed against both Alasdair MacIntyre's *After Virtue*, 204–25, and Charles Taylor's *Sources of the Self*, 47–52.

101. The following passage—which I have quoted several times in the course of this essay—puts the point as eloquently as any I have read, and does so, moreover, in explicit reference to Homer:

"The strange nostalgia for a completely integrated society, which so dominates the thinking of such seemingly disparate commentators on the *Iliad* as Redfield and Havelock [we should want to add MacIntyre, and Taylor, and even Nietzsche to this list], should here be mentioned. . . .

"It must be said about these readings that they contradict the poem's own focus, which is on Achilles' refusal to live within the heroic code. Furthermore, the *Iliad* presents Achilles as paradigmatic rather than perverse: all heroes feel about themselves pretty much as he does. In *short, the* Iliad *tells us very forcefully that social institutions are no consolation for individual deprivation. . . .*

"*The nostalgia of the critics for an integrated society is not even ratified for a time before the Trojan War.*"

(W. Thomas MacCary, *Childlike Achilles*, 29–30, emendation mine).

102. Charles Taylor, *Sources of the Self*, 37. See also 42.

103. This is said against MacIntyre, too, in *Three Rival Versions of Moral Enquiry*, 229.

104. Taylor's later book, *The Ethics of Authenticity* (Cambridge, MA: Harvard University Press, 1992), 94, 120–21, nicely confirms much of what I have been arguing here. There, we find what I am pleading for here: a no-nonsense attitude to spit on our hands and get on with the serious business of living, here and now. Taylor says that he is now far more interested in finding "subtler languages" (81–91) in the fight "against fragmentation" (109–21), than in crassly "knocking" the achievements of our own day and age.

Regrettably, the misleading language of "inwardness" as a uniquely modern phenomenon, persists (26–28).

AFTERWORD:
A POST-MORTEM ON
POST-MODERNITY

> I wish to speak a word for Nature, for absolute free-
> dom and wildness, as contrasted with a freedom and culture
> merely civil—to regard man as an inhabitant, or a part and
> parcel of Nature, rather than a member of society.
> I wish to make an extreme statement. If so I may make
> an emphatic one, for there are enough champions of civi-
> lization: the minister and the school-committee and every
> one of you will take care of that.
>
> —Thoreau, "Walking"

I

In a remarkable portrait entitled, appropriately enough for my purpose, *The Condition of Postmodernity*,[1] David Harvey refers to what he calls "the travails of space-time compression." That is, for him, the key to unlocking the mystery of our modernness.[2] It is an oft-told tale by now, an all-too-familiar portrait to anyone who has made it through *this* book. Our world has grown geographi-cally smaller, somehow; technology and the development of global markets have seen to that. In fact, our world has grown *too* small, and therefore too com-plicated. The "erosive" modern forces of cosmopolitanism and technical so-phistication have punched their way through the thick stone walls of the ancient Greek *polis*. The barbarians, MacIntyre warns us, are already inside the gates, and may well be here to stay. If that is true of our "modern" sense of space, then how much more true is it of our perceptions of *time*. I worried about both of these claims, especially the temporal one, in the fifth chapter, and I worry about them still. These antimodern self-portraits, this image of "compression," speak to no environment that I know quite so well as the academic. Most scholars do exist in a frenetic never-never land where time and space are singularly "com-pressed." Large parts of this book emerge from my deep concern about the ways in which academic knowledge is manufactured.[3] In short, we all decide—the truth of the matter is that we are *told* this in so many different reviews by so

233

many different people, that we finally take it on as an academic orthodoxy—
that certain ideas are unquestionable. We define what it is to be "modern" with
a certain set of scholarly assumptions, and just enough apocalyptic posturing to
make it all marketable, and then we pass off our own very distinctive institutional concerns as "just the way things are." Then we nominate that peculiarly
unsettled feeling as "modern."

Harvey acknowledges four, loosely speaking (and when the topic is "postmodernism," the language is always pretty loose),[4] "postmodern" responses to
this modern dilemma of spacelessness, timelessness, and, well, breathlessness.
First and foremost comes a sort of fatalistic despair, a wringing of the hands in
the face of the enormity and apparent inevitability of it all. Harvey calls this a
withdrawal "into a kind of shell-shocked, blasé, or exhausted silence."[5] But the
only real candidates for this most extreme of postmodern postures come in the
form of two films by Wim Wenders, *Paris, Texas* and *Wings of Desire* (the latter film seems profoundly enchanted and romantic, not shell-shocked at all). It
is not clear that anyone could, or would, or does actually live like this. These
are films and fictions, not facts. Here, again, we see the peculiar danger of
equating narrative with critical enquiry. We are spoonfed a contrivance, the
playful depthlessness of the high tech era. That is but one more modernist fa-
ble. It is the very attitude which kept Miniver Cheevy, complaining all the
while, glued to his barstool.

This same attitude *can* take a more devil-may-care approach, attempting,
as Harvey has it, "to ride the tiger of time-space compression through constitution of a language and an imagery that can mirror and hopefully command
it."[6] He mentions Nietzsche in this regard, the latest and most antimodern of
Nietzsche's many masks, the bullying philosopher of the will to power.[7] This
revelling in destruction, in the amorality of Nature (a Nature rather different, in
its way, from the one Thoreau admired), clearly does have an appeal in any
number of postmodern writers, like Baudrillard, who claim to be carrying on in
a Nietzschean idiom. It is not quite this simple. As I tried to show in the first
chapter, Nietzsche will not come to any very eloquent defense of *our* antimodernism. His philology was *un*modern music of a very different sort, and his
*anti*modernism seems to be a direct violation of his own better philological in-
stincts. Those who try, like MacIntyre, to make him simply *the* philosopher of
the will to power (and hence, *the* philosopher of our modernity) rely too heavily by far on notes which Nietzsche never saw fit to publish,[8] and ideas with
which he wrestled, but never resolved to his own satisfaction. Nietzsche's
philology, as I tried to suggest, can provide critical leverage *against* this excessive antimodernism.

A third response to the problems which modernity poses, and "the grand
narrative" which comes from living in an increasingly (so we say) global vil-

lage, Harvey defines as "the progressive angle to postmodernism which emphasizes community and locality, place and regional resistances, social movements, respect for otherness and the like." This curious version of "postmodern" resistance—resistance to the erosive forces of our modernity—might better be called *pre*modern. It is the very kind of thing, grounded in the same suspicion of overarching Enlightenment metanarratives, which MacIntyre, and Hauerwas, and a host of other antimodernists share. Call it postmodern, call it premodern; it hardly matters. The point is that it is *anti*modern to the core, and that is precisely where I have tried to engage it. Whence this philosophical disaffection with the here and now? That is the alienation which lies at the heart of the tragic posture.

My reaction to this vast literature, and to this complex "problem of modernity," also seems to have a place in Harvey's scheme. He calls it "a freewheeling denial of the complexity of the world," and "a penchant for the representation of it in terms of highly simplified rhetorical propositions."[9] I have puzzled over that challenge, puzzle over it still. There is nothing "freewheeling" about my denials, I hope. For it seems to me that the "highly simplified rhetorical propositions" are coming from the other side, from those who have been arguing all along that Homer's world is *nothing* like ours, that the "erosive" forces of globalism and Enlightenment universalism have conspired to change it all. They have colluded in the manufacture of that "modern" cultural artifact we now call "the individual." So we are told. That, as I tried to show in the last chapter, is the highly simplified rhetoric of antimodernism.

There is an alternative to these perspectives, it seems to me, and I have devoted this book to its description. It will require continuing to read Homer, among other so-called classics. It will require an historical imagination. It will require travel—*into the past*. My "alternative" is, in large part, the refusal to grant the word 'modern' its current status as a proper noun. It is worthy of careful study, the process whereby the term 'modern' came to achieve its status as a proper noun, and I hope to return to this idea in a subsequent book. It appears that the word comes into English usage in the latter half of the sixteenth century.[10] I made much of this fact in the fifth chapter. It derives indirectly from the late Latin *hodiernus*, "here and now," originally implying contemporaneity, and nothing more—much as the word *modo* meant "now."[11] When the Aberdeen Register of 1555 refers to "our maist gracious quene *moderne*," they were *not* making a judgment about her politics, her style of dress, or anything else. They simply meant to say that she is our queen, here and now. It is *we* who have adopted the term as a definitive adjective, at times nearly as a proper noun (Chaplin's film *Modern Times* is highly instructive). Modernity, so say we latter-day "moderns," is a crisis, a problem to be solved, a decisive moment of *ending*. When "modernity" is posited—as a problem, a precise *temporal* problem—at the beginning, then there really are only two coherent alternatives, two ways of bringing this apocalyptic story to its end:

1. retreat into some romanticized form of *pre*modernity.
2. the mad dash forward into the vagaries of *post*modernism.

The former is an idyll; the latter a concept too sketchy as yet to be meaningful. If indeed 'modern' means simply "here and now," then the label '*post*modern' becomes simply the most self-serving and specious "afterword" of them all. Modernity is, as Jürgen Habermas rightly notes, "an unfinished project,"[12] "Today" always is. But that is so for the simple reason that we are always, *always* here and now.

Whether we move forward or backward, we are still moving away from the center, away from our selves, away from the here and now. That is, the gospel of Miniver Cheevy, the counsel of Quixotism. It is a form of antimodernism I refuse to take too seriously. Henry David Thoreau had some insightful and profound advice on that score. The soundest response to our contemporary antimodern discontent would be to learn how to bake bread, to keep a large garden, to read one good book (rather than twenty mediocre ones), to remember the fonder and happier "ethics" of the dinner-party, of friendship . . . and always, always, to take time for the solitude of a walk.

> If you are ready to leave father and mother, and brother and sister, and wife and child and friends, and never see them again,—if you have paid your debts, and made your will, and settled your affairs, and are a free man, then you are ready for a walk.[13]

We have a lovely idiom in English, "to take the time." It is a sober counsel, indeed. Time flies, and we will lose it if we do not "take" it. We are as capable of "taking" time now as ever we were, if we take it for ourselves, seize hold of it, even steal it when we have to. Our inability to see or say these things is where we are failing, in the academy, and now increasingly outside of it.

II

I have not dealt very long upon postmodernism. I hope that I have now made it a little clearer why. Its "weighty language"[14] is too noun-heavy, and its rhetoric is temporally obsessed. We talk . . . about how to talk. We talk about talking. We read about reading. We study how best to study. And we never quite turn to the tasks at hand.[15]

Postmodernism is perhaps the most faddish of all the afterwords I have examined, and therefore the least compelling of the two forms of antimodernism I have been discussing. It does not simply misread the past; it ignores it. My attention in this book has been drawn to the much more troubling, because much more popular, kinds of *pre*modern solutions offered by MacIntyre and Hauerwas, and increasingly, by our politicians. I spend more time with them because I have learned so much from them, and also because my tentative suggestions (not "solutions," for there are none; the "problem" such as it is does not require "solutions") about bread-baking and gardening, of friendship and love and long walks—*in a word, the taking of time*—may seem to be very much like what Alasdair MacIntyre calls a "practice"[16] or a "craft,"[17] and what Stanley Hauerwas calls "the ethical significance of the trivial"[18] or "discipleship."[19] They are not, exactly.

On the one hand, these practices are not grounded in the spurious narrative of decline and fall, the antimodern myth of decadence which insists that we are somehow coming to an end, here and now. Secondly, my views stand at an infinite remove from their curious brand of antiliberalism. To the degree that political Liberalism teaches the *penultimacy* of the *polis*, I am indeed an unabashed "Liberal." I find Thoreau's portrait of naturalism and the moral life both richer and more nuanced (except in his curious discussion of "civil disobedience") than many of our latter-day Aristotelians'. I find it truer too to that stunning aesthetic moment which was Classical Athens. Even so traditional, so encyclopedic, a thinker as Aristotle himself knew that there is a crucial difference between something being merely "traditional" and its being "good." As he is quick to remind us:

> Archaic laws [*nomous*] were much too simple and barbaric. The Greeks, for instance, used to carry swords, and bought their women from one another. And there are lingering archaisms still to be found in various customs [*nomimōn*] roundabout. In Cyme, for instance, there is a law for homicide, whereby the accused, if he assembles a certain number of witnesses from his own family, will be liable to the very murder-charge from which he is running.
>
> In short, all people [*holos*] seek, not tradition [*patrion*], but the good [*t'agathon*].[20]

To say all that represents a marked refusal of the romanticized—now tarnished and trivialized—concept of a "tradition." Here, I suspect, is the greatest difference that being *un*modern, rather than *anti*modern, makes. And that word, 'tradition,' is a word which I suppose catches in my throat at least as painfully as the words 'community' and 'modern' do today. We have cheapened them all through academic overuse.

The classics—Homer is without a doubt one "classic" author, and Sophocles is another—seem to me to tell a slightly different tale. The individual is the
non plus ultra for any "tradition" worthy of the name, and remains the standard
by which it may best be measured. Self-sufficiency is a crucial political virtue. It
was Nietzsche's insight, and later his excess, to focus upon this eminently classical insight. "My religion," he says, "if I can still call it that, lies in the creation
of genius."[21] Now this brand of individualism is still a world away from insisting that we are all alone in the universe. Thoreau lived in a hut he built with his
own hands, on the outskirts of a town, not in a desert or cave or mountaintop. He
stayed tantalizingly close to the marketplace. He went away to learn how to
walk—to learn more about seasons, about Nature's rhythms, and to experiment
with *time*—not merely to be alone. As "individuals" we each must learn to manage that never-ending, cyclical movement between the marketplace and the
mountaintop. Our latter-day Aristotelians, and our antimodern posturers, have all
but forgotten the necessity of the mountaintop. An individual resides within a
context—it is never enough merely to ride off into the sunset at day's end—and
the individual always participates as a member of some various moral communities. Communities, not a single community—this is where MacIntyre and
Hauerwas are most misleading. 'Culture' and 'tradition' are almost always monolithic in their work, just as are their portraits of the Homeric and early Christian
past. It is always left to the individual to appropriate culture, to evaluate it, and
to make it a living thing. In a word, to *listen* to it. To do so *takes time*. No one of
us—thank God—accepts all that we are told, anymore than we believe all that
we read, or parrot all that we hear. This postured nostalgia is too much with us,
and we moderns have indeed "our own crucial myth of classical culture."

> A tradition is, after all, like love; we "crystallize" it, endow it with the
> perfections it must have in order to justify our need and our love. And classi-
> cal Greek culture has for some time stood in relation to modern culture as a
> measure of our fall from grace and innocence. . . . To our modern dissonance,
> the Greeks play the role of old tonality, the abiding image of a great human-
> ity. They are our lost power, lost wholeness, the pure *presence* and continuity
> of reality our culture has lost.
>
> Against a need like this and a myth like this, argument may be futile. But
> we should not, I think, be allowed to mythologize unawares. If we first de-
> prive classical culture of its true turbulence in order to make ourselves a myth
> of what we have lost, and then hedge that myth with false ritual, we are de-
> priving ourselves of that community of interest and danger that makes the
> twentieth century true kin to the Greeks. We deprive ourselves, in short, of ac-
> cess to what the past can teach us in order to take only what we want.[22]

A tradition is like love—there is no insight more worthy of Martha Nussbaum's
passionate writing about the Greeks. And we have been in the habit, for some

time now, of telling ourselves that there is no kiss so sweet as a first kiss—that is MacIntyre's and Hauerwas' nostalgic affair. The "tragedy" of love, we are told, resides in an unhappy ending of sorts, in the inevitable fact that the passion *must* dwindle, even where the love endures. Marriage itself is a "practice," an obligation and a vow, more than anything else. The passion is what's missing. We are all trying to get back to a paradise of first kisses and fonder hopes which is gone for good.

If we fail to take the risk inherent in an erotic commitment, if we do not dare to open ourselves to its dangers, its risks, *and* its high delight, if we remain content to read the past solely in the purer light of our nostalgic fantasies, then we fail to do justice to the present, *our* "modernity." Here and now is where our passions lie. I have not been at all interested in debunking Greece. My own feelings for her run just as deep, and are just as romantically inclined. They are, in the best sense, passionate. I hope to devote a subsequent book to discussing that, by focusing in upon Greece's greatest legacy, her aesthetic legacy: the literature of *tragedy* and *erotics*. My perspective derives from a profound respect for the manner in which the Greeks attempted to negotiate their disputes— erotic and political alike, even turning some of them into poetry—not from the naïve assumption that they did not have any. I have learned enormously from both Hegel and Nietzsche, each of whom, in his own way, sought to refine this Romantic myth of harmonious origins which German-speaking philhellenes—beginning with Winckelmann—had done so much to popularize.[23] We still hear a critical word of warning from Nietzsche, which is, at the same time, an enduring challenge:

> To *surpass* Greek culture through our own achievements—that is the task. But to do that, it must first be known![24]

As Nietzsche should have been the first to add—although oddly enough, he made it the mainstay of his later method[25]—there is no myth so dangerous, so subversive, as the myth of *decadence*: a quixotic longing for what the past had in abundance, a sentimental education in what we have lost. If the past was a little less innocent, then we are probably less corrupt; if the past was a little less peaceful, then certainly our own conflicts and confusions are not so desperate. In a word, if there was no magical beginning—just a very, very good one—then we surely are not living "afterwards," at the end.

Notes

1. David Harvey, *The Condition of Postmodernity: An Enquiry into the Origins of Cultural Change* (Oxford: Basil Blackwell, 1990).

2. For more in this vein, see Anthony Giddens' *The Consequences of Modernity* (Stanford: Stanford University Press, 1990), 1–21.

3. I am heartened to see Alasdair MacIntyre, for his part, increasingly aware of how important the *locus* of this debate—within the university—is for the way in which it is conducted. See *Three Rival Versions of Moral Enquiry: Encyclopedia, Genealogy, Tradition* (South Bend, IN: University of Notre Dame Press, 1990), 6–8. He identifies the self-serving rhetoric of *specialization*, the increasing *departmentalization* of academic debate, and the intransigent *refusal to listen* (and hence to change one's mind) as aspects of the modern university which have combined to corrupt its soul. Much to my dismay, he also lists the ideology of *universalism* as the most crippling, and "encyclopedic," aspect of the modern universe-ity. That, I think, is the crucial difference between us, and to my mind it changes everything. In any analysis of "the modern university," in Nietzsche's world and in our own, the important word is 'university,' not 'modern.'

4. Part of the problem seems to be that the term means different things in philosophical, artistic, cinematic, and architectural circles. It has also become something of a fad, a *French* fad, and that faddishness has made the discourse even sloppier. As Harvey is the first to admit: "No one agrees as to what is meant by the term, except, perhaps, that 'postmodernism' represents some kind of reaction to, or departure from, 'modernism.' Since the meaning of modernism is also very confused, the reaction or departure known as 'postmodernism' is doubly so." (Harvey, *The Condition of Postmodernity*, 7).

5. Harvey, *The Condition of Postmodernity*, 350.

6. *Ibid.*, 351. All subsequent quotations in this discussion come from the same page.

7. *Ibid.*, 273–74.

8. I grant that I may seem to have done the same thing myself, by making so much of the unpublished essay, *Wir Philologen*. There is a crucial difference between the two projects, however. Nietzsche gave up the enormous project of "Unmodern Observations" because he simply did not have the time or energy to complete all thirteen essays. He gave up on the will to power because it was an idea which could not be formulated in the systematic terms he had envisioned. For more on this failed systematicity, see James J. Winchester, *Nietzsche's Aesthetic Turn: Reading Nietzsche After Heidegger, Deleuze and Derrida* (Albany: SUNY Press, 1994) ix-xiv, 9–69.

9. "Travel," he is quick to add (and this one stings), "even imaginary and vicarious, is supposed to broaden the mind, but it just as frequently ends up confirming prejudices." I suppose that much depends on *how* one travels, with what expectations, and *where* one goes. What is clear enough, however, is that *not* travelling at all dooms one in advance to a kind of parochial thinking. As Twain put the matter:

> Travel is fatal to prejudice, bigotry, and narrow-mindedness, and many of our people need it sorely on these accounts. Broad, wholesome, charitable views of men and things

cannot be acquired by vegetating in one little corner of the earth all one's lifetime. (*The Innocents Abroad* [New York: Airmont Publishing Company, 1967], 443)

Compare Descartes, who warned:

One who spends too much time travelling eventually becomes a stranger in his own country; and when one is too curious about the practices of past ages one usually remains quite ignorant about those of the present.
[This passage from the *Discourse on Method* is quoted by Louis Dupré in *Passage to Modernity: An Essay in the Hermeneutics of Nature and Culture* (New Haven: Yale UP, 1993) 157].

10. *The Oxford English Dictionary*, 2nd ed. (Oxford: Clarendon Press, 1989), IX.947–49.

11. Louis Dupré, *Passage to Modernity*: 145–46.

12. Jürgen Habermas, "Modernity: An Incomplete Project," in H. Foster, ed., *The Anti-Aesthetic: Essays on Postmodern Culture* (Port Townshend, WA: Bay Press, 1983), 3–15. I should be careful to add that Habermas, while the spokesperson for a position I appreciate very much, shares too many modernist prejudices finally to make the case he wants to make. He is, even more than George Steiner, an *academic's* academic. And, like Steiner, he cannot grant such primacy to the "problem" of modernity without being predetermined to some form of its solution. That is to say, while Habermas is not antimodern, he grants the point far too quickly that "modernity" is precisely the problem we need to be talking about.

13. Henry David Thoreau, "Walking," in *Walden, and Other Writings of Henry David Thoreau*, ed. Brooks Atkinson (New York: The Modern Library, 1950), 598.

14. See David H. Hesla's "Postmodernism's Weighty Language" and the energetic replies it prompted in *Soundings* 75.2/3 (1992): 215–53.

15. See my "Against Positions: Notes on the Relation Between Moral Vision and Moral Debate" in *Soundings* 78.3/4 (1995) 501–518.

16. Alasdair MacIntyre, *After Virtue,* 2nd ed. (South Bend, IN: University of Notre Dame Press, 1984) 187.

17. MacIntyre, *Three Rival Versions of Moral Enquiry*, 61.

18. Stanley Hauerwas, *Christian Existence Today: Essays on Church, World, and Living in Between* (Durham, NC: The Labrynth Press, 1988), 253–66.

19. Stanley Hauerwas, *After Christendom? How the Church Is to Behave if Freedom, Justice, and a Christian Nation Are Bad Ideas* (Nashville, TN: Abingdon Press, 1991) 93–107. The practices he equates with discipleship are bricklaying, quilting, and yes, gardening—but Hauerwas emphasizes their *social* character, whereas I think they are important because they alter our interaction with *time*.

20. Aristotle, *Politics* 1268b39, translation mine.

21. *Wir Philologen*, 5[22]; *Sämtliche Werke*: *Kritische Studienausqabe in 15 Bänden* (Berlin: Walter de Gruyter, 1967–1977), VIII, 46.

22. William Arrowsmith, "A Greek Theater of Ideas," *Arion, First Series*, 2.3 (1963): 56.

23. Vassilis Lambropoulos, *The Rise of Eurocentrism*: *Anatomy of Interpretation* (Princeton: Princeton University Press, 1993), 49–61.

24. *Wir Philologen*, 5[167]; *Sämtliche Werke*, VIII.88.
Hegel, at roughly the same age of twenty-five, ventured a remarkably similar remark. See his *Early Theological Writings,* trans. T. M. Knox (Philadelphia: University of Pennsylvania Press, 1948), 149; and also *The Philosophy of History* trans. J. Sibree (New York: Dover Publications, 1956), 6.

25. "Nothing has preoccupied me more profoundly than the problem of decadence— I had reasons. 'Good and evil' is merely a variation of that problem. Once one has developed a keen eye for the symptoms of decline [*Niedergang*], one understands morality too, understands what is hiding behind its holiest names and values—namely, *empty* life, the will to an end, utter fatigue. Morality negates life." *The Case of Wagner*, 1888 preface; *Sämtliche Werke*, VI.11–12.

SELECT BIBLIOGRAPHY

Ammerman, Nancy T. *Baptist Battles: Social Change and Religious Conflict in the Southern Baptist Convention*. New Brunswick, NJ: Rutgers University Press, 1990.

———. *Bible Believers: Fundamentalists in the Modern World*. New Brunswick, NJ: Rutgers University Press, 1987.

Aristotle. *Metaphysics*. Translated by Richard Hope. Ann Arbor, MI: University of Michigan Press, 1952.

———. *Nicomachean Ethics*. Translated by Martin Ostwald. Indianapolis, IN: Library of the Liberal Arts, 1962.

———. *Poetics*. Translated by Gerald F. Else. Ann Arbor, MI: University of Michigan Press, 1965.

———. *Politics*. Translated by Ernest Barker. Oxford: The Clarendon Press, 1946, 1958.

———. *Rhetoric*. Translated by George A. Kennedy. New York: Oxford University Press, 1991.

Bellah, Robert N., Richard Madsen, William M. Sullivan, Ann Swidler, and Stephen M. Tipton. *Habits of the Heart: Individualism and Commitment in American Life*. Berkeley: University of California Press, 1985.

Berger, Peter. *The Sacred Canopy: Elements of a Sociological Theory of Religion*. Garden City, NY: Doubleday, 1967.

Blumenberg, Hans. *The Legitimacy of the Modern Age*. Translated by Robert M. Wallace. Cambridge, MA: MIT Press, 1983.

Borgman, Albert. *Crossing the Postmodern Divide*. Chicago: University of Chicago Press, 1992.

Butler, Eliza M. *The Tyranny of Greece over Germany*. New York: Macmillan, 1935.

Casey, John. *Pagan Virtue: An Essay in Ethics*. Oxford: The Clarendon Press, 1990.

Derrida, Jacques. *Éperons/Spurs: The Styles of Nietzsche*. Translated by Barbara Harlow. Chicago: University of Chicago Press, 1978.

Douglas, Mary and Steven Tipton, eds. *Religion and America: Spiritual Life in a Secular Age*. Boston: Beacon Press, 1982.

Dupré, Louis. *Passage to Modernity: An Essay in the Hermeneutics of Nature and Culture*. New Haven: Yale University Press, 1993.

Farnsley, Arthur E., II. *Southern Baptist Politics: Authority and Power in the Restructuring of an American Denomination*. University Park, PA: Pennsylvania State University Press, 1994.

Ferry, Luc and Alain Renaut. *Heidegger and Modernity*. Translated by Franklin Philip. Chicago: University of Chicago Press, 1990.

Foucault, Michel. *The Archaeology of Knowledge* and *The Discourse on Language*. Translated by A.M. Sheridan Smith (New York: Barnes & Noble, 1972, 1993).

———. *The Birth of the Clinic: An Archaeology of Medical Perception*. Translated by A. M. Sheridan Smith. New York: Vintage Books, 1973.

———. *Discipline & Punish: The Birth of the Prison*. Translated by Alan Sheridan. New York: Vintage Books, 1973.

———. *The History of Sexuality, Vols. I–III*. Translated by Robert Hurley. New York: Vintage Books, 1978.

———. *The Order of Things: An Archaeology of the Human Sciences*. New York : Vintage Books, 1970.

Giddens, Anthony. *The Nation-State and Violence*. Berkeley: University of California Press, 1985.

———. *The Consequences of Modernity*. Stanford: Stanford University Press, 1990.

Gilman, Sander, ed. *Conversations With Nietzsche: A Life in the Words of His Contemporaries*. Trans. David J. Parent. New York: Oxford University Press, 1987.

Goldmann, Lucien. *The Philosophy of the Enlightenment*. Translated by Henry Maas. Cambridge, MA: MIT Press, 1968, 1973.

———. *The Hidden God: The Tragic Vision in Pascal's Pensées and the Tragedies of Racine*. Translated by Philip Thody. Atlantic Highlands, NJ: Humanities Press, 1964, 1977.

Gunton, Colin E. *The One, the Three and the Many: God, Creation and the Culture of Modernity*. Cambridge: Cambridge University Press, 1993.

Habermas, Jürgen. *Communication and the Evolution of Society*. Translated by Thomas McCarthy. Boston: Beacon Press, 1976, 1979.

———. *Knowledge and Human Interests*. Translated by Jeremy Shapiro. Boston: Beacon Press, 1968, 1971.

————. *Legitimation Crisis*. Translated by Thomas McCarthy. Boston: Beacon Press, 1973, 1975.

————. *The Philosophical Discourse of Modernity*. Translated by Frederick Lawrence. Cambridge, MA: MIT Press, 1985, 1987.

————. *The Theory of Communicative Action*. 2 Vols. Translated by Thomas McCarthy. Boston: Beacon Press, 1981, 1984, 1989.

————. *Toward a Rational Society*. Translated by Jeremy Shapiro. Boston: Beacon Press, 1968, 1970.

Hatfield, Henry Caraway. *Winckelmann and His German Critics, 1755–1781: A Prelude to the Classical Age*. New York: King's Crown Press, 1943.

Hauerwas, Stanley. *After Christendom? How the Church Is to Behave If Freedom, Justice and a Christian Nation Are Bad Ideas*. (Nashville, TN: Abingdon Press, 1990).

————. *Against the Nations: War and Survival in a Liberal Society*. New York: Winston Press, 1985.

————. "Can Aristotle Be a Liberal? Or, Nussbaum on Luck." *Soundings* 72.4 (1989): 675–91.

————. *A Community of Character*. South Bend, IN: University of Notre Dame Press, 1981.

————. *Dispatches from the Front: Theological Engagements With the Secular*. Durham, NC: Duke University Press, 1994.

————. *Naming the Silences: God, Medicine and the Problem of Suffering*. Grand Rapids, MI: William B. Eerdmans Publishing Company, 1990.

————. *The Peaceable Kingdom*. South Bend, IN: University of Notre Dame Press, 1983.

————. *Suffering Presence: Theological Reflections on Medicine, the Mentally Handicapped, and the Church*. South Bend, IN: University of Notre Dame Press, 1986.

————. *Truthfulness and Tragedy*. South Bend, IN: University of Notre Dame Press, 1977.

————. *Unleashing the Scripture: Freeing the Bible from Captivity to America*. Nashville, TN: Abingdon Press, 1993.

————. *Vision and Virtue*. South Bend, IN: University of Notre Dame Press, 1974.

Horton, John and Susan Mendus, eds. *After MacIntyre: Critical Perspectives on the Work of Alasdair MacIntyre*. Notre Dame, IN: University of Notre Dame Press, 1994.

Jaegar, Werner. *Aristotle: Fundamentals of His Development*. London: Oxford University Press, 1934, 1967.

————. *Early Christianity and Greek Paideia*. Cambridge, MA: Harvard University Press, 1961.

————. *Paideia: The Ideals of Greek Culture*. 3 Vols. Translated by Gilbert Highet. New York: Oxford University Press, 1939, 1945.

————. *The Theology of the Early Greek Philosophers*. Translated by Edward S. Robinson. Westport, CT: Greenwood Press, 1947, 1960, 1980.

Johnson, Paul. *The Birth of the Modern: World Society, 1815–1830*. New York: Harper-Collins, 1991.

Kaufmann, Walter. *Nietzsche: Philosopher, Psychologist, Antichrist*. 4th ed. Princeton: Princeton University Press, 1974.

————. *Tragedy and Philosophy*. Princeton: Princeton University Press, 1968, 1979.

Kerr, Walter. *The Decline of Pleasure*. New York: Simon & Shuster, 1962.

————. *Tragedy and Comedy*. New York: Simon & Shuster, 1967.

Lawrence, Bruce B. *Defenders of God: The Fundamentalist Revolt Against the Modern Age*. San Francisco: Harper & Row, 1989.

Lindbeck, George. *The Nature of Doctrine: Religion and Theology in a Postliberal Age*. Philadelphia: The Westminster Press, 1984.

Löwith, Karl. *From Hegel to Nietzsche: The Revolution in Nineteenth Century Thought*. Translated by D. E. Green. New York: Doubleday, 1967.

MacCary, W. Thomas. *Childlike Achilles: Ontogeny and Phylogeny in the Iliad*. New York: Columbia University Press, 1982.

MacIntyre, Alasdair. *After Virtue*. 2nd ed. South Bend, IN: University of Notre Dame Press, 1984.

————. *Against the Self-Images of the Age: Essays on Ideology and Philosophy*. South Bend, IN: University of Notre Dame Press, 1978.

————. "Ancient Politics and Modern Issues," *Arion, Second Series*, 1.2 (1974): 425–30.

————. *Hegel: A Collection of Critical Essays*. New York: Doubleday, 1972.

————. "How Virtues Become Vices: Values, Medicine and Social Context." In *Evaluation and Explanation in the Biomedical Sciences*, edited by H. T. Engelhardt and S. Spicher, 97–121. Dordrecht: D. Reidel Publishing Company, 1975.

————. *Herbert Marcuse: An Exposition and a Polemic*. New York: Viking Press, 1970.

————. *Marxism and Christianity*. South Bend, IN: University of Notre Dame Press, 1968, 1984.

———. "Pascal and Marx: On Lucienn Goldmann's *Hidden God*," Reprinted in his *Against the Self-Images of the Age: Essays on Ideology and Philosophy*, 76–87. South Bend, IN: University of Notre Dame Press, 1978.

———. "Relativism, Power, and Philosophy," In *After Philosophy*, edited by Kenneth Baynes, James Bohman, and Thomas McCarthy, 385–411. Cambridge, MA: MIT Press, 1987.

———. *A Short History of Ethics*. New York: Macmillan, Collier Books, 1966.

———. *Three Rival Versions of Moral Enquiry: Encyclopedia, Genealogy, and Tradition*. South Bend, IN: University of Notre Dame Press, 1990.

———. *The Unconscious*. London: Routledge & Kegan Paul, 1958.

———. *Whose Justice? Which Rationality?* South Bend, IN: University of Notre Dame Press, 1988.

Marty, Martin and R. Scott Appleby, eds. *Fundamentalisms Observed*. 2 Vols. Chicago: University of Chicago Press, 1991, 1994.

Mazower, Mark, *Inside Hitler's Greece: The Experience of Occupation, 1941–1944*. New Haven: Yale University Press, 1993.

Nietzsche: Sämtliche Werke, Kritische Studienausgabe in 15 Bänden. Berlin: Walter de Gruyter Verlag, 1980.

Nietzsche, Friedrich. *The Antichrist* [1888]. Translated by H. L. Mencken. Torrance, CA: The Noontide Press, 1980.

———. *Beyond Good and Evil: Prelude to a Philosophy of the Future* [1886]. Translated by Walter Kaufmann. New York: Random House, Vintage Books, 1966.

———. *Beyond Good and Evil* [1888]. Translated by Helen Zimmern. New York: The Modern Library.

———. *The Birth of Tragedy* and *The Case of Wagner* [1872, 1888]. Translated by Walter Kaufmann. New York: Random House, Vintage Books, 1967.

———. *The Birth of Tragedy* and *The Genealogy of Morals* [1872, 1887]. Translated by Francis Golffing. New York: Doubleday, Anchor Books, 1956.

———. *Daybreak* [1881]. Translated by R. J. Hollingdale. Cambridge: Cambridge University Press, 1982.

———. *Ecce Homo* [1888]. Translated by R. J. Holiingdale. New York: Penguin Books, 1979, 1982.

———. *The Future of Our Educational Institutions* and *Homer and Classical Philology* [1871]. Translated by J. M. Kennedy. In *The Complete Works of Friedrich Nietzsche*, edited by Oscar Levy. New York: Russell & Russell, 1964.

————. *The Gay Science* [1882]. Translated by Walter Kaufmann. New York: Random House, Vintage Books, 1974.

————. *Human, All-Too-Human* [1878, 1879]. Translated by Marion Faber. Lincoln: University of Nebraska Press, 1984.

————. *On the Genealogy of Morals* and *Ecce Homo* [1887, 1888]. Translated by Walter Kaufmann. New York: Random House, Vintage Books, 1969.

————. *Philosophy in the Tragic Age of the Greeks* [1873]. Translated by Marianne Cowan. Chicago: Henry Regnery Company, 1962.

————. *Thus Spoke Zarathustra* [1883, 1885]. Translated by Walter Kaufmann. New York: Viking Press, 1966.

————. *Twilight of the Idols* [1887]. Translated by Walter Kaufmann. In *The Portable Nietzsche*, 463–563. New York: Viking Press, Penguin Books, 1954, 1982.

————. *Untimely Meditations* [1873–1876]. Translated by R. J. Hollingdale. (Cambridge: Cambridge University Press, 1983).

————. "We Classicists." Translated and edited by William Arrowsmith. In *Unmodern Observations*, 305–87. New Haven: Yale University Press, 1990.

————. *The Will to Power*. Translated by Walter Kaufmann and R. J. Hollingdale. New York: Random House, Vintage Books, 1967.

————. *Wir Philologen* [1875]. Translated by William Arrowsmith. *Arion, Second Series*, 1.2 (1974): 279–380.

Nussbaum, Martha Craven. *Aristotle's De Motu Animalum*. Princeton: Princeton University Press, 1978.

————. *The Fragility of Goodness: Luck and Ethics in Greek Tragedy and Philosophy*. New York: Cambridge University Press, 1986.

————. *Love's Knowledge: Essays on Philosophy and Literature*. Oxford University Press, 1990.

————. "Non-Relative Virtues: An Aristotelian Approach." *Midwest Studies in Philosophy* 13 (1988): 32–53.

————. "Shame, Separateness, and Political Unity: Aristotle's Criticism of Plato." In *Essays on Aristotle's Ethics*, edited by Amelie O. Rorty, 395–435. Berkeley: University of California Press, 1980.

————. *The Therapy of Desire: Theory and Practice in Hellenistic Ethics*. Princeton: Princeton University Press, 1994.

Nussbaum, Martha Craven with Amelie O. Rorty. *Essays on Aristotle's De Anima*. Oxford: Clarendon Press, 1992.

Placher, William. *Unapologetic Theology: A Christian Voice in a Pluralistic Conversation.* Louisville, KY: Westminster/John Knox Press, 1989.

Redfield, James M. *Nature and Culture in the Iliad: The Tragedy of Hector.* Expanded Edition (Durham, NC: Duke University Press, 1994).

Rorty, Amelie O., ed. *Essays on Aristotle's Ethics.* Berkeley: University of California Press, 1980.

Rosen, Stanley. *The Ancients and the Moderns: Rethinking Modernity.* New Haven: Yale University Press, 1989.

Ross, W. D. *Aristotle.* London: Methuen & Company, 1923, 1956.

Ruprecht, Louis A. Jr. "After Virtue? On Distorted Philosophical Narratives." *Continuum* 3 (1994): 9–34.

———."Against Positions: Notes on the Relation Between Moral Vision and Moral Debate." *Soundings* 78.3/4 (1995) 501–518.

———. "In the Aftermath of Modernism: On the Postures of the Present and Their Portrait of the Past." *Soundings* 75.2/3 (1992): 255–85.

———. "Mark's Tragic Vision." *Religion and Literature* 24.3 (1992): 1–25.

———. "Martha Nussbaum: On Tragedy and the Modern Ethos." *Soundings* 72.4 (1989): 589–605.

———. "Nietzsche's Vision, Nietzsche's Greece" *Soundings* 73.1 (1990): 61–84.

———. *Tragic Posture and Tragic Vision: Against the Modern Failure of Nerve.* New York: Continuum Press, 1994.

Sass, Louis A. *Madness and Modernism: Insanity in the Light of Modern Art, Literature, and Thought.* San Francisco: Harper Collins, 1992.

Snell, Bruno. *The Discovery of Mind: The Greek Origins of European Thought.* trans. T.G. Rosenmeyer, New York: Oxford University Press, 1953.

Steiner, George. *After Babel: Aspects of Language and Translation.* New York: Oxford University Press, 1974.

———. *Antigones.* New York: Oxford University Press, 1986.

———. "Antigones." The Twelfth Jackson Knight Memorial Lecture, delivered at the University of Exeter, 2 March 1979.

———. *In Bluebeard's Castle: Some Notes Toward a Redefinition of Culture.* New Haven: Yale University Press, 1971.

———. *The Death of Tragedy.* New York: Hill and Wang, Dramabooks, 1961.

————. *George Steiner: A Reader*. London: Penguin Books, 1984.

————. "Real Presences." The Leslie Stephen Memorial Lecture. Cambridge University Press, 1986.

————. *Real Presences*. Chicago: University of Chicago Press, 1989.

————. "Why English?" The English Association Presidential Address, July, 1975.

Steiner, George and Robert Fagles, eds. *Homer: A Collection of Critical Essays*. Englewood Cliffs, NJ: Prentice-Hall, 1962.

Stout, Jeffrey. *Ethics After Babel: The Languages of Morals and Their Discontents*. Boston: Beacon Press, 1988.

Taylor, Charles. *The Ethics of Authenticity*. Cambridge, MA: Harvard University Press, 1992.

————. *Hegel*. New York: Cambridge University Press, 1975.

————. "Justice After Virtue." In *After MacIntyre: Critical Perspectives on the Work of Alasdair MacIntyre*, edited by John Horton and Susan Mendus, 16–43. Notre Dame, IN: University of Notre Dame Press, 1994.

————. *Sources of the Self: The Making of the Modern Identity*. Cambridge, MA: Harvard University Press, 1989.

Toulmin, Stephen. *Cosmopolis: The Hidden Agenda of Modernity*. Chicago: University of Chicago Press, 1990.

Walzer, Michael. *Spheres of Justice: A Defense of Pluralism and Equality*. New York: Basic Books, 1983.

Weil, Simone. "l' Iliade, ou, La Poème de la Force." In *La Source Greque*, 11–43. Paris: Editions Gallimard, 1953.

————. *Gravity and Grace*. Translated by Arthur Mills with an introduction by Gustave Thibon. New York: G. P. Putnam's Sons, 1952.

————. *Intimations of Christianity Among the Ancient Greeks*. Translated variously. London: Routledge & Kegan Paul, 1957, 1987.

————. *The Need for Roots*. Translated by Arthur Wills with a preface by T. S. Eliot. New York: Octagon Books, 1984.

Winchester, James J. *Nietzsche's Aesthetic Turn: Reading Nietzsche After Heidegger, Deleuze and Derrida*. Albany: SUNY Press, 1994.

Wolff, Robert Paul, Barrington Moore, and Herbert Marcuse. *A Critique of Pure Tolerance*. Boston: Beacon Press, 1965.

INDEX

Achilles, 40, 41, 42, 43, 72, 73, 82, 95,
    98, 103, 104, 105, 106, 107, 108,
    109, 111, 113, 169, 211–8, 219–23
Acropolis, 15
Adam, 135, 137
Aegean, xii, 34, 38
Aegina, 38–41, 42, 43, 45, 47, 48, 49,
    51, 52, 61n.84
Aeneas, 219
Aeschylus, 28, 38
aftermath, 6, 120n.62, 201, 207, 209,
    223, 226n.33
Agamemnon, 42, 73, 107, 212–6, 219,
    220, 221
Agora, 15
Aiakos, 40, 41
Aiakidai, 40, 41
Ajax, 41, 42, 43, 98, 204, 214, 216–8
Alexander the Great, 9
Alexandrian culture, 33, 34, 181
Alexandrian Empire, 7, 184
American Academy of Religion, 165
American School of Classical Studies, ix
Anankê, 102
anti-American, 67, 127, 129, 146, 147
anti-Christian (see also Nietzsche,
    Friedrich)
  Christianity and, 11
antidecadent, 95
Antigone, 82, 222
antiliberalism, 82, 237
antimodern, 3, 10, 15–16, 44, 45, 49,
    51–52, 53, 67, 82, 97, 98, 106, 109,
    112, 113, 127, 129, 131, 133, 134,
    140, 146, 148, 211, 236, 237, 238
  antipagan, 144, 145
  Christian, 128

foundationalism and, 148–9
fundamentalism and, 166, 169, 178,
    183
Hellenism and, 115, 184, 223
modernism and, 10, 146–7, 182, 202,
    205, 234, 235
narrative, 132, 142
theology, 145, 146
antimodernism. See antimodern
anti-worldly, 131, 141
Aphaia, 36, 37, 40, 42, 59n.70
apocalyptic, 8, 128, 131, 133, 139, 170,
    178, 180, 203, 205, 207, 208, 222,
    223
apocalypticism. See apocalyptic
Aquinas, Saint Thomas, 68, 72, 75, 76,
    115n.1
aretê, 212
Arianism, 144
Aristophanes, 28
Aristotle, 5, 7, 14, 17, 29, 67, 68, 69, 70,
    74–82, 91, 98, 99, 105, 107, 112,
    113, 114, 127, 130, 131, 134, 140,
    146, 148
  as encyclopediast, 80, 88n.71, 93, 168
  doctrine of "the mean," 69, 71,
      85nn.25, 28
  epic and tragedy, 108
  "great-souled man" in, 13,
      18n.15, 76
  happiness in, 72, 85n.31, 100–102,
      149n.6
  looking to the end, 101–102
  on living "after virtue," 100
  "political animal" in, 70–77, 82,
      84n.21, 104, 167, 228n.63
  tradition in, 237